LOPE DE VEGA STUDIES 1937-1962

A CRITICAL SURVEY AND ANNOTATED BIBLIOGRAPHY

COMPILERS

1937-38: Arthur M. Fox, Queen's University at Kingston
1939-40: Edward Glaser, University of Michigan
1941-42: James A. Castañeda, Rice University
1943-44: Raymond R. MacCurdy, University of New Mexico
1945-46: Carlos Ortigoza, Indiana University
1947-48: Walter Poesse, Indiana University
1949-50: Arnold G. Reichenberger, University of Pennsylvania
1951-52: Ramon Rozzell, Arkansas State Teachers College
1953-54: Helen L. Sears, Wells College
1955-56: K.-L. Selig, University of Texas
1957-58: Alan S. Trueblood, Brown University, and
Donald R. Larson, Princeton University
1959-60: Richard W. Tyler, University of Texas
1961: Gerald E. Wade, University of Tennessee
1962: Gerald E. Wade, University of Tennessee, and
Jack H. Parker, University of Toronto

* * * * *

Chairman of Spanish 3, MLA, for the Quadricentennial Year:
Myron A. Peyton, College of Wooster

LOPE DE VEGA STUDIES
1937-1962

A CRITICAL SURVEY
AND ANNOTATED BIBLIOGRAPHY

A Project of
The Research Committee of the *Comediantes*
(Spanish Group Three of the Modern Language Association of America)
in observance of
The Quadricentennial Year

General Editors

JACK H. PARKER
UNIVERSITY OF TORONTO

ARTHUR M. FOX
QUEEN'S UNIVERSITY AT KINGSTON

Published for the Committee by University of Toronto Press

Copyright, Canada, 1964, by
University of Toronto Press
Printed in Canada

Reprinted in 2018
ISBN 978-1-4875-8732-1 (paper)

PREFACE

Almost thirty years have passed since the literary world last paused to pay homage to Spain's greatest dramatic poet, Lope Félix de Vega Carpio (1562-1635). On that earlier commemorative occasion, the tercentenary of Lope's death, an extensive tribute of publications dealing with his life and works issued forth from both scholarly and popular presses in Spain and abroad. At the close of the tercentenary a valuable service to Lopean scholarship was performed by William L. Fichter in summing up and evaluating the significant contributions to the field of Lope de Vega studies during the period immediately prior to 1935 and down to the end of 1936.[1] Now, a quarter of a century later, despite an interlude of nearly a decade in which the hispanists' world was torn first by Civil War in Spain and then by World War II, much progress in Lopean studies can be observed; for the quadricentennial of Lope's birth the Comediantes (Spanish Group Three of the Modern Language Association of America) have deemed it a fitting and useful tribute to the memory of the Fénix de los Ingenios to undertake as a group project a continuation of Professor Fichter's survey, taking stock of what has been accomplished from 1937 to 1961, and down through the Quadricentennial Year, 1962.

This volume is an experiment in scholarly cooperation. The members of the Research Committee of MLA Spanish Group Three, appointed by Myron A. Peyton, Chairman for the Quadricentennial Year, have worked diligently as individuals on assigned portions of the project. Preliminary criteria were established for the guidance of all, but a certain individuality in style and method will be observed from unit to unit, according to resources available in each instance and to personal preference and interpretation, especially in the critical surveys and in annotations.

The bibliographical system evolved, after a great deal of sorting and re-sorting, is an alphabetical arrangement, going from the general to the particular, with "Editions" preceding "Studies." However, to present a picture of the evolution of editions, book reviews and studies of individual works, the internal treatment in these cases is chronological. With the provision of cross-references within the various sub-sections, the Editors believe that Indexes — so highly desirable on every occasion, it is true — are not essential in the present volume. Works frequently attributed to Lope are included,

---

1. "The Present State of Lope de Vega Studies," Hisp, XX(1937), 327-52.

although we recognize that the attribution in many cases is doubtful if not definitely erroneous (e.g., La Estrella de Sevilla) in the light of modern scholarship. With regard to the inclusion of unpublished works, it was decided to list doctoral but not masters dissertations. In verifying and amplifying these listings, the Editors are especially indebted to Walter Poesse's compilation "Disertaciones lopescas" (Hispanó, No. 18, 1963, 77-89) and to the anonymous catalogue of "Tesis doctorales de interés literario de la Universidad de Madrid" (RL, XXI, Nos. 41-42, 1962, 107-16). In the case of published works, newspaper material has normally been omitted.

It is gratifying to Lope de Vega scholars to note the ever-increasing number of available bibliographical aids. In addition to older manuals by Foulché-Delbosc and Barrau-Dihigo and by Fitzmaurice-Kelly, and the more recent bibliographies by Homero Serís and by José Simón Díaz, there are the serial bibliographies of a general nature in RFE, RL, ZRP, etc., and, for theses, the listings in Hisp and MLJ, as well as the résumés provided by DA. Of great help are the PMLA annual compilations (which expanded in 1957 to include international coverage), the SP annual bibliography of the Renaissance, the BCom semi-annual bibliography of foreign publications on the Comedia and The Year's Work in Modern Language Studies published by the Modern Humanities Research Association. For Lope in particular, we have Tiemann's work for Germany, the Simón Díaz-Juana de José Prades Ensayo (1955; with the Nuevos estudios, 1961) and Robert B. Brown's bibliographical study of Lope's comedias históricas, tradicionales y legendarias, of 1958. Announced by Warren T. McCready is a projected bibliografía temática of studies on Golden Age dramatists for the years 1850-1950, which will be an extremely valuable contribution to Comedia studies in general and to Lope de Vega studies in particular. To this compilation the Editors are already indebted for several items which Dr. McCready has generously placed at their disposal.

The Editors wish to express their appreciation to Mrs. E. V. Thomas, M.A., University of the West Indies, Trinidad, for her painstaking work in sorting the fichas as they came from the various compilers. To the Committee on Humanities and Social Sciences Research of the University of Toronto and to the Arts Research Committee of Queen's University at Kingston, thanks are hereby rendered for financial assistance for the preparation of the manuscript for publication. The cooperation of Miss Francess G. Halpenny and Miss B. E. Plewman, of the Editorial Offices of the University of Toronto Press, is acknowledged with much gratitude. The work of Mrs. T. B. Barclay, M.A., who provided invaluable assistance in typing the manuscript with great care for photographic reproduction, cannot be too highly praised.

Lopistas are asked to send to the Editors comments, corrections and additions, to supplement lacunae in the present work, for in a field as vast as Lope de Vega studies we do not presume to completeness or perfection.

Toronto, Canada
June, 1964

J. H. P.
A. M. F.

TABLE OF CONTENTS

PREFACE	v
ABBREVIATIONS	ix

THE YEARS 1937-1961

CRITICAL SURVEY		3
ANNOTATED BIBLIOGRAPHY		
<u>Editions</u>: General		22
Drama — A. General		23
B. Individual Plays		25
Poetry — A. General		35
B. Individual Poems		38
Prose — Individual Prose Works		40
<u>Studies</u>: General, including Biography		43
Drama — A. General		70
B. Individual Plays		109
C. The <u>Arte nuevo</u>		149
D. The <u>Peregrino</u> Lists		151
Poetry — A. General		152
B. Individual Poems		158
Prose — A. General		171
B. Individual Prose Works		171

THE QUADRICENTENNIAL YEAR 1962

COMMENTARY	181
BIBLIOGRAPHY	184

ABBREVIATIONS

Acad.	Academia, Academy	CCLC	Cuadernos del Congreso por la Libertad de la Cultura
Anon.	Anonymous		
Archiv	Archiv für das Studium der neueren Sprachen und Literaturen	CHA	Cuadernos Hispanoamericanos
		Chapt.	Chapter
AUC	Anales de la Universidad de Chile	CL	Comparative Literature
		Clás.	Clásica(s), Clásico(s)
BA	Books Abroad	Clás. Cast.	Clásicos Castellanos
BAE	Biblioteca de Autores Españoles	Clav	Clavileño
		CMLR	Canadian Modern Language Review
BBMP	Boletín de la Biblioteca Menéndez Pelayo	Col.	Colección, Collection
BCom	Bulletin of the Comediantes	CSIC	Consejo Superior de Investigaciones Científicas
BEPIF	Bulletin des Études Portugaises et de L'Institut Français au Portugal		
		Cuad.	Cuadernos
		DA	Dissertation Abstracts
BFE	Boletín de Filología Española	Dept.	Department
BH	Bulletin Hispanique	Diss.	Dissertation
BHR	Bibliothèque d'Humanisme et Renaissance	Doct.	Doctoral
		EAm	Estudios Americanos
BHS	Bulletin of Hispanic Studies (until 1948: Bulletin of Spanish Studies)	Ed(s).	Edición(es), edited (by), edition(s), editor(s)
		Edit.	Editorial(es)
Bib.	Biblioteca, Bibliothèque	Fac.	Faculdade, Facultad, Faculty
Bol.	Boletim, Boletín		
BRAE	Boletín de la Real Academia Española	FiR	Filologia Romanza
		FMod	Filologia Moderna

Govt.	Government	PMLA	Publications of the Modern Language Association of America
GSLI	Giornale Storico della Letteratura Italiana		
		PQ	Philological Quarterly
Hisp	Hispania	PSA	Papeles de Son Armadans
Hispanó	Hispanófila	Pseud.	Pseudonym
HR	Hispanic Review	Pub(s).	Publicación(es), publication(s) (of), published (by), publisher, publishing
Imp.	Imprenta		
Inst.	Institute, Instituto		
KFLQ	Kentucky Foreign Language Quarterly	PULC	Princeton University Library Chronicle
Lang(s).	Language(s)	QQ	Queen's Quarterly
LanM	Les Langues Modernes	RAE	Real Academia Española
Lit(s).	Literario(s), literatura(s), literature(s)	RBFilol	Revista Brasileira de Filologia
		RBN	Revista de Bibliografía Nacional
LM	Letterature Moderne		
LR	Les Lettres Romanes	RBPH	Revue Belge de Philologie et d'Histoire
M.-B.	Morley-Bruerton		
MLA	Modern Language Association of America	Repub(s).	Republication(s), republished (by)
MLF	Modern Language Forum	Rev.	Review(s), Revista, Revue
MLJ	Modern Language Journal		
MLN	Modern Language Notes	RF	Romanische Forschungen
MLQ	Modern Language Quarterly		
MLR	Modern Language Review	RFE	Revista de Filología Española
MP	Modern Philology		
Nac.	Nacional	RFH	Revista de Filología Hispánica
N.d.	No date	RH	Revue Hispanique
NL	Les Nouvelles Littéraires	RHM	Revista Hispánica Moderna
No.	Number, número		
NRF	Nouvelle Revue Française	RIE	Revista de Ideas Estéticas
NRFH	Nueva Revista de Filología Hispánica	RJ	Romanistisches Jahrbuch
NS	Die neueren Sprachen	RL	Revista de Literatura
O.s.	Old style		

RLC	Revue de Littérature Comparée	TAE	Teatro Antiguo Español
RLMC	Rivista di Letterature Moderne e Comparate	TDR	Tulane Drama Review
		Trans.	Translated (by), translation, translator
RLR	Revue des Langues Romanes		
RNC	Revista Nacional de Cultura (Caracas)	UCPMP	University of California Publications in Modern Philology
RomN	Romance Notes		
RPh	Romance Philology	Univ.	Universidad(e), University
RR	Romanic Review	Unpub.	Unpublished
RUBA	Revista de la Universidad de Buenos Aires	Vol(s).	Volume(s)
		VR	Vox Romanica
SFr	Studi Francesi	ZRP	Zeitschrift für romanische Philologie
Soc.	Sociedad, Society		
SP	Studies in Philology		

THE YEARS 1937—1961

Critical Survey

1937 — 1961

1937-1938

The tragic events in Spain during the years under review are underlined by the paucity of Lope items from Peninsular sources. The gap in publication of RFE reflects the times: although Vol. XXIV bears the date 1937, it was not published until some years later; Vol. XXV is dated 1941. From Barcelona in 1937, however, we have the first editions of two well-known literary histories, Ángel Valbuena Prat's Historia de la literatura española, and in a more restricted field Guillermo Díaz-Plaja's manual on La poesía lírica española, both giving due consideration to Lope within their respective limitations of space. From Bilbao in 1938 we have the title Lope de Vega y clave de "Fuenteovejuna" by Esteban Calle Iturrino, and bearing a Madrid imprint of the same year there is María del Pilar Oñate's El feminismo en la literatura española, which includes Lope's theatre and La Dorotea in its purview. Abroad, no major works on Lope de Vega appeared in these years, other than a reprint of Hugo A. Rennert's Life, but valuable reviews of important works published in the fruitful preceding period of the Lope de Vega tercentenary continued to appear, and these reviews have been included in our bibliography. At the same time there was a surprising number of new articles in the various areas of Lope studies, attesting that the vein had not been worked out by the abundant tercentennial production.

In noting the accomplishments of Lopean scholarship during the years 1937-38 it is fitting to pay tribute to William L. Fichter's excellent survey of the state of Lope de Vega studies at that time (Hisp, XX, 327-52), already mentioned above. In addition to that appraisal, ranging over the whole field, Dr. Fichter provided a detailed examination of one topic in a subsequent article, "Recent Research on Lope de Vega's Sonnets" (HR, VI, 21-34).

In an article entitled "Objective Criteria for Judging Authorship and Chronology in the Comedia" (HR, V, 281-85), S. Griswold Morley gave the rationale of the methods of investigation which he had long been pursuing and which, with the collaboration of Courtney Bruerton, were soon to bear fruit in the epoch-making Chronology of Lope de Vega's "Comedias" (1940). Questions of versification, chronology and authenticity in the Comedia were the subjects of many of the articles which appeared in the 1937-38 period. There were three by Messrs. Morley and Bruerton, either singly or in collaboration, and no fewer than five by J. Homero Arjona; there was one each by Harry W. Hilborn, J. A. van Praag and Francisco de B. San Román. The foregoing enumeration for our two-year period testifies to the number of hispanists far and near whose researches over the years contributed indirectly to the Morley-Bruerton Chronology.

Of the studies of Lope's drama that were published in the period under review most extensive was a series of lectures by E. Kohler on "L'Art dramatique de Lope de Vega," which appeared in Revue des Cours et Conférences in nine instalments. Others were J. Homero Arjona's "El disfraz varonil en Lope de Vega" (BH, XXXIX, 120-45); Joseph Gregor's Das spanische Welttheater; Francis C. Hayes' "The Use of Proverbs as Titles and Motives in the Siglo de Oro Drama: Lope de Vega" (HR, VI, 305-23); Charlotte M. Lorenz's "Seventeenth Century Plays in Madrid from 1808-1818" (HR, VI, 324-31); and Eva R. Price's "The Peasant Plays of Lope de Vega" (MLF, XXII, 214-19). The abiding significance of Lope's Comedia was questioned by William C. Atkinson in A Handbook to the Study and Teaching of Spanish, edited by E. Allison Peers, and the conformist character of the Comedia in plot and idea was related by Rudolph Schevill to the destruction of Erasmian inquiry in "Erasmus and the Fate of a Liberalistic Movement Prior to the Counter Reformation" (HR, V, 103-23).

General titles on Lope that appeared were José de la Riva Agüero's Lope de Vega, which included material on Lope's Peruvian Amarilis, and Alfonso Reyes' oft-reprinted "Silueta de Lope de Vega." Lope received attention also in A. F. G. Bell's Castilian Literature, Ralph S. Boggs' Outline History of Spanish Literature, I. L. McClelland's The Origins of the Romantic Movement in Spain and Eugen G. Winkler's Gestalten und Probleme. For poetry, there were Benedetto Croce's "Poesia di Lope" (La Critica, XXXV, 241-55), W. L. Fichter's "Two Sonnets Attributed to Lope de Vega" (HR, VI, 345-46), and articles on the history of the décima by Juan Millé y Giménez (HR, V, 40-51) and Dorothy Clotelle Clarke (HR, VI, 155-58). A. K. Jameson contributed two articles, "The Sources of Lope de Vega's Erudition" (HR, V, 124-39), dealing with the historical and scientific allusions in the Jerusalén conquistada, Isidro, Dragontea and Hermosura de Angélica, and "Lope de Vega's La Dragontea: Historical and Literary Sources" (HR, VI, 104-19), describing Lope's distortion of the facts in elevating the subordinate Amaya to the position of a national hero. Aspects of Lope's relations with the New World were discussed in another pair of articles, Irving A. Leonard's "More Conjectures regarding the Identity of Lope de Vega's 'Amarilis indiana'" (Hisp, XX, 113-20), and "Notes on Lope de Vega's Works in the Spanish Indies" (HR, VI, 277-93), which presented evidence of Lope's popularity with the reading public and theatre-goers in the New World.

In the area of comparative studies we have F. de Figueiredo's "Camões e Lope" (RLC, XVIII, 160-71); C. Guerrieri Crocetti's "Lope de Vega e l'Italia" (Pensiero e Poesia, pp. 61-86); Ezio Levi's "Roma e Lope de Vega" (Atti del IV Congresso Nazionale di Studi Romani, IV, 263-69); C. Looten's "Rapports littéraires entre la Néerlande et l'Espagne" (RLC, XVII, 613-50); and Eugenio Mele's "Lope de Vega, Merlin Cocai e Luciano" (GSLI, CXII, 323-28).

1939-1940

The highlight of this period is, without any doubt, Morley and Bruerton's Chronology of Lope de Vega's "Comedias" (MLA Monograph Series, XI, 1940). The authors of this classic and absolutely indispensable tool for the Lope scholar have, over the years, seen a complete justification of their use of quantitative data in the analysis of Lope's metrical art. Their conclusions have been corroborated by later discoveries and, as Fichter so rightly put it in his review of the book, "this excellent product of long and painstaking scholarly collaboration" is a landmark in the whole history of Lope studies.

Tiemann's Lope de Vega in Deutschland (1939), which surveyed Lope in Germany over the years 1629-1935, is very useful. Drawing upon rich sources in Germany and Austria, it provides a great deal of information on lopeana, and has been highly praised by its reviewers. The second volume of Amezúa's Lope de Vega en sus cartas (1940) continued the Epistolario, the first volume of which was published in 1935, and concluded the introductory material. (The letters proper will appear in 1941 and 1943.) This vast compilation, with illuminating documentation, provides invaluable insights into the personalities of Lope and of his associates. Karl Vossler's Lope de Vega und sein Zeitalter, originally published in Munich in 1932, and translated into Spanish in 1933 by Ramón de la Serna, appeared in its second Spanish printing in 1940. It provides valuable background material.

In the year 1939 the Comedia's comic servant received attention in an article by Arjona in HR (VII, 1-21) and in a review in ZRP (LIX, 124-25) of Maria Heseler's Studien zur Figur des Gracioso (Göttingen dissertation of 1933). Fichter, Hainsworth and Halstead studied, with perspicacity, problems of authenticity, Lope in France and Lope's attitude toward astrology and astronomy, respectively. Blecua in the same year brought forth the Ebro edition of Lope's Poesía lírica, which included eleven selections not already found in Montesinos' edition in Clás. Cast.

1940 saw the publication of J. A. Moore's thesis (Pennsylvania, 1937) on the "Romancero" in the Chronicle-Legend Plays, and of Ruth A. Oppenheimer's thesis-edition (Hamburg, 1938) of Santiago el verde, in TAE, 9. Dale, Morby and Wilson contributed articles on games and social pastimes, La batalla del honor and contemporary manners, in HR (VIII, 219-41), BH (XLII, 236) and BHS (XVII, 3-23 and 88-102), respectively. Ramón Gómez de la Serna wrote an "ensayo de simpatía" on El caballero de Olmedo for the Rev. Cubana (XIV, 38-59), wherein also appeared Carolina Poncet's reflections on the Belardo line in Peribáñez, "a la iglesia me acogí" (XIV, 78-99).

An outstanding edition of a comedia, long attributed to Lope, but now generally denied to him by modern critics, is that of La Estrella de Sevilla, by Reed, Dixon and Hill (1939). Although intended as a text-book for classroom purposes, it is thoroughly scholarly in treatment.

1941-1942

In this period, biographical studies were greatly enriched by Amezúa's publication of the first volume of Lope's letters (Vol. III of the Epistolario). Owing to the personal, unguarded nature of this correspondence, we now not only feel a more authentic acquaintance with the Fénix, but we also see a dimension of the man not revealed in the works he created for the public at large. His subservience as an adulator, the vehemence of his passions, his cynicism and, at times, cruelty, may not always correspond to romantic biographical notions concerning Lope, but they are extremely significant facets of his personality. Amezúa's Epistolario establishes itself as a monumental landmark in studies of Lope, and this third volume seems definitely to be the outstanding triumph of the 1941-42 period.

It is interesting to note the great frequency with which the Morley-Bruerton Chronology was used as a tool in Lope de Vega studies during this period. Most reviewers were impressed by the great value this work would have in clearing up much of the mystery surrounding doubtful attributions. They saw this successful study and interpretation of versification as an inspiration and point of departure for further study of Lope's comedias. Fichter's review (RR, XXXIII, 202-11) constitutes in itself an important contribution to chronology studies, as does his article on "New Aids for Dating Undated Autographs..." (HR, IX, 79-90).

Little work of a critical or interpretative nature was accomplished in 1941-42. However, the groundwork for much serious investigation was laid by Arco y Garay's La sociedad española en las obras dramáticas de Lope de Vega, a colossal undertaking, premiado by the Royal Spanish Academy. This exhaustive classification of an immense number of passages (some 5,000) provides a lively and interesting picture of early 17th-century Spain as known and portrayed by Lope in his plays.

Entrambasaguas suggested Leandro Fernández de Moratín, Feijóo and Sarmiento as exceptions to the universally accepted 18th-century disregard and contempt for Golden Age drama in "El lopismo de Moratín" (RFE, XXV, 1-45) and in "Lope de Vega, Feijóo and Sarmiento" (Correo Erudito, II, 179-82). And with regard to editions of Lope's writings, we find some commendable work. The scholarly edition of Peribáñez by John M. Hill and Mabel M. Harlan, in their text-book Cuatro comedias (New York, 1941), provides a good brief introduction and a wealth of textual notes. The Romancero espiritual, edited by Luis Guarner (Valencia, 1941), is the first complete critical edition of this work. Most other editions of this period, aimed as they were at a wide reading public (there is even a children's edition), have relatively little critical interest.

Numerous articles were published in these years, dealing mainly with literary history and Lope biography. An interesting event, reported in this period, was the reopening of Lope de Vega's house, which had been restored before the outbreak of the Civil War.

1943-1944

In these years, there appeared a model critical edition of a Lope play: William L. Fichter's El sembrar en buena tierra (MLA General Series, XVII, 1944). The late Claude E. Anibal paid fitting tribute to this outstanding contribution to Lope scholarship in the following words: "Mr. Fichter's exemplary patience in research, his long-standing and intimate acquaintance with the Comedia of Lope and his contemporaries, his fine sense of values, and his editorial integrity and meticulousness combine to make this book in many respects a model of its kind" (RR, XXXVII, 252-68). The Introduction (35 pages), the Text (autograph MS, 1616, British Museum), the Notes (84 pages), indeed the whole monograph, from cover to cover, should be carefully studied by every lopista.

Eduardo Juliá Martínez edited, also in 1944, the controversial "different" text of El caballero de Olmedo (attributed to Cristóbal de Morales); El castigo sin venganza came forth from the Madrid "Centro de Estudios sobre Lope de Vega;" and Blecua added to the Ebro collection with an edition of Peribáñez. (The previous year had seen another Peribáñez: the Hachette Aubrun-Montesinos volume, with an excellent introduction.) In 1944, too, Joaquín de Entrambasaguas, in the Rev. de Bibliografía Nac., laid plans for an as yet unfulfilled desideratum: "una edición de las Obras completas de Lope."

The final volume of Amezúa's significant Epistolario was published in 1943; and numerous articles of value appeared in the learned journals: for example, Morby on "tragedia" and "tragicomedia" in Lope (HR, XI, 185-209), Casalduero on form and meaning of Fuenteovejuna (RFH, V, 21-44), Fichter and Sánchez Escribano on "A mis soledades voy..." (HR, XI, 304-13), Pierce on La Jerusalén conquistada (BHS, XX, 11-35); and, for 1944, Peers on mysticism in Lope's religious verse (BHS, XXI, 133-45, and continued in the following year) and María Goyri de Menéndez Pidal on Lope's Romancero (Mediterráneo, No. 5, 209-15).

1945-1946

In these critical years — the last of the Second World War and the first of the post-war period — Lope de Vega studies in general touched a low point. The year 1945 was brightened however by the appearance of Una colección manuscrita y desconocida de comedias de Lope de Vega Carpio, a wonderful hallazgo (as the first chapter is entitled) by Agustín González de Amezúa y Mayo.

This book describes the five manuscript volumes made by a scribe, "un tal Ignacio de Gálvez," in 1762, the first four of which contain copies of thirty-two of Lope de Vega's plays. The importance of this discovery can be measured by the fact that it supplies the text of three lost comedias and the place and date of all thirty-two, sixteen of which were previously undated. The transcription of the original seems to have been so perfect as to provide almost with certainty the correct text, as can be observed from Amezúa's listing of the variants in the Gálvez text and the Academy text side by side.

Two books were published in 1946 by Joaquín de Entrambasaguas: <u>Estudios sobre Lope de Vega</u>, Vol. I, and <u>Vivir y crear de Lope de Vega</u>, Vol. I. The first one includes a reprint, with important additions, of "Una guerra literaria del Siglo de Oro," an outstanding contribution for the understanding of Lope's dramatic art. The other volume contains a biography of Lope, which does not contribute anything new, but is superior in content, form and style to the first biography written by Entrambasaguas (<u>Vida de Lope de Vega</u>, Barcelona, 1936; reprinted in 1942).

Also in 1946 appeared Federico Carlos Sainz de Robles' edition of Lope's <u>Obras escogidas</u>, Vol. I, containing thirty-nine <u>comedias</u>, and Vol. II, a selection of lyric, religious and epic poetry, prose and novels. Although providing a collection of so many of Lope's writings in two volumes of convenient size and handsome format, the editing leaves much to be desired. Ignoring the painstaking work of recent scholars in questions of authenticity and textual accuracy, the editor has relied to too great an extent on personal taste and uncritical opinion.

Argentina contributed a noteworthy book on Lope's drama: Marcos A. Morínigo's <u>América en el teatro de Lope de Vega</u>, a scholarly work dealing with all aspects of the <u>Indias</u> in Lope's plays. North American articles on the drama include Morley's short study of <u>El acero de Madrid</u> (<u>HR</u>, XIII, 166-69) and Fichter's dating of <u>Santiago el verde</u> (<u>HR</u>, XIII, 243-44). French scholars, writing in <u>BH</u>, contributed useful notes on <u>mise en scène</u> (Baulier, XLVII, 57-70), on the date of <u>El ejemplo de casadas</u> (Kohler, XLVII, 79-91), on chronology (Bataillon, XLVIII, 227-37) and on the sources of <u>Pobreza no es vileza</u> (Saunal, XLVIII, 239-46). Other contributions were "Un auto de Lope de Vega rechazado," by Montoto (<u>BRAE</u>, XXV, 429-33) and "The Spanish Peasant in the Drama of Lope de Vega," by Kathleen Gouldson (<u>Liverpool Studies in Spanish Literature</u>, pp. 63-89).

Studies of Lope's poetry were more numerous. Among the more outstanding were Lapesa on <u>La Jerusalén</u> (<u>BRAE</u>, XXV, 111-36), Peers on mysticism (<u>BHS</u>, XXII, 38-43) and Barbazán on "Una edición ignorada de un romance..." (<u>Bibliografía Hispánica</u>, V, 157-67). Among reprints of little-known editions are Alfay's <u>Poesías varias</u>, which contains a <u>romance</u> by Lope thought to have been lost, and Janner's <u>La glosa en el Siglo de Oro</u>, which includes six rare <u>glosas</u> by Lope, accompanied by critical notes. Articles of less value are Zabala's "Sobre una fisonomía inicial del romance de Lope <u>De pechos sobre una torre</u>" (<u>RBN</u>, VI, 311-24), because its reconstruction lacks factual support, and Balbín Lucas' "La primera edición de <u>La Dragontea</u>" (<u>RBN</u>, VI, 355-56), which provides a reprint of an unknown communication dealing with the epic poem, but lacks the research necessary to prove the author's hypothesis.

In the period 1945-46, two outstanding editions, printed previously, received much attention from reviewers: Fichter's <u>El sembrar en buena tierra</u> and Juliá Martínez' <u>El caballero de Olmedo</u>. A new critical edition was Richard W. Tyler's <u>La corona de Hungría</u>, an unpublished doctoral dissertation. Other dissertations, likewise unpublished, were those by Ruth Horne (a study of <u>El peregrino en su patria</u>) and by Marcel David (a study of Lope's vocabulary).

Several well-known <u>comedias</u> by Lope appeared in popular editions in Spain, Mexico and Britain. Among the titles favoured by reprinting were <u>El Amor enamorado</u>, <u>El caballero de Olmedo</u>, <u>La dama boba</u>, <u>Fuenteovejuna</u>, <u>El mejor alcalde el rey</u>, <u>La niña de plata</u>, <u>Peribáñez</u>, <u>El remedio en la desdicha</u> and <u>El villano en su rincón</u>. <u>La moza de cántaro</u> was translated into Russian.

1947-1948

Perhaps it is because the years 1947-48 followed so closely the end of World War II that little of real worth in the field of Lopean scholarship was produced in this period. A number of articles appeared, many of them subjective and, therefore, more interesting than important. Bataillon, Bruerton, Morley, Tiemann and Wagner continued their usual dependable (but during these years, small) additions to our store of knowledge of the <u>Fénix</u> and his works. One of the most valuable studies is that of Montoto on the words used by Lope "que no figuran en el Diccionario de la Real Academia Española" (<u>BRAE</u>, XXVI, 281-95, 443-57; continued in later vols.). Another is the "Addenda" by Morley and Bruerton (<u>HR</u>, XV, 49-71) to their <u>Chronology</u> of 1940.

Lopean scholarship was enriched by the editing of two more of the autograph plays: T. Earle Hamilton's <u>El cardenal de Belén</u> and Henry W. Hoge's <u>El príncipe despeñado</u>. Hamilton's edition is disappointing because of its lack of annotation; Hoge's, a doctoral dissertation, was not published until 1955. Apart from these, there were several editions of a few of Lope's other plays, not one of which can be considered of true, significant or lasting value.

Strangely enough, the three most significant works in book form were reprintings. One is the second volume of the <u>Estudios</u> of Entrambasaguas, its appearance welcome not only because it made more accessible some of the scattered works of this indefatigable <u>lopista</u>, but also because of the material that he added. The second is a convenient edition of Lope's <u>cartas</u> by Ángel Rosenblatt, a two-volume work of a smaller format than that of Amezúa. The third is Vossler's <u>Lope de Vega und sein Zeitalter</u>, with very few changes, however, from the edition of 1932.

Four doctoral dissertations in the United States were devoted to Lope during the years 1947-48; one is the Hoge edition mentioned above; the others treat of aspects of his drama also (the <u>dama</u> by Frances Whatley, the rustic by Beth W. Noble, and the concept of the city state by Perry J. Powers). None of the three, so far as the writer is aware, has been published in whole or in part, although all three made a significant contribution.

In this quadricentennial volume, it is fitting to honour the efforts of early <u>lopistas</u>. The work of two nineteenth-century English hispanists was appraised in 1947-48: Baron Holland, by Bruce W. Wardropper (BHS, XXIV, 259-68), and John R. Chorley, by J. C. J. Metford (BHS, XXV, 247-59). Both studies are well done and informative.

During the period 1947-48, we might say that there were no failures, primarily because nothing of great significance was attempted. But there were no great triumphs either.

1949-1950

In 1949-50, two general articles on Lope de Vega appeared in Dictionaries of Spanish Literature: the one by Zamora Vicente is based on expert literary scholarship; the other by Sainz de Robles, although too encomiastic, is valuable for the attention paid to the non-dramatic works. Entrambasaguas skilfully presented the contrast between Cervantes' timelessness and Lope's 17th-century hispanidad (AUC, CVIII, 235-44). The same author's study (Rev. Bibliográfica y Documental, IV, 5-30) of the assessment which the esthetic Manual of Blair and Munárriz made of Lope de Vega is a significant contribution, not only to the history of Lope appreciation, but to neo-classic poetic and dramatic theory in general. Espino Gutiérrez' speculations (BBMP, XXV, 84-98) on Lope's classicism and romanticism are generalities of limited value.

In the field of Lope's biography, we have two erudite studies by María Goyri de Menéndez Pidal. The first (NRFH, IV, 347-90) tries to identify Celia with Micaela de Luján, thereby pre-dating the Lope-Micaela relationship from 1599 (Castro) to 1593. However, in 1952, Morley and Bruerton's article, "Lope de Vega, Celia y Los comendadores de Córdoba" (NRFH, VI, 57-68), will effectively refute Doña María's argumentation. In the other study Doña María sets a date for Isabel de Urbina's death, September 15 or 20, 1594. Also, Cecilio Barberán described Lope's house, rooms, furniture and garden in its restored stage (Rev. de Educación Nac., X, 33-48), and Ximénez de Sandoval, by intuition, rather than by documentation, reconstructed a sentimental biography of Lope's daughter, Micaela, the nun (Escorial, XX, 633-67).

We note one metrical and two linguistic studies. In a monograph, Segura Covarsí defined Lope's position in the history of the Petrarchan canzone; Montoto brought to a conclusion his vocabulario (BRAE, XXIX, 135-49, 329-38) and Sloman offered a scholarly study on the phonology of the Moorish jargon used in Lope's plays (MLR, XLIV, 207-17).

In drama, reprints of general import appeared. Menéndez Pelayo's introductions to the plays edited for the Academy Edition were published in six volumes as part of the National Edition of Menéndez Pelayo's Obras completas. The usefulness of these well-known studies was enhanced by the addition of an important index. Valbuena Prat's excellent manual in the Labor series, Literatura dramática española, was re-issued. We mention here, because it seems to be of general interest, Werner's study on the gracioso, the major part of which is dedicated to Cervantes (Gymnasium und Wissenschaft, pp. 196-230).

Three scholars studied Lope's views on certain topics as found in his comedias. The most extensive is Herrera García's series of three articles on Spanish nobility, a storehouse of first-hand information on the subject (Escorial, XIX, 509-47, etc.). Miss Sears summarized the findings of her dissertation on Fortune and Fate in a few densely informative pages (BCom, II, No. 1, 1-3); and Miss Bomli drew on Lope's life and work in her monograph on the position of the woman in Spain during the Golden Age.

Dates of plays were determined in studies by Bruerton and Tyler. The former put the composition of Peribáñez between 1605 and 1608, on the basis of versification (HR, XVII, 35-46). Tyler fixed the date of seven plays, in two Notes, on internal evidence (MLN, LXV, 375-79 and HR, XVII, 250-51). In this connection we must mention Poesse's important contribution to our knowledge of what has been called "objective criteria" for determining Lope's authorship. In his monograph, Poesse observed the internal line structure of thirty plays preserved in autograph manuscript, applying the statistical methods developed by Morley.

There appeared seven source studies. One comprised only a few pages in Moore's monograph on the legend of Romeo and Juliet, in which he rejected any purported "lost" source for Castelvines y Monteses. The other six were detailed investigations. One, Bruerton's study of La quinta de Florencia as the "source" of Peribáñez, dealt rather with the fluctuating treatment of what we would call the Peribáñez or Fuenteovejuna theme, the violation of peasant honour by a wilful overlord (NRFH, IV, 25-39). Bataillon's masterful study of El villano en su rincón showed the complex interplay of existing stories, the traditional topos, Spanish monarchical veneration, and the diplomatic and dynamic constellation of the moment of composition (Feb., 1614 — Oct., 1615); in short, una comedia de circunstancias. It is a source study fused with critical evaluation (BH, LI, 5-38 and LII, 397). Hoge's article succeeded in establishing more exactly the chronical sources of El príncipe despeñado, and in addition, studied the autograph and editions of the play as well as the play's relationship to other comedias composed about the same time (PMLA, LXV, 824-40). The publications by Malkievics-Strzalkowa (26-page study, Cracow), Vernet (Cuad. de Lit., V, 17-36) and Campos (Rev. de Indias, IX, 731-54) are solid pieces of research establishing the sources, respectively, of El rey sin reino, El gran duque de Moscovia and El nuevo mundo descubierto por Colón. The title of the Campos article promised more than it gave, but what it gave was solid. The articles by Schulte-Herbrüggen (AUC, CVIII, 5-94), Toledano (Escorial, XX, 737-44) and Wilson (BH, LI, 125-59) are best considered as "criticism," although Bataillon's study of El villano en su rincón could be treated just as well here as under source studies. Schulte-Herbrüggen promised in the title a study of Lope's dramatic art, but actually he dealt only with two plays, El postrer godo de España and La vida y muerte del rey Bamba. His work is of value for the study of these two <u>comedias</u>, but it failed in its avowed subject owing to serious bibliographical deficiencies. We agree with Toledano, who argued against Menéndez Pelayo that the commander in <u>Peribáñez</u> is a sincere, passionate lover, but not a villain as is his counterpart in <u>Fuenteovejuna</u>. Wilson, although more incidentally, voiced the same opinion in his analysis of imagery and structure in <u>Peribáñez</u>, contrasting peasant language and noble language. Wilson's article is one of the best purely critical studies in the field.

Lope's <u>autos</u> received attention during this period. Wardropper finds Lope's sacramental drama "sterile" except when Lope chose an essentially lyrical theme (<u>PMLA</u>, LXV, 1196-1211). Pérez Gómez reported on the rejection of Lope's <u>Auto de la Virgen</u>, commissioned by the City of Seville, on grounds of an error in the legend of the Virgen de los Reyes as presented in the <u>auto</u> (<u>BH</u>, IX, 93-94). Fr. Manuel Penedo published records of payment made to Lope by the City Council for <u>autos</u> written by him (<u>Rev. Bibliográfica y Documental</u>, IV, 313-17). A brief note by Gonzalo Menéndez Pidal discussed the name of Pedro Carbonero (<u>BH</u>, VIII, 53-54); Valbuena Prat spoke of <u>La Estrella de Sevilla</u> and of Lope's mythological plays (<u>Clav</u>, I, No. 4, 26-28); and Ley considered as possible tragedies <u>El caballero de Olmedo</u> and <u>El castigo sin venganza</u> (<u>Clav</u>, I, No. 4, 9-12).

As for poetry, the most comprehensive study was Borghini's book on Lope's epic poems evaluated according to the principles of Crocian esthetics. It is an indispensable introduction to Lope's epic work. Dámaso Alonso contributed two articles on Lope's poetry. The first dealt with Marino as imitator of Lope and sympathetically discussed the difficult distinction between the terms originality, imitation and plagiarism, as understood in the seventeenth century (<u>RFE</u>, XXXIII, 110-43, etc.). The topic of the second article is Lope's competition with Góngora's esoteric poetry (<u>Clav</u>, I, No. 2, 10-15). Peers settled the problem of mysticism in Lope's poetry: Lope is sincerely religious, but not a mystic in the strict sense of the term (<u>Estudios dedicados a Menéndez Pidal</u>, I, 349-58).

In prose, two studies were devoted to <u>La Dorotea</u>. Durand emphasized the element of parody in this novel, in an essayistic article (<u>RNC</u>, XI, 65-79). Morby thoroughly investigated the recurrences of the Elena Osorio theme, the "matter of Dorotea," until it took final artistic form in <u>La Dorotea</u> (<u>HR</u>, XVIII, 108-25 and 195-217). This article is one of the most perceptive critical studies, based on sound research, in the field. For another novel, López Estrada discussed the indebtedness of Tirso's <u>La fingida Arcadia</u> to Lope's <u>Arcadia</u> (<u>Tirso de Molina por Revista Estudios</u>, pp. 303-20). The López Estrada article belongs more to Tirso than to Lope bibliography.

1951-1952

In 1951-52, there were no outstanding editions of Lope's plays, but a considerable number were reprinted (e.g., Aguilar, <u>Obras escogidas: Teatro</u>). Kohler brought out a second edition, somewhat improved, of

El perro del hortelano, and an edition of El mejor mozo de España (by García Mercadal) presents a clearly printed text. Greer rendered a valuable service by reproducing so meticulously the autograph of El piadoso aragonés; but lacking any study of the play itself and notes to elucidate the text, this edition falls short of the high standard set previously by Fichter's edition of El sembrar en buena tierra. The spate of trivial editions of Fuenteovejuna continued with the appearance of three more, only one of which (Ebro) meets even the meagrest requirements of the classroom. The publication of seven individual editions in as many years, and inclusion in several collections requiring reprinting, would seem to attest to the enduring popularity of Fuenteovejuna. If this is true, it is strange that a masterpiece so widely read goes unedited in a manner that befits it.

For the non-dramatic works, Entrambasaguas remedied a need by replacing his 1935 edition of the Jerusalén conquistada with another reproduction of the 1609 princeps, containing Lope's own notes. Entrambasaguas presented some villancicos which had been attributed to Lope in a unique volume of 1794 (RJ, V, 275-84). Here the curious will be interested, if not esthetically rewarded.

No new facts about Lope's life were made known. However, there was some disputation over one significant detail of Lope's biography, which has a bearing on the chronology of both his plays and his poetry. In an article of 1950 María Goyri de Menéndez Pidal had argued for an earlier date for the Lucinda period of Lope's life and writings. This is now controverted by Morley and Bruerton (NRFH, VI, 57-68). There is no better place to mention a peak of achievement for this period by Morley; his objective, thorough and painstaking study of Lope's pseudonyms and literary disguises constitutes a sine qua non for the seeking of autobiographical allusions in all of Lope's writings.

In that long troublesome problem of the numerous comedias that Lope might or might not have written, Fichter laid the groundwork for another objective criterion for establishing a canon of Lope's authentic ones. Based on the incomplete knowledge we have of orthoëpy, Fichter tested some of Lope's doubtful plays in the light of his use of syneresis, etc. (Homenaje a Archer M. Huntington, pp. 143-53). With zealous labour Sloman would remove La selva confusa from the limbo of doubtful Lope and set it squarely in the Calderonian canon (HR, XX, 134-48). Heaton, twenty years before, had been convinced that the play belonged to Lope. From the anonymity of the romancero nuevo o artístico, Sra. Pidal claimed five ballads for Lope (Filología, III, 185).

No small progress was made in the matter of Lope's chronology. Thornton Wilder, a scholar and practical man of the theatre, threw new light on the order of plays in the Peregrino lists (Festgabe für Karl Reinhardt, pp. 194-200). By internal evidence, Tyler proposed dates for nine more plays (BCom, IV, No. 2, 2-3, and MLN, LXVII, 170-73) and Arjona for one (HR, XX, 313-15).

Lope and his sources received considerable attention. Although little really new regarding the sources per se was brought out, interesting and valid articles were contributed by Echegaray (BH, LIII, 13-33), Macrí (LM, III, 515-43) and Martin (MLN, LXVI, 238-41). Other studies concerned themselves more with how Lope used his sources. Amado Alonso (Thesaurus, VIII, 1-24), Anderson-Imbert (Asomante, VIII, 17-22) and Metford (BHS, XXIX, 78-86) exhibited sources already known and then proceeded to analyse what Lope created from them. In so doing, they revealed his inventive skill, his ability to create vivid stage personalities and his mastery of stage craftsmanship.

Wölfflin's Principles in Spanish Drama, by Roaten and Sánchez Escribano, offers a formal analysis of Fuenteovejuna. It limits itself mainly to a consideration of the elements of the plot and does not attempt to make valuation judgments. Morínigo made another contribution to "American" studies through his article on "Indigenismos americanos" in Lope (RNC, XII, 72-95). And for Lope's prose, Morby presented an insight into Lope the scholar, and revealed, on a reduced scale, how Lope employed the display of pedantry as part of the technique of composing La Dorotea (HR, XX, 108-22).

For Lope's poetry, there came a boon in the second edition of Dámaso Alonso's Poesía española, with its useful index to all of his poems and to all of the aspects of his poetry which the author analyses. Of the reprinted materials found in this period, one deserves mention: Estudios sobre Lope de Vega, by the outstanding lopista, José F. Montesinos, to whom credit must go for initiating the analysis of Lope's methods and achievements as a lyric poet. Of rather negligible value were the portions of several books which were too general, subjective or biased to add much to our understanding of El Fénix.

1953-1954

The years 1953 and 1954 did not produce any major studies on Lope de Vega. Perhaps the greatest contribution to Lope scholarship was the completion of the publication of the Jerusalén conquistada by Entrambasaguas. This edition, with its carefully edited text and excellent critical study, had been badly needed for a long time. Another well-edited text is that of the play Los Ramírez de Arellano, with metrical study and notes by Diana Ramírez de Arellano, who, of course, had a great personal interest in this genealogical play.

No new biographical material was unearthed, with the exception of a new portrait, described in Atlante, II, 107-08, by González de Amezúa, and a document discussed by Sánchez Marino in which Lope petitioned for the legitimization of a son who has not been identified (Anales Cervantinos, III, 380). The life and loves of Lope continued to attract biographers and popularizers. A superior kind of popular treatment was that by Ricardo del Arco, who contributed an excellent chapter on Lope to the Historia general de las literaturas hispánicas, edited by Guillermo Díaz-Plaja.

An outstanding study on the Comedia was Wardropper's Introducción al teatro religioso del Siglo de Oro. Although fewer than twenty pages of the volume are devoted to Lope, Wardropper's conclusions, based upon detailed analysis of three of his autos sacramentales, have significance for his dramatic production as a whole. Other elements of Lope's theatre which were analysed included the motives for action, by Carlos Ortigoza, whose Los móviles de la "Comedia" treats of Lope in one of its chapters; theatrical irony in Peribáñez, by Roberto G. Sánchez (Clav, V, No. 29, 17-25); the meaning and structure of Fuenteovejuna, by G. W. Ribbans (BHS, XXXI, 150-70); and phonology by Tomás Navarro (Archivum, IV, 45-52). All of these studies resulted in new understanding or increased appreciation of Lope's dramatic technique, except Navarro's, which, as he commented, would have to be extended to more works of Lope and also to works of other authors of the same period before the results could be significant.

Both Sánchez and Ribbans challenged earlier assumptions: the first, regarding the lyrical and social value of Peribáñez; and the second, the nonessential character of the secondary plot in Fuenteovejuna. Other studies which challenged or refuted earlier theses were Arjona's study of El lacayo fingido, which showed convincingly, by means of rhyme and orthoëpy, that the extant play by this title is not Lope's play (SP, LI, 42-53); Avalle-Arce's "Dos notas a Lope de Vega," the second of which argued that Cubillo de Aragón's Tragedia del duque de Berganza does not deal with the same story as Lope's El duque de Viseo, which uses only three of the same characters and has an entirely different point of view (NRFH, VII, 426-32); Leavitt's defence of Feliciana in "A Maligned Character in Lope's El mejor alcalde el rey" (BCom, VI, No. 2, 1-3); and Bataillon's two articles showing that Pedro Carbonero was an outlaw whose exploits were known proverbially in the sixteenth century, but who was not associated with the siege of Granada until Lope made this association (RPh, VII, 26-34, and BH, LV, 375-77). Stiefel's suggestion that Tirso de Molina was indebted to Lope's La ocasión perdida and El secretario de sí mismo was submitted to examination by Gerald E. Wade in "The Literary Sources of El castigo del penséque of Tirso de Molina," and found to be true (South Atlantic Studies for Sturgis E. Leavitt, pp. 81-96).

In other studies of the drama in this period, van Dam clarified an obscure allusion in El bastardo Mudarra in the Academy edition by reference to the autograph of the play (RJ, VI, 342-43). Likewise, Reichenberger took advantage of the publication of the autograph of El piadoso aragonés to study the accuracy of the Academy edition, the handling of the original by the censor and the autor, and Lope's manner of composing (HR, XXI, 302-21). An amusing contribution to Lope chronology was offered by Thornton Wilder in "Lope, Pinedo, Some Child Actors and a Lion" (RPh, VII, 19-25). Arjona compared Lope's Amar, servir y esperar and Castillo Solórzano's El socorro en el peligro, which have identical plot, characters and names of characters, and showed that Lope was the borrower in this instance (RR, XL, 257-62). José Luis Micó Buchón analysed El divino africano (Humanidades, VI, 105-17).

With regard to Lope's non-dramatic literature, Morby made two small contributions to Dorotea scholarship with his discoveries of an early version of the Dorotea story in El Isidro (HR, XXI, 145-46) and of a miniature canzoniere of praise for Marta de Nevares in La Dorotea (RPh, VI, 289-93). Glaser found that Lope's attitude toward the Portuguese, especially the house of Braganza, varied and was much less admiring in his letters than in his poetry (BRAE, XXXIV, 387-411). J. H. Parker, in a study of the Orfeo en lengua castellana, which he believed Lope either wrote or approved, found culto devices in this work, but only half as many as in Juan de Jáuregui's Orfeo (RR, XL, 3-11). He concluded that Lope's criticism was directed against the excessive use of such devices. Inez Macdonald analysed La Gatomaquia (Atlante, II, 27-44) and Leo Spitzer related Al triunfo de Judit to the medieval trionfo and to pictorial representations of the story of Judith (MLN, LXIX, 1-11).

Lope de Vega continued to attract candidates for advanced degrees. Besides the studies by Ortigoza and Ramírez de Arellano, already mentioned, which originated as doctoral dissertations, a number of unpublished doctoral theses belong to these years: Charles L. Adams analysed traditional and novelesque elements in the development of plot in the dated plays, William F. Heald compared plot patterns of Lope and Shakespeare, Cecilia Ross prepared a critical edition of La hermosa Ester, Consuelo W. Seymour analysed popular elements and the idea of justice in Lope's comedias and Oscar M. Villarejo studied relations between Lope and the Elizabethan and Jacobean drama. In Paris, as mémoires, Christiane Jouisse compared plays of Lope with refundiciones of the same plays by Moreto, and Jeannine Pascal selected plays by Lope and Tirso that had similar themes and compared them. Both studies demonstrated major differences in dramatic technique between the dramatists compared and contrasted.

1955-1956

In 1955-56, for drama, Arjona continued his research with a most painstaking study of Lope's rhyming habits and technique in the autograph comedias (HR, XXIII, 108-28). Arjona's investigation, positivistic and scientific, was highly successful and effective, and revealed an excellent criterion for the establishment of authorship. For the analysis of individual plays, two articles on Fuenteovejuna, by Spitzer (HR, XXIII, 274-92) and Wardropper (SP, LIII, 159-71), deserve to be singled out. Devoted to style analysis, they applied this technique to the study of the organic and structural unity of the work. And from the number of comedias associated in some way with Lope treated in 1955-56, it is evident that continuing interest in the dramatist was very strong. Examples of this are the investigation of the "debate amoroso" in Amar sin saber a quién by Miss Bravo-Villasante (RL, VII, 193-99); reference to La campana de Aragón by Simón Díaz (RL, VII, 30-49); the discussion of the date of El cuerdo en su casa, with allusion to "bigoteras," by William E.

Wilson (BCom, VII, No. 2, 29-31); the analysis of the Biblioteca de Palacio MS of *Las ferias de Madrid*, with a comparison with the Cotarelo edition, by Bruerton (BH, LVII, 56-69); the comparison of Lope's *La hermosa Ester* with Pinto Delgado's *Poema de la reyna Ester* by Fishlock (BHS, XXXII, 81-97); an addition to Leavitt's previous note on *El mejor alcalde el rey* by Sloman (BCom, VII, No. 2, 17-19); a play analysis and source study of *El niño inocente de la Guardia* by Glaser (BHS, XXXII, 140-53); a study of the source of *La quinta de Florencia* by Leighton (NRFH, X, 1-12); and a discussion of the authorship of *El príncipe melancólico* by Arjona (HR, XXIV, 42-49). Hoge printed his thesis-edition of *El príncipe despeñado* and Sheppard edited, as an unpublished doctoral dissertation, *El villano en su rincón*. Likewise, as doctoral theses, Lionetti wrote on Ariosto's influence on Lope's plays and Marín produced his later-to-be-published study of *La intriga secundaria*.

Lope and modern psychology caught the attention of three critics: Fucilla (BCom, VII, No. 2, 22-23), Arjona (BCom, VIII, No. 1, 5-6) and Bousfield (American Psychologist, X, 828). Arjona did a serious study of false Andalusian rhymes in Lope's theatre (HR, XXIV, 290-305) and Adams entered into the problem of a motif-index with special reference to Lope (BCom, VII, No. 1, 1-3).

For poetry, Entrambasaguas continued his publications on "villancicos a los Misterios del Rosario" attributed to Lope (RL, VII, 3-18, and IX, 72-81) and Montesinos treated the history of a *romance* by Lope: *Una estatua de Cupido* (Symposium, IX, 1-18). Pierce devoted attention to the *Jerusalén conquistada* (BHS, XXXIII, 93-98) and Powers studied *Las lágrimas de la Madalena*, making reference to imagery (CL, VIII, 273-90).

The years 1955-56 are important for research on *La Dorotea*. Besides the edition by Blecua, Morby dealt with proverbs in the work (RPh, VIII, 243-59) and Trueblood wrote an article of fundamental importance on "The Case for an Early *Dorotea*" (PMLA, LXXI, 755-98). Re-evaluating the problem of the creative process and artistic genesis of Lope's novel, Trueblood threw new light on this complex work.

Special mention should be made of the José Simón Díaz-Juana de José Prades *Ensayo de una bibliografía de ... Lope de Vega*, which, in spite of certain shortcomings, was a valiant attempt to bring together a vast amount of Lope material.

1957-1958

Scholarly activity relating to Lope in 1957-58 presents contrasting pictures in the dramatic and non-dramatic areas of his production. The results attained by direct research on his plays were less striking than the gain in understanding of the nature of his drama as a whole. In the non-dramatic area, the noteworthy achievements came in studies of particular and often very limited aspects, and in one major edition rather than in work of broad scope.

Two articles stood out for their clear exposition of the newer methods of analysis of Spanish plays developed and effectively applied by British scholars, methods which take into account critical techniques applied by students of the drama in other areas and ages and are based on a consideration of stylistic, thematic, moral and historical factors. The principles set forth in A. A. Parker's The Approach to the Spanish Drama of the Golden Age suit especially well a formalized drama like that of Calderón, but their results are also illuminating when applied to Lope's best plays. Parker emphasizes the central importance of theme as a unifying factor and a key to meaning, theme conveyed directly through action subservient to moral purpose and worked out by means of dramatic casuality. More restricted in approach, but similarly illuminating, was Wardropper's "Poetry and Drama in Calderón's El médico de su honra" (RR, XLIX, 3-11). Viewing Golden Age plays as dramatic poetry, the author suggests that they are best understood when action, character and dialogue are seen as subservient to poetic rather than dramatic effect. They are to be looked upon as extensions of metaphor by dramatic means. One will locate the dominant patterns of imagery and explore their implications in order to grasp the play's structure and meaning. Although in Lope's case this approach tends to underestimate the importance of his strong "sense of theatre" and the histrionic bent of his imagination, it has the virtue of drawing attention to an aspect of his theatre whose importance is not always seen.

A third work of the greatest value for the general orientation of the student of Lope was Cioranescu's El barroco o el descubrimiento del drama. This masterly monograph, free of preconceived ideas, subjects the still ill-defined phenomenon of the baroque to the most searching and sensible re-examination and in the process sheds light on the nature and extent of Lope's affinities with it. The approach is stylistic, formalistic and thematic rather than ideological. The baroque is seen as a dynamic art that seeks to capture life in movement, action and complexity, under the guidance of wit, not imagination, with an uneasy awareness of contrast and conflict and nostalgia for a lost equilibrium. Doubt lies at the heart of the baroque drama. In the Spanish theatre, however, within the characteristic baroque dualism, doubt rarely becomes truly problematical since the "metaphysical criterion" can always provide a definitive resolution.

Turning to Lope scholarship proper, one has no hesitation in singling out Morby's edition of La Dorotea not only as the crowning achievement of 1957-58, but as a permanent landmark. The introductory study and the copious penetrating and all-embracing annotation bring to this difficult work the same type of painstaking imaginative scholarship as characterizes the best critical editions of Lope's creations in other genres. The central importance of the acción en prosa in Lope's vast production makes the accomplishment particularly significant and the complexity and difficulty of La Dorotea makes this well-indexed edition a valuable reference work.

While the study of Lope's theatre saw no comparable achievement, two valuable new instruments in this area deserve special mention.

Understanding of the nature and functioning of the unity of action was greatly advanced (in print) by the systematic analyses in Marín's La intriga secundaria en el teatro de Lope de Vega, which reveals a surprisingly consistent procedure and in its inductive approach provides a sound basis for grasping how Lope actually conceived of the unity of action and how much importance he attached to it. A helpful tool for the scholar working in one segment of Lope's theatre is Brown's careful and thorough Bibliografía de las comedias históricas, tradicionales y legendarias de Lope de Vega.

Certain items relating to individual comedias deserve mention. Correa's distinction between vertical and horizontal honour proved a sensitive critical tool when applied to Peribáñez (HR, XXVI, 188-99). In Cappelletti's "Notas sobre tres dramas y una epopeya de la libertad" (Universidad, No. 36, 237-49), the timeliness of Fuenteovejuna was revealed by linking the play to an up-to-date analysis of the implications of liberty. Camus' lively translation of El caballero de Olmedo into vigorous French prose expressly tailored to the needs of modern actors underscored the vitality of the play, while his moving foreword pointed out that the fresh world of Lope's theatre, with its dynamic, decisive and committed characters, has much to say to the "ashen" Europe of today. Among editions of individual plays, that of El cardenal de Belén by Elisa Aragone deserves particular mention.

In the field of Lope's lyric verse, the brief article by Peter Dunn, "Some Uses of Sonnets in the Plays of Lope de Vega" (BHS, XXXIV, 212-22), opened up a fertile field for study and employed an original and suggestive method of analysis to bring out a variety of dramatic functions which sonnets fulfil. Glaser's Estudios hispano-portugueses demonstrated in the case of two lyrical sonnets the fruitful results that can be attained by a skilful use of a detailed stylistic and historical analysis. Palm's remarks on Lope's letras and ballads, accompanying his translation into German, however unpretentious and unsystematic, abound in acute suggestive insights. In the area of Lope's less purely lyrical verse, Müller-Bochat's study of his "triumph" poetry shed a great deal of light on Lope's relationship to his predecessors and to the manifestations of this traditional motif in plastic and pictorial art.

Valuable as these contributions are, viewing the picture from 1957-58, it is evident that major work remains to be done in the whole area of Lope's lyric and shorter non-dramatic verse. A much closer approximation needs to be made towards the establishment of a canon of Lope's ballad production as a precondition for a study of its formal, stylistic and other characteristics. Lope's art of the sonnet, detailed study of the themes, techniques and style of particular sonnet collections, a broad re-examination of longer lyrics like those reflecting the vicissitudes of his last years — this is merely a sampling of some directions scholarly activity could take in this area.

1959-1960

The chief contributions to Lope de Vega studies in 1959-60 seem to be largely of an analytical nature, wherein some aspect of Lope was studied or examined, as distinct from exclusively factual treatments, editions and translations of texts, and the like. To a greater or lesser degree, this is true of what we have in writings by Arjona, Artman, Boorman, Casalduero, Gaos, Glaser (especially regarding La hermosa Ester, in Sefarad, XX, 110-35), Guerrieri Crocetti, Iventosch, López Navío, May, Morby, Oliver, Parker, Rosendorfsky, Rovner, Sanzoles, Sinicropi and Yates.

Not many dissertations were completed, but the critical edition of La villana de Getafe by Gunda S. Kaiser (unpublished doctoral dissertation) is noteworthy. For biography, an article by McCready, "Lope de Vega's Birth Date and Horoscope" (HR, XXVIII, 313-18), was an important and timely contribution, anticipating the quadricentennial by sufficient time to set celebrations on the newly-established date, December 12, new style. McCready, in rejecting November 25, pointed to Pérez de Montalván's confusing of two saints' names, and appealed to astrological data found in Lope's writings.

Several well-known and older articles and books were re-issued or appeared in different forms; e.g., Casalduero's "Fuenteovejuna" (TDR, IV, 83-107) and Spitzer's "Fuenteovejuna" and "Al triunfo de Judit" (Romanische Literaturstudien), as well as the Colección Austral edition of La Dorotea and of Peribáñez and La Estrella de Sevilla, the Colección Crisol edition of four plays and the Blecua edition of Poesía lírica. In the latter connection, it is gratifying to note that Lope, the poet, was not entirely neglected in favour of Lope, the dramatist, however much the two overlap each other. Still on the subject of editions, it would of course be visionary in the extreme to expect every biennium to produce works of the stature of the Fichter edition of El sembrar en buena tierra, or the Morby edition of La Dorotea. In fact, one is tempted to suggest that these two contributions and the Morley-Bruerton Chronology are probably the outstanding achievements of the quarter-century with which our whole survey is concerned.

1961

The year 1961 produced several doctoral dissertations on some aspect of Lope, attesting to the interest he continued to evoke in university graduate studies. Both editions and studies of themes were involved; for example, Scungio's critical edition of La discordia en los casados (with a study of Lope's use of Italian novelle as source material for his plays), Pianca's paleographic edition of Don Lope de Cardona, Hawley's critical edition of Las hazañas del Cid, Ziomek's paleographic edition of La nueva victoria de D. Gonzalo de Córdoba, Fox's critical edition of El poder en el discreto (with a subject index of illustrative anecdotes in the comedias novelescas y costumbristas) and McCready's study of La heráldica en las obras de Lope de Vega y sus contemporáneos.

The spate of editions of El villano en su rincón, with accompanying studies, was due to the play's being prescribed for the Spanish secondary school course leading to the bachillerato. Of the half-dozen editions, by various lopistas in Spain, and by various publishing houses there, perhaps the best is the one by Zamora Vicente; and, among the accompanying studies, Entrambasaguas' Lope de Vega y su tiempo is an authoritative monograph on Lope for pupils of secondary school age, as is the Correa Calderón-Lázaro, Lope de Vega y su época. A biography, Zamora Vicente's Lope de Vega: Su vida y su obra, provides an adequate and well-written account for the general reader. Among works printed in translation, Jill Booty's Five Plays, edited by Pring-Mill, is worthy of favourable comment, and Schroeder's refundición of El anzuelo de Fenisa, for "modern" acting, furnishes an interesting version.

The Morley and Tyler Los nombres de los personajes en las comedias de Lope de Vega: Estudio de onomatología, in two volumes, was a high point of the year; and the Pérez and Sánchez Escribano Afirmaciones de Lope de Vega sobre preceptiva dramática (the printing of the Pérez dissertation of 1957) made a creditable doctoral thesis generally available. Simón Díaz and Juana de José Prades are to be congratulated on their supplement (Nuevos estudios) to the earlier Lope bibliography (1955); and Ruth Lundelius did the Comedia a real service by giving us a practical and very readable account of Physical Aspects of the Spanish Stage in the Time of Lope de Vega.

Soons produced a keen analysis of El caballero de Olmedo in his "Towards an Interpretation..." (RF, LXXIII, 160-68), and also studied, with perspicacity, Fuenteovejuna as an historical play in its relation to manierismo (RF, LXXIII, 339-46). The outstanding Lope article of the whole year was without doubt McCrary's "Fuenteovejuna: Its Platonic Vision and Execution" (SP, LVIII, 179-92), where the play is called a "reconstruction of history according to the canons of a normative Platonic vision." Zamora Lucas edited Lope's Poesías preliminares de libros (from books written by Lope's friends), and Morby's edition of La Dorotea (1958) continued to receive enthusiastic reviews; but poetry and prose were generally neglected.

In anticipation of the quadricentennial of Lope's birth, many studies were "in progress" and nearing completion, intended as homenajes to the Fénix in 1962.

Annotated Bibliography

EDITIONS

GENERAL

Vega Carpio, Lope Félix de. *Obras escogidas*. Tomo primero: *Teatro*. Tomo segundo: *Poesías líricas, Poemas, Prosa, Novelas*. Ed. Federico Carlos Sainz de Robles. Madrid, Aguilar, 1946. Pp. 1723, 1965. 2nd ed.: 1952-53; Tomo tercero: *Teatro* (additional plays), 1955. (Later eds. published.)
Rev: Vol. I (2nd ed.): E. A. Peers, *BHS*, XXIX(1952), 170-71.
Vol. I contains *Estudio preliminar*: "Retrato, horóscopo, vida y transfiguración de Lope de Vega," "La obra de Lope de Vega," "Bibliografía de Lope de Vega." The *Comedias* are preceded by a "Nota preliminar." *BAE* and *RAE* texts are followed. The edition lacks scholarly value, and problems are handled in an arbitrary manner; e.g., the authorship of *La Estrella de Sevilla*, which Sainz de Robles insists is by Lope, but which most critics believe to have been written by some other dramatist.

------. *El caballero de Olmedo, seguido de una antología lírica y dramática* (*Fuenteovejuna, La dama boba*). Ed. Guillermo Díaz-Plaja. Barcelona-Buenos Aires, La Espiga-Editorial Ciordia, 1961. Pp. 246. (Clás. de Siempre, 6.)
Contains a prologue and footnotes to *El caballero de Olmedo*. The *antología* consists of selections from Lope's lyric and dramatic poetry, and from his prose.

------. *Peribáñez y el comendador de Ocaña, El mejor alcalde el rey, El castigo sin venganza, La Estrella de Sevilla, La Dorotea* (2 vols.), *Los comendadores de Córdoba, La noche de San Juan*. 8 vols. Madrid, Hernando, 1934-35. (Bib. Universal, 185-92.)
Rev: W. L. Fichter, *HR*, V(1937), 188-89.

------. *El villano en su rincón, Poesías, Antología dramática*. Ed. Guillermo Díaz-Plaja. Barcelona-Buenos Aires, La Espiga-Editorial Ciordia, 1961. Pp. 226. (Clás. de Siempre, 1.)
Contains a prologue and footnotes to *El villano en su rincón*, with selections from Lope's lyric and dramatic poetry, and from his prose.

DRAMA

A. GENERAL

Teatro clásico español. Buenos Aires, El Ateneo, 1958. Pp. 1219. (Clás. Inolvidables.)
    Includes La dama boba and Fuenteovejuna.

Vega, Lope de. Cancionero teatral. Ed. J. Robles Pazos. Baltimore, Johns Hopkins Univ. Press, 1935. Pp. 114.
  Rev: C. E. Anibal, MLN, LII(1937), 291-94.
    "An unpretentious collection of 138 songs from various plays of Lope de Vega" (Anibal).

------. Comedias. Ed. Luis Garner. 2 vols. Barcelona, 1956.

------. Comedias. Tomo I: El remedio en la desdicha, El mejor alcalde el rey. Ed. J. Gómez Ocerín and R. M. Tenreiro. Nueva ed. Madrid, Espasa-Calpe, 1960. Pp. 272. (Clás. Cast., 39.)
    Merely a re-issue of the well-known edition of 1920. The introduction, notes and pagination are the same.

------. Sus comedias más famosas. Buenos Aires, El Ateneo, 1951. Pp. 750. (Clás. Inolvidables.)
    Contains: "Silueta de Lope de Vega," by Alfonso Reyes; El arte nuevo de hacer comedias and eight comedias: Fuenteovejuna, El mejor alcalde el rey, El caballero de Olmedo, Peribáñez, La Estrella de Sevilla, El villano en su rincón, La dama boba, La niña de plata and the auto sacramental, La siega. No textual notes.

------. Five Plays: Peribáñez, Fuenteovejuna, The Dog in the Manger, The Knight from Olmedo, Justice without Revenge. Trans. Jill Booty; ed. R. D. F. Pring-Mill. New York, Hill and Wang, 1961. Pp. xli, 278. (Mermaid Dramabook.)
    A review by Juana de José Prades (RL, XIX, 1960, 312-13) praises the introduction, but objects to the at times too free translation which misses the spirit of the original.

------. Teatro. Ed. Luis Santullano. Mexico, Orión, 1945. Pp. 238. (Col. Lit. "Cervantes", 10.)
    Contains: Peribáñez, Fuenteovejuna, El mejor alcalde el rey. The prologue deals in general terms with Lope's life and works. Not a critical edition, but merely reproduces the BAE texts.

------. El amor enamorado, El caballero de Olmedo. Buenos Aires-Mexico, Espasa-Calpe, 1946. Pp. 160. (Col. Austral, 638.)
    Not a critical edition. Makes popularly accessible El amor enamorado (Acad., VI).

------. El caballero de Olmedo, La niña de plata. Madrid, Imp. Diana, 1948.

------. Richter..., nicht Rächer! (<u>El castigo sin venganza</u>), <u>Die kluge Närrin</u> (<u>La dama boba</u>), <u>Die schlaue Susanne</u> (<u>La discreta enamorada</u>), <u>Das Unmöglichste von allem</u> (<u>El mayor imposible</u>), <u>Der verhexte Wald</u> (<u>La selva confusa</u>), <u>Die beiden Tellos</u> (<u>Los Tellos de Meneses</u>). 6 vols. Berlin, Widukind-Verlag, 1941. Pp. 127, 146, 197, 174, 138, 129.

------. <u>La dama boba</u>, <u>La niña de plata</u>. Buenos Aires-Mexico, Espasa-Calpe, 1946. Pp. 214. (<u>Col. Austral</u>, 574.) (Later eds.)
Not a critical edition. No notes. <u>BAE</u> text.

------. <u>La Estrella de Sevilla</u>, <u>Peribáñez</u>, <u>El caballero de Olmedo</u>, <u>Fuenteovejuna</u>. Ed. Federico Carlos Sainz de Robles. Madrid, Aguilar, 1948. Pp. 636. (<u>Col. Crisol</u>, 32.) (Later eds.)

------. <u>Fuenteovejuna</u>, <u>La Estrella de Sevilla</u>. In <u>Diez comedias del Siglo de Oro</u>, ed. Alpern and Martel, New York, Harper, 1939, pp. 73-234.

------. <u>Fuenteovejuna</u>, <u>La Estrella de Sevilla</u>, <u>Peribáñez y el comendador de Ocaña</u>. New York, Doubleday, 1961. Pp. 273.

------. <u>Fuenteovejuna</u>, <u>El mejor alcalde el rey</u>. Ed. César Bunster. Santiago, Chile, Edit. Universitaria, 1955.
Rev: E. García, <u>AUC</u>, CXIV(1956), 168-69.

------. <u>Fuenteovejuna</u>, <u>El mejor alcalde el rey</u>, <u>El perro del hortelano</u>. Barcelona, Cisne, 1940. Pp. 160. (<u>Teatro selecto clás.</u>, 3.)

------. <u>Fuenteovejuna</u>, <u>Peribáñez y el comendador de Ocaña</u>. Madrid, Taurus, 1959. Pp. 266. (<u>Ser y Tiempo</u>. <u>Temas de España</u>, 6.)
Texts only.

------. <u>Fuenteovejuna</u>, <u>Peribáñez</u>, <u>El mejor alcalde el rey</u>. Ed. Pedro Henríquez Ureña. Buenos Aires, Losada, 1938. Pp. 262.
Contains a short introductory essay and a few textual notes.

------. <u>Fuenteovejuna</u>, <u>Peribáñez y el comendador de Ocaña</u>, <u>El mejor alcalde el rey</u>, <u>La Estrella de Sevilla</u>. In Sainz de Robles, <u>El teatro español: Historia y antología (desde el siglo XIV al XIX)</u>, II, Madrid, Aguilar, 1942, pp. 69-447.

------. (<u>Fuenteovejuna</u> and <u>El robo de Elena</u>) Fontovejuna et L'Enlèvement d'Hélène (suivi de <u>La Dévotion à la Croix</u> et <u>La vie est un songe</u>, par Calderón). Paris, Mazenod, 1959. Pp. 224. (<u>Col. Les Écrivains célèbres</u>.)

------. *El mejor alcalde el rey, Fuenteovejuna*. Buenos Aires-Mexico, Espasa-Calpe, 1942. (Col. Austral.)

------. *La moza de cántaro, El caballero de Olmedo*. Adaptación para niños de A. J. M. Madrid, Aguilar, 1961. Pp. 112.

------. *Peribáñez, El caballero de Olmedo, La dama boba*. Ed. Guillermo de Torre. Barcelona, Éxito, 1951. Pp. lxxii, 371. (Clás. Jackson, 13.)

------. *Peribáñez y el comendador de Ocaña, La Estrella de Sevilla*. Madrid, Espasa-Calpe, 1938. Pp. 225. (Col. Austral, 43.) (Later eds.)

------. *Peribáñez, La Estrella de Sevilla, El caballero de Olmedo*. Madrid, Nuevas Edit. Unidas, 1958. Pp. 358.

------. *La prueba de los amigos*, ed. L. B. Simpson; *La batalla del honor*, ed. R. K. Spaulding; *El cordobés valeroso Pedro Carbonero*, ed. M. A. Zeitlin; *El desdén vengado*, ed. I. A. Leonard. Berkeley-Madrid, Univ. of California Press-Gráficas Reunidas, 1934-35. Pp. 145, 141, 148, 157. (*Autógrafos de Lope de Vega Carpio*.)
Rev: W. L. Fichter, HR, V(1937), 84-87.

------. The above *autógrafos*, plus *El bastardo Mudarra*. Ed. S. G. Morley. 1935. Pp. 151.
Rev: William J. Entwistle, MLR, XXXII(1937), 641-43; E. Allison Peers, BHS, XVI(1939), 159-60.

------. *El remedio en la desdicha, El villano en su rincón, La siega*. Ed. José María Mohedano. Madrid, S.A.E.T.A., 1945. Pp. 320.

B. INDIVIDUAL PLAYS

------. *El anzuelo de Fenisa*. Recast by Juan Germán Schroeder. Madrid, Alfil, 1961. Pp. 104. (Col. Teatro, 310 Extra.)
A very modest and inexpensive edition, with a short foreword commenting on the play's history and aesthetic qualities. The editor states that "la presente refundición, atenta a la comprensión popular, ha pretendido conseguir la máxima agilidad y un acercamiento en diversos momentos escénicos al gusto e imperativos estéticos de nuestros días, para que con ello alcanzase una acogida que nos la devolviese del injusto olvido." The *refundición* was presented in Madrid on Mar. 3, 1961.

------. *El arauco domado*. Ed. A. de Lezama. Santiago de Chile, Zig-Zag, 1953.

------. El Brasil restituido. Ed. José Maria Viqueira Barreiro, with a study of "El lusitanismo de Lope de Vega." Coimbra, Coimbra Editora, 1950. Pp. vi, 351.
Rev: João Maio, Brotéria, LII(1951), 119-20 (uncritical); A. G. R., HR, XIX(1951), 370-71 (poor edition, value consists mainly in the collection of Lope's views on Portugal); María Goyri de Menéndez Pidal, NRFH, IV(1951), 412-13 (of the same opinion).

------. El caballero de Olmedo. Ed. José M. Blecua. Zaragoza, Ebro, 1941. (Clás. Ebro.) (Later eds.)

------. El caballero de Olmedo. Ed. Joaquín de Entrambasaguas. Barcelona, Horta, 1948. Pp. 113.
Rev: Matilde López Serrano, Rev. Bibliográfica y Documental, III (1949), 306-07 ("Uno de los más bellos resultados bibliográficos del año 1948").
Bibliophile ed. of 110 copies.

------. Le Chevalier d'Olmedo. Trans. Albert Camus. Paris, Gallimard, 1957. Pp. 208.

------. El caballero de Olmedo. Madrid, Alfil, 1961. Pp. 102. (Col. Teatro, 295 Extra.)
An inexpensive edition, with a short page of comment on the play's history, and a brief biography of Lope.

------. El caballero de Olmedo. Mexico, Helio, 1961. Pp. 250.

------(?). El caballero de Olmedo (attributed to Cristóbal de Morales). Ed. Eduardo Juliá Martínez. Madrid, CSIC, 1944. Pp. 216. (Rev. de Bibliografía Nac., Anejo 2.)
Rev: María Jiménez Salas, Arbor, III(1945), 171-73; William L. Fichter, HR, XIV(1946), 264-70.
In his review, Fichter gives an account of this early Caballero de Olmedo (1606), written by an obscure author, and which inspired Lope's famous work. E. J. M. edits the MS for the first time, and attributes it to Cristóbal de Morales. Fichter is not convinced by the arguments brought forward, but concludes that "Although further work remains to be done on Cristóbal de Morales, Sr. Juliá Martínez has rendered a service in bringing together the known material and in having attempted an initial approach to the play."

------. El cardenal de Belén. Ed. T. Earle Hamilton, Lubbock, Texas Tech. Press, 1948. Pp. xii, 139.
Rev: Arnold G. Reichenberger, Hisp, XXXIII(1950), 283-84 (generally favourable; but offers many suggestions for improved punctuation, and points out minor flaws in the text); Mabel Margaret Harlan, HR, XIX(1951), 269-74 (substantially along the same lines as the foregoing review; offers still more emendations in punctuation).

A paleographic ed. of the autograph in the Biblioteca Medicea
Laurenziana, Florence. Includes an extensive discussion of
the marks "for the guidance of the compositor."

------. El cardenal de Belén. Ed. Elisa Aragone. Zaragoza, Ebro,
    1957.
  Rev: J. J. Perlado, RL, XI(1957), 238-39.
  A student edition. Originally a doctoral thesis, University of
    Florence. Excellent prologue and helpful notes.

------. El castigo del discreto, "together with a Study of Conjugal
    Honor in (Lope's) Theater." Ed. William L. Fichter. New York,
    Inst. de las Españas, 1925. Pp. 283.
  Rev: Ludwig Pfandl, ZRP, LVIII(1938), 738-40.
  A highly praised edition and study.

------. El castigo sin venganza. Ed. Joaquín de Entrambasaguas.
    Madrid, Centro de Estudios sobre Lope de Vega, 1944.

------. La corona de Hungría, with "An Introductory Study of the
    Treatment of the Reina Sevilla Legend in the Theater of Lope
    de Vega." Ed. Richard W. Tyler. Unpub. doct. diss., Brown
    Univ., 1946. Pp. 198.
  Based on the autograph MS. Comparison with Los pleitos de
    Ingalaterra, "The earlier play from which much of La corona is
    copied." The discussion of the legend refers to eleven of
    Lope's plays, largely from the point of view of whether or not
    a champion defends the accused woman, in a combat judiciare.

------(?). La cruz en la sepultura. Ed. H. C. Heaton. New York,
    New York Univ. Press, 1948. Pp. xi, 61.
  Rev: A. G. Reichenberger, Hisp, XXXII(1949), 404-05; E. W. Hesse,
    HR, XVIII(1950), 184-85.
  "Provisionally edited from a rare suelta," attributed on differ-
    ent occasions to Ruiz de Alarcón, Lope and Calderón. H. C. H.
    would, at most, give "a hesitant assignment of the play to
    Lope." Heaton believes that this play, probably by an unknown
    dramatist, was later refurbished by Calderón as La devoción de
    la cruz, but the reviewers believe that the suelta is Calderón's
    La devoción in an earlier, defective version. La cruz en la
    sepultura is almost certainly not by Lope.

------. La dama boba. Ed. Francisco Tolsada. Zaragoza, Ebro, 1945.
    Pp. 146. (Bib. Clás. Ebro, 61.)
  A good popular edition, with an introduction on Lope's life and
    times, the characteristics of his Comedia, an analysis of the
    play, and a brief bibliography.

------. La dama boba. Ed. Isidoro Montiel. Madrid, Castilla, 1948.
    Pp. 229. (Bib. Clás. Castilla, 5.)

The introduction contains a general discussion of Lope's women and the dramatist's attitude toward women. There is an analysis of the play, its characters and of Lope's dramatic technique. The text is said to follow the autograph, but does not do so very well. There are some 56 pages of notes.

------. La dama boba. In Teatro clásico español (1958). See Editions — Drama — General.

------. Del monte sale (quien el monte quema). Ed. Emilio LeFort Peña. Buenos Aires, La Facultad, 1939. Pp. 220. (Doct. diss., Univ. of Minnesota, 1935.)
 Rev: Enrique Anderson-Imbert, Sur, X(1940), 83-85; Raúl Moglia, RFH, II(1940), 186-90.
 A paleographic edition. Introduction, pp. 11-89; text, pp. 93-203; notes, pp. 207-14.

------. La discordia en los casados, with "A Study of Lope de Vega's Use of Italian Novelle as Source Material for his Plays." Ed. Raymond L. Scungio. Unpub. doct. diss., Brown Univ., 1961.

------. (La discreta enamorada?) Preríkoná milenka. Trans. Vítazoslav Hecko. Bratislava, Diliza, 1959. Pp. 112. (Bib. cídaje.)

------. (El doctor simple?) Doctors All. A One-Act Farce after Lope de Vega. By Moritz Adolf Jagendorf. New York, Samuel French, 1937. Pp. 27.

------(?). Don Gil de la Mancha. Ed. Paul F. Larenow. Unpub. doct. diss., Univ. of New Mexico, 1955. (DA, XV, 1846.)
 Decides against Lope's authorship.

------. Don Lope de Cardona. Ed. Alvin Hugo Pianca. Unpub. doct. diss., Univ. of Wisconsin, 1961. (DA, XXI, 3790.)
 MS 17, 417, Biblioteca Nacional.

------. Los embustes de Celauro. Ed. Joaquín de Entrambasaguas. Zaragoza, Ebro, 1942. Pp. 142.
 Rev: J. M. Alda Tesán, RFE, XXVI(1942), 123-25.
 This edition makes available one of Lope's lesser known plays. Assigning it to a group dealing with "temas de la vida familiar y casera," Entrambasaguas considers as a principal factor in its merit "la exaltación de lo cotidiano."

------(?). La Estrella de Sevilla. Ed. Reed, Dixon and Hill. Boston, Heath, 1939. Pp. xxxix, 269.
 John M. Hill's outstanding introduction states that the author of La Estrella de Sevilla would appear to be an Andalusian of high dramatic ability.

------. (<u>Fuenteovejuna</u>.) <u>The Sheep Well</u>. Trans. John Garrett
   Underhill. In <u>Poetic Drama: An Anthology of Plays in Verse
   from the Ancient Greek to the Modern American</u>, ed. Alfred
   Kreymborg, New York, Modern Age Books, 1941, pp. 424-48.
  Many passages are rendered in prose.

------. <u>Fuenteovejuna</u>. Ed. E. Allison Peers. Liverpool, Inst. of
   Hispanic Studies, 1946. Pp. vii, 98. (<u>Plain Text Series</u>, 11.)

------. <u>Fuenteovejuna</u>. Ed. William Smith Mitchell. London, Bell,
   1948. Pp. 169. (<u>Bell's Spanish Classics</u>.)
  Rev: Raymond R. MacCurdy, <u>Hisp</u>, XXXIII(1950), 178 (an ed. for
   students, providing much background material. Editor missed
   Anibal's "Historical Background...," <u>PMLA</u>, 1934); Gerald E.
   Wade, <u>MLJ</u>, XXXV(1951), 82-83 ("There are all too few notes,"
   and of these, "too many ... are inaccurate." "On the whole,
   one must regretfully conclude that the text is not done well
   enough to meet the standards for an acceptable text-book of
   the <u>Comedia</u>.").

------. <u>Fuenteovejuna</u>. Paris, Les Ordres de Chevalerie, 1948. Pp.
   200.
  With brief introduction by Jean Camp. Printed on heavy paper,
   with large type. A "library," rather than a scholarly edition.
   Attractively illustrated by Carlos Fontseré. Spanish text.

------. <u>Font-aux-Cabres</u>. Adapted by Jean Cassou and Jean Camp.
   Paris, Les Ordres de Chevalerie, 1948.
  This was the version presented at the Sarah Bernhardt Theatre
   and at the Théâtre du Peuple, Paris, in 1937-38. (See M. M.
   du Gard, <u>Les Nouvelles Littéraires</u>, Feb. 12, 1938.)

------. <u>Fuenteovejuna</u>. Ed. Ariel Ángel Dasso. Buenos Aires, Marcos
   Sastre, 1951. Pp. 102.
  Rev: J. Ibáñez, <u>Rev. Javeriana</u>, XXXVIII(1952), 60; J. Mendes,
   <u>Brotéria</u>, LVIII(1954), 377-78.
  Eight pages of introduction are devoted to Lope's biography and
   a plot summary. There are some brief notes of a lexical
   nature, but the real difficulties of the text are passed over.
   Small format.

------. <u>Fuenteovejuna</u>. Ed. Tomás García de la Santa. Zaragoza,
   Ebro, 1951. Pp. 108. (<u>Bib. Clás. Ebro</u>, 84.)
  One of the better editions in the collection. The introduction
   is fully adequate for the aims of the volume, and the editor
   has made use of American scholarship in the matter of sources,
   chronology and bibliography of texts. Follows the <u>Dozena
   parte</u>. The notes leave something to be desired.

------. <u>Fuenteovejuna</u>. Ed. Eugène Kohler. Strasbourg, Heitz, 1952. Pp. 142.
  Rev: C. V. Aubrun, <u>BH</u>, LIV(1952), 442; Eva Seifert, <u>VR</u>, XIII(1954), 417-18.
    There are twelve pages of introduction devoted to a biographical sketch of Lope and comments on the play. Unfortunately, the text follows the Acad. edition. The volume contains a table of versification (with more lines than the figures given by M.-B., <u>Chronology</u>) and forty-eight concise notes.

------. (<u>Fuenteovejuna</u>.) <u>Maayan Ha-Kevasim</u>. Hebrew trans. by Rafael Eliaz. Tel Aviv, Ha-kibbuz ha-meuhad, 1955. Pp. 254.

------. <u>Fuenteovejuna</u>. Ed. Eva Seifert. Halle, 1956.
  Rev: Wilhelm Berger, <u>NS</u>, VII, new series (1957), 443-44; G. Sobejano, <u>RF</u>, LXIX(1957), 176-80.

------. <u>Fuenteovejuna</u>. Buenos Aires, 1957. Pp. 158.

------. <u>Fuenteovejuna</u>. In <u>Masterpieces of the Spanish Golden Age</u>, ed. Ángel Flores, New York, Reinhart, 1957, pp. 235-86.
  English version by Ángel Flores and Muriel Kittel.

------. <u>Fuenteovejuna</u>. Mexico, Novara, 1958.

------. <u>Fuenteovejuna</u>. In <u>Teatro clásico español</u> (1958). See Editions — Drama — General.

------. <u>Fuenteovejuna</u>. Trans. Dominique Aubier. Paris, 1958. (<u>Col. Répertoire pour un Théâtre populaire</u>.)

------. <u>Fuenteovejuna</u>. Madrid, Escelicer, 1959. Pp. 88. (<u>Col. Teatro</u>, 220.)
  Text, and one page containing a few lines of comment.

------. <u>Fuenteovejuna</u>. In <u>The Classic Theatre</u>, ed. Eric Bentley, III, New York, Doubleday, 1959, pp. 161-231.
  English version by Roy Campbell.

------(?). <u>Las hazañas del Cid, y su muerte, con la tomada de Valencia</u>. Ed. Don Hawley. Unpub. doct. diss., Univ. of Iowa, 1961. (<u>DA</u>, XXII, 2793.)

------. <u>La hermosa Ester</u>. Ed. Cecilia Ross. Unpub. doct. diss., Univ. of California, 1952.

------. <u>El mejor mozo de España</u>. Ed. J. García Mercadal. Madrid, Aguado, 1951. Pp. 170. (<u>Col. Más Allá</u>, 37.)
  The introduction is a rather faithful reproduction of Menéndez Pelayo's study in the Acad. ed. No notes.

------. Los melindres de Belisa. Ed. Henriette C. Barrau. Amsterdam, H. J. Paris, 1933. Pp. 278.
  Rev: Wolfgang Wurzbach, ZRP, LVII(1937), 770-72.

------. El molino. Barcelona, Edit. Juventud, 1944. Pp. 207.

------. (La moza de cántaro.) Russian trans. by L. T. Schepkenoy-Koupernek. Moscow-Leningrad, Government Pub., 1946. Pp. 167.

------. La nueva victoria de don Gonzalo de Córdoba. Ed. Henryk Ziomek. Unpub. doct. diss., Univ. of Minnesota, 1961. (DA, XXII, 568.)
  Paleographic ed. of the autograph MS of Oct. 8, 1622. With variants. Includes a study of historical aspects. (See 1962 publications.)

------. (El nuevo mundo descubierto por Cristóbal Colón.) The Discovery of the New World by Christopher Columbus. Trans. Frieda Fligelman. Berkeley, Gillick Press, 1950. Pp. 62.
  Rev: Ramon Rozzell, Hisp, XXXV(1952), 376-77.

------. (El nuevo mundo descubierto por Cristóbal Colón.) French trans., 1953. See Studies — Drama — Individual Plays.

------. Las paces de los reyes y judía de Toledo. Ed. James A. Castañeda. Unpub. doct. diss., Yale Univ., 1958.
  See 1962 publications.

------. El palacio confuso, with "A Study of the Menaechmi Theme in Spanish Literature." Ed. Charles Henry Stevens. New York, Inst. de las Españas, 1939. Pp. xcii, 138. (Doct. diss., New York Univ., 1938.)
  Rev: G. Cirot, BH, XLII(1940), 178-80; W. L. Fichter, RR, XXXI(1940), 398-403; John M. Hill, HR, VIII(1940), 364-67.
  Includes the transcription of the text, notes, a detailed bibliography and a lengthy introduction.

------. Peribáñez. Trans. Eva R. Price. Redlands, California, Fine Arts Press, 1938.

------. Peribáñez y el comendador de Ocaña. In Cuatro comedias, ed. John M. Hill and Mabel M. Harlan, New York, Norton, 1941, pp. 1-177. (Reprinted: 1956.)
  Rev: Sturgis E. Leavitt, MLJ, XXV(1941), 896-97; W. J. Entwistle, MLR, XXXVII(1942), 101-02; H. C. Heaton, HR, X(1942), 73-79 (objects to the acceptance of "emendations" of past editors); of reprint, A. G. Reichenberger, HR, XXV(1957), 77-78.
  The edition is scholarly; the introduction and notes are excellent.

------. <u>Peribáñez y el comendador de Ocaña</u>. Ed. Charles V. Aubrun
and J. F. Montesinos. Paris, Hachette, 1943. Pp. xlix, 206.
Rev: W. J. Entwistle, <u>MLR</u>, XLIII(1948), 281-83.
Contains an excellent introduction.

------. <u>Peribáñez y el comendador de Ocaña</u>. Ed. J. M. Blecua.
Zaragoza, Ebro, 1944.

------. <u>Peribáñez y el comendador de Ocaña</u>. Ed. Juan Loveluck.
Santiago de Chile, Zig-Zag, 1954.

------. <u>El perro del hortelano</u>. Ed. E. Kohler. Paris, Les Belles
Lettres, 1951. Pp. lxix, 281. (<u>Texte d'Étude</u>, 4, Faculté des
Lettres, Univ. de Strasbourg.)
Rev: <u>Índice Cultural Español</u>, No. 67 (1951), 69-71; C. V. Aubrun,
<u>BH</u>, LIII(1951), 339-40; Ramon Rozzell, <u>HR</u>, XXI(1953), 164-69;
Ángel Valbuena Briones, <u>Clav</u>, V, No. 29 (1954), 78.
A <u>nouvelle édition critique</u>. A tremendous improvement over the
1934 edition. The introduction has profited from W. L.
Fichter's review. There are, however, some puzzling remarks
made in the section <u>Transmission du texte</u>; and it is not made
clear what the base text of the present one is. The copious
notes are placed on the page opposite the page of text to
which they correspond; many of them merely translate the
Spanish passage into French.

------. <u>Pies ogrodnika</u> (<u>El perro del hortelano</u>). Polish trans. by
Tadeuz Peiper. Warsaw, Panstw. Instytut Wydawn, n.d. Pp. 194.

------. <u>El piadoso aragonés</u>. Ed. James N. Greer. Austin, Univ. of
Texas Press, 1951. Pp. xi, 166. (<u>Univ. of Texas Hispanic
Studies</u>, 3.)
Rev: W. C. Atkinson, <u>BHS</u>, XXIX(1952), 120-21; C. V. Aubrun, <u>BH</u>,
LIV(1952), 95-96; J. de Entrambasaguas, <u>RL</u>, I(1952), 484-85; J.
García Arauz, <u>Arbor</u>, XXII(1952), 444-45; A. V. P., <u>Clav</u>, III,
No. 13 (1952), 74; A. G. Reichenberger, <u>HR</u>, XXI(1953), 351-53.
Based on the autograph of Aug. 17, 1626. Includes a commentary
on every peculiarity of the MS, Lope's afterthoughts, his modes
of correcting, and the censor's and <u>autor</u>'s alterations. There
is no study of the play itself or notes to explain the meaning
of the text.

------. <u>El poder en el discreto</u>. Ed. Arthur M. Fox, "together with
a Subject Index of Illustrative Anecdotes in (Lope's) <u>Comedias
novelescas y costumbristas</u>." Unpub. doct. diss., Univ. of
Toronto, 1961. Pp. lx, 270.
The dissertation bears out in detail the description of its
title. The text is taken from the autograph of May 8, 1623.
There are paleographic notes and others explanatory of the text.

The anecdotes total 117, and come from 59 *comedias*. An introduction explains what the author is trying to do and how he plans to achieve it. The dissertation gives evidence of careful workmanship throughout.

------. El príncipe despeñado. Ed. Henry H. Hoge. (Doct. diss., Univ. of Wisconsin, 1948.) Bloomington, Univ. of Indiana Press, 1955. Pp. x, 188. (Indiana Univ. Publications, Humanities Series, 33.)
Rev: R. R. MacCurdy, Hisp, XXXVIII(1955), 386-87; Margaret Crosland, MLR, LI(1956), 465; R. W. Tyler, MLQ, XVII(1956), 89-91 (objects to the citing of plays considered to be of doubtful authenticity by M.-B.); M. S. Carrasco Urgoiti, RHM, XXIII(1957), 59-60 (the edition is considered most praiseworthy); A. G. Reichenberger, HR, XXV(1957), 71-74 (the editor's work is highly commended despite a few errors in the notes, which the reviewer corrects. Reichenberger would evaluate the play more highly and sees the honra theme rather than the depiction of regicide as its principal interest); Ramon Rozzell, NRFH, XII(1958), 416-19 (the careful establishing of the text and the editor's introduction are praised; the absence of a critical evaluation of the work is regretted. Amplifications of and additions to the editor's notes are offered.).
Some minor changes and omissions occur in the printed version. These omissions include pages of criticism (cf. reviewers' comments) and the synopsis, as well as the quotations in the section on sources and some of the commentary. Some of the material omitted is to be found in the editor's article in PMLA, LXV(1950), 824-40. (See Studies — Drama — Individual Plays.)

------. Los Ramírez de Arellano. Ed. Diana Ramírez de Arellano. Madrid, Inst. de Estudios Madrileños, 1954. Pp. 298. (Doct. diss., Univ. of Madrid, 1952.)
Rev: Elena Catena de Vindel, RL, VI(1954), 419-21; A. Carballo Picazo, Clav, VI, No. 32 (1955), 73-74.
This "Contribución al estudio de las comedias genealógicas de Lope de Vega" is a very good edition, with attention directed especially to the genealogical character of the play.

------. El remedio en la desdicha. Ed. J. W. Barker. Cambridge, England, Cambridge Univ. Press, 1951. Pp. xxi, 116. (Reprint of 1931 ed.)

------. Santiago el verde. Ed. Ruth A. Oppenheimer. Hamburg, Preilipper, 1938. Pp. 205. (Doct. diss. in German, Univ. of Hamburg, 1938.) Published, in revised form, in Spanish: Madrid, CSIC, 1940. Pp. 220. (TAE, 9.)

Rev: J. A. T., RFE, XXIV(1937), 414-18 (the review compares this
German edition unfavourably with the forthcoming Spanish ed.);
W. L. Fichter, HR, VII(1939), 357-59.
The German version has as subtitle: "eine Comedia von Lope de
Vega Carpio, zum ersten Mal nach der Handschrift des Britischen
Museums kritisch herausgegeben mit einer Studie und
Anmerkungen." The Spanish version devotes pp. 143-209 to a
detailed discussion of the play, and provides a bibliography
and an index.

------. El sembrar en buena tierra. Ed. William L. Fichter. New
York, Modern Language Association of America (London, Oxford
Univ. Press), 1944. Pp. xiv, 247. (MLA General Series, Vol.
XVII.)
Rev: Ashley Dukes, Theatre Arts, XXIX(1945), 255b; W. J. Entwistle,
MLR, XL(1945), 323 ("the edition of the text, the notes and
the introduction are wholly commendable"); Mabel M. Harlan,
HR, XIII(1945), 355-58 ("in providing Hispanists with the text
of Lope's El sembrar en buena tierra, and with the abundant
critical apparatus that goes with it, Professor Fichter has
made an admirable contribution of further definitiveness on a
number of points"); Merle I. Protzman, Hisp, XXVIII(1945),
458-60; C. E. Anibal, RR, XXXVII(1946), 252-68 ("Mr. Fichter's
exemplary patience in research, his long-standing and intimate
acquaintance with the Comedia of Lope and his contemporaries,
his fine sense of values, and his editorial integrity and
meticulousness combine to make this book in many respects a
model of its kind. The MLA, aided by a grant from the Hispanic Society, has made it Volume XVII of its General Series.
It is the first work in Spanish literature to be there
included, and one hopes, in view of the great number of
seventeenth-century Spanish dramas which still cry eloquently
for lebensraum, that it will not be the last. But it will be
properly difficult for subsequent editors to compete with the
quality of this auspicious inauguration."); Raúl Moglia, RFH,
VIII(1946), 158-62; E. A. Peers, BHS, XXIII(1946), 159; M.
Puente Ojea, RFE, XXX(1946), 431-33.
An outstanding critical edition, as the reviews indicate.

------. La siega. Ed. José Fradejas Lebrero. Tetuán, Cremades,
1958. Pp. 87. (Bib. Clás. Bachillerato, 10.)
A useful students' edition of this auto. There is a schematic
introduction to Lope and to this work, and an even more
schematic introduction to the drama of the Golden Age.

------. La villana de Getafe. Ed. Gunda Sabina Kaiser. Unpub.
doct. diss., Univ. of Wisconsin, 1958. (DA, XIX, 2634.)
The play is dated as late 1613 or early 1614, because of "evidence found in Lope's correspondence with the Duke of Sessa."
An appendix deals with the life of the autor, Pedro de Valdés,
and Jerónima de Burgos, his wife, and Lope's sometime mistress.

------. *El villano en su rincón*. Ed. Douglas Claire Sheppard. Unpub. doct. diss., Univ. of Wisconsin, 1955. (DA, XVI, 341.)
"Lope manages to superimpose upon his comedia de costumbres rurales a comedia filosófica with overtones of the auto sacramental a lo profano."

------. *El villano en su rincón*. Ed. José Luis Aguirre. Valencia, Cosmos, 1961. Pp. 192.
An edición escolar, with the conventional type of introduction and notes. The attempt to include some additional passages from Lope is not very successful.

------. *El villano en su rincón*. Ed. José Manuel Blecua. Zaragoza, Ebro, 1961. Pp. 117. (Bib. Clás. Ebro.)
Surprisingly complete for such an inexpensive edition. Includes temas de trabajo escolar.

------. *El villano en su rincón*. Ed. Díaz-Plaja. 1961. See Editions — General.

------. *El villano en su rincón*. Ed. Entrambasaguas. 1961. See Studies — Drama — Individual Plays.

------. *El villano en su rincón*. Ed. Alonso Zamora Vicente. Madrid, Gredos, 1961. Pp. 174.
A carefully prepared textbook. Adequate bibliography, and a valuable and complete discussion of the play's sources.

The great number of ediciones escolares of *El villano en su rincón* in 1961 was inspired by the Spanish secondary school prescription for the bachillerato.

POETRY

A. GENERAL

Alfay, Josef. *Poesías varias de grandes ingenios españoles*. Ed. José M. Blecua. Zaragoza, Institución "Fernando el Católico" (CSIC), 1946. Pp. xv, 223.
Reprint of an anthology published by Alfay in 1654, in Zaragoza. Includes two poems attributed to Lope: "Soneto de Lope de Vega contra los cultos" (p. 54), and a décima satírica against Juan Ruiz de Alarcón (p. 81). The most valuable contribution is, however, a romance by Lope, "desconocido hasta hoy" (p. xii), which begins "Famoso Guadalquiví" (p. 167).

Buchanan, Milton A. (ed.). *Spanish Poetry of the Golden Age*. Toronto, Univ. of Toronto Press, 1942. Pp. i, 149. (Revised and reprinted, 1947.)
Lope de Vega: pp. 69-75; notes, 137-38.

Hesse, Everett W. (ed.). *Spanish Verse of the Sixteenth and Seventeenth Centuries*. Madison, Wisconsin, College Typing Co., 1950. Pp. 261.
  Lope de Vega: pp. 190-213.

Janner, Hans. (ed.). *La glosa en el Siglo de Oro: Una antología*. Madrid, 1946. Pp. 95. (Col. Ene.)
  Rev: Otis H. Green, *HR*, XV(1947), 408; Samuel Gili Gaya, *NRFH*, II(1948), 199 ("La peculiaridad española de este tipo de poetización había sido señalada, entre otros, por Lope de Vega...").
  The volume contains an essay on the *glosa* and its evolution in the Golden Age, and critical notes. Lope is represented by *glosas* XXVI-XXXI (pp. 49-57), two of which are by "Maestro Burguillos."

Moreno Báez, Enrique (ed.). *Antología de la poesía lírica española*. Madrid, Rev. de Occidente, 1952. Pp. lxiii, 565.
  Rev: M. Darbord, *BH*, LV(1953), 102.
  Includes Lope de Vega, pp. 251-65. There are no explanatory notes, but the introduction is very good.

Perry, Janet H. (ed.). *The Heath Anthology of Spanish Poetry*. Boston, Heath; London, Harrap; n.d. Pp. 468.
  Lope de Vega: pp. 256-67.

Rivers, Elias L. (ed.). *36 Spanish Poems*. Boston, Houghton Mifflin, 1957. Pp. vi, 72.
  Lope de Vega: pp. 48-49.

Roncaglia, Aurelio (ed.). *Poesia d'amore spagnola d'ispirazione melica popolaresca dalle "kharge" mozarabiche a Lope de Vega*. Modena, 1953.
  Rev: W. Cardoso, *RBFilol*, I(1956), 238-45; M. F. Alatorre, *NRFH*, XI(1957), 404-06.
  The care with which the seventy selections of this anthology are presented and studied, and the rich bibliography, make this an excellent guide for the student. The selections from Lope are *canciones populares*, folk songs, and not artistic adaptations of folk songs as suggested by the editor.

Sainz de Robles, Federico Carlos. *Historia y antología de la poesía castellana (del siglo XII al XX)*. Madrid, Aguilar, 1946. Pp. 1719. (2nd ed.: 1950.)
  Rev: M. Crowther, *BHS*, XXIV(1947), 63-65.
  Sainz de Robles includes several of Lope's poems whole or in part, and makes a brief study of them (pp. 103b-105b).

Tettenborn, P. D. (ed.). *Spanish Lyrics of the Golden Age*. London, Bell, 1952. Pp. 208.

Rev: E. C., <u>BHS</u>, XXIX(1952), 125.
    Lope de Vega: pp. 142-56. There is a brief introduction, but no notes.

<u>Translations from Hispanic Poets</u>. New York, Hispanic Society of America, 1938. Pp. xvi, 271.
    Includes four lyrics by Lope: pp. 64-72.

Vega, Lope de. <u>Cancionero divino</u>. <u>Antología de lírica sagrada</u>. 2nd ed.: Madrid, Bolaños y Aguilar, 1947. (1st ed.: Madrid, 1935.)

------. <u>Cardos del jardín de Lope</u>. <u>Sátiras del "Fénix"</u>. Ed. Joaquín de Entrambasaguas. Madrid, CSIC, 1942. Pp. 72.
  Rev: J. A. T., <u>RFE</u>, XXVI(1942), 370.
    Satires "Contra unos cómicos," "Contra don Luis de Góngora," and "Contra los preceptistas aristotélicos" (main attack aimed at Cristóbal Suárez de Figueroa and Torres Rámila).

------. <u>Flor nueva del "Fénix"</u>. <u>Poesías desconocidas y no recopiladas de Lope de Vega</u>. Ed. Joaquín de Entrambasaguas. Madrid, CSIC, 1942. Pp. 193.
  Rev: J. A. T., <u>RFE</u>, XXVI(1942), 121-22.
    "Poesías amorosas," "Sonetos a diferentes asuntos," "Epístolas" and "Elegías."

------. <u>Lieder und Romanzen</u>. Ed. Erwin W. Palm. Munich, Piper Verlag, 1958. Pp. 60.
    Twenty-eight <u>letras</u> and <u>romances</u> are translated into German, with a "Nachwort" (pp. 44-60), which stresses the fusion of traditional and mannered elements with fresh ones and brings out Lopean echoes in 20th century poets.

------. <u>Lírica</u>. Ed. Eugenio Nada. Barcelona, Montaner y Simón, 1943.

------. <u>Poesía lírica</u>. Ed. José Manuel Blecua. Zaragoza, Ebro, 1939. Pp. 126. (<u>Bib. Clás. Ebro</u>, 2.) (Later eds.)
  Rev: Enrique Terzano, <u>RFH</u>, III(1941), 183.
    Includes eleven selections not found in the Montesinos <u>Clás. Cast.</u> vols. 68 and 75. Good notes.

------. <u>Poesías líricas</u>. Ed. Agustín Millares Carlo. Mexico, Secretaría de Educación Pública, 1947.

------. <u>Poesías líricas</u>. Ed. José F. Montesinos. 2 vols. Madrid, Espasa-Calpe, 1951-52. (<u>Clás. Cast.</u>, 68, 75.)
    Substantially the same as the 1925-26 edition. The <u>Adiciones y enmiendas</u> of vol. 2 (1926) have been incorporated into the text.

------. *Poesías líricas*. 4th ed. Madrid, Espasa-Calpe, 1957. Pp. 168. (*Col. Austral*.)

------. *Poesías preliminares de libros*. Ed. Florentino Zamora Lucas. Madrid, CSIC, 1961. Pp. 73. (*Cuad. Bibliográficos*, 2.)
    A continuation and amplification of F. Cerdá's *Colección de las obras sueltas ... de Lope de Vega*. 82 poems of various types written by Lope from 1582 on as part of the preliminaries of books published by friends. Following each poem is the title of the book (and its author) in which the poem originally appeared.

------. *Poesías religiosas*. Mexico, Edit. Mexicanas, 1957. Pp. 140. (*Bib. Religiosa*.)

------. *Poésies et Chansons*. Trans. Mercedes Guillén and G. L. Mano. Paris, 1955.

------. *Poésies lyriques*. Trans. E. Vandercammen and F. Verhesen. Paris, Les Lettres, 1951. Pp. 109. (*Col. Parallèle*.)
    Lope's theatre has enjoyed a great vogue in France, but his poetry has been neglected. In 1910, there appeared a prose translation by M. H. Barthe in his *Morceaux choisis de Lope de Vega*. The 1951 volume is a careful poetic translation by two French poets; the 24 selections also appear in the original.

------. *Sus mejores poesías*. Barcelona, Bruguera, 1954. Pp. 126. (*Col. Laurel*, 9.)

B. INDIVIDUAL POEMS

Vega, Lope de. "Canción. *Castilla la Vieja*." *CHA*, No. 23 (1951), 281-82.
    "Naranjitas tiraba la niña / en Valencia por Navidad..."

------. *La Dragontea*. 2 vols. Madrid, Museo Naval, 1935 (not pub. until 1941).
    Rev: Joaquín de Entrambasaguas, *RFE*, XXV(1941), 127-29.
    Originally conceived as a 3-volume project (I: Text; II: *Repertorio* of pertinent documents in the MSS collection of the Museo Naval; III: *El vocabulario marítimo de Lope en "La Dragontea"*). Vol. III was lost during the Civil War. Radically modernized spelling.

------. *La Dragontea*. Ed. Dorothy Reeves Breen. Unpub. doct. diss., Univ. of Illinois, 1936. (Abstract, 19 pp., dated 1941.)
    Includes "Sources and Models," "Characters" and "Critical Estimate." Although literary value is denied the work, it is conceded that it has "definite value in the field of Spanish colonial history."

------. *La Gatomaquia*. Ed. Agustín del Campo. Madrid, Castilla, 1948. Pp. 245. (Bib. Clás. Castilla, 3.)

  A very small format, on Bible paper. The prologue contains a general discussion of Lope and the work. The notes are based on those of Rodríguez Marín (1935) and are extensive.

------. *La Jerusalén conquistada*. In Frank Pierce (ed.), The Heroic Poem of the Spanish Golden Age: Selections, New York, Oxford Univ. Press, 1947. Pp. xx, 231.

  The editor reproduces 90 of the some 6,000 stanzas of the poem. In his general introduction, he expresses the opinion that Lope was not gifted, intellectually or temperamentally, for the epic. He calls the poem diffuse and revealing little of Lope's genius, but in spite of its being generally condemned, it contains some passages of lyrical and heroic inspiration. There is a brief discussion of the poem's content, a select bibliography and notes on the selections given. A good, but incomplete, contribution to a neglected genre.

------. *La Jerusalén conquistada*. Epopeya trágica. Ed. Joaquín de Entrambasaguas. 3 vols. Madrid, CSIC, 1951-54. Pp. 515, 507, 420.

  Rev: I. S. Révah, BEPIF, XVIII(1954), 186; María S. Carrasco Urgoiti, RHM, XXI(1955), 155; Martín de Riquer, FiR, II(1955), 220-21; John Van Horne, HR, XXV(1957), 69-71.

  Vols. I and II contain the text, which is a faithful reproduction of the first edition (1609); Lope's own notes (references to sources and allusions) are included. Vol. III is the estudio crítico. The reviews are enthusiastic, and the entire edition is an important contribution to Lope de Vega scholarship.

------. *Romancero espiritual*. Ed. Luis Guarner. Valencia, Bernés, 1941. Pp. xl, 180. (2nd ed. revised: Romancero espiritual y Rimas sacras, Madrid, Castilla, 1949.) (Later eds.)

  Rev: (of 1st ed.): Juan Antonio Tamayo, RFE, XXVI(1942), 119-21; A. Lumsden, BHS, XXI(1944), 100-02.

------. *Soliloquios amorosos de un alma a Dios*. Ed. María Antonia Sanz Cuadrado. Madrid, Castilla, 1948. Pp. 222. (Bib. Clás. Castilla, 4.)

  The extensive prologue deals with Lope's religious life and attitude. According to the editor, Lope exalted the Catholic faith in his works even in his "moralmente más relajados" periods. She adds that he was an extraordinarily religious poet. There are 56 pages of informative notes.

------. *Sonetos*. Ed. Manuel Arce. Santander, La Isla de los Ratones, 1960. Pp. 75. (Col. Clás. Inolvidables, 1.)

An attractive small volume. The prologue calls Lope, Góngora and Garcilaso the greatest Spanish sonneteers. An "anticipado homenaje" for the 400th anniversary. Includes the famous "Soneto de repente" from La niña de plata, four sonnets from La Arcadia, twenty from the Rimas humanas, seven from the Rimas sacras, two from La Dorotea and six from the Rimas del licenciado Burguillos.

PROSE

INDIVIDUAL PROSE WORKS

Vega, Lope de. Las aventuras de Pánfilo. Cuento de espantos. Ed. Alfonso Reyes. 2nd ed. Mexico, 1957. Pp. 19. (Col. La Flecha.)
A new edition of the episode from Book V of El peregrino en su patria, which Borrow called the best ghost story in Spanish literature.

------. Epistolario. Ed. Agustín G. de Amezúa. 4 vols. Madrid, RAE, 1935-43. Pp. xiv, 524; 734; xcviii, 406; 398. (Vols. I, 1935, and II, 1940, are entitled Lope de Vega en sus cartas: Introducción al Epistolario de L. de V. C.; Vols. III, 1941, and IV, 1943, are entitled Epistolario de L. de V. C.)
Rev: Joaquín de Entrambasaguas, RFE, XXV(1941), 251-72 (of I, II); RBN, II(1941), 370-71 (of III); Juan Antonio Tamayo, RFE, XXVI(1942), 136-42 (of III).
A fundamental, and monumental, work (a fifth volume was planned). The first vol. deals with Lope's association with the Duque de Sessa, and the second with biographical data gleaned from their correspondence. Vols. three and four contain letters. Amezúa's comments throughout are illuminating. In all, an invaluable contribution to studies of several aspects of the Golden Age and of personalities of the day.

------. Cartas completas. Ed. Ángel Rosenblatt. 2 vols. Buenos Aires, Emecé, 1948. Pp. 472, 488. (Bib. Emecé de Obras Universales.)
Rev: H. K. L., BA, XXIII(1949), 285.
A reprinting, in 2 small volumes, of letters originally published by Amezúa. One letter (432 bis) has been added to the 809. The spelling has been modernized and a few changes in dates made. Two passages omitted by Amezúa "por razones personales" have been restored. A very helpful índice de nombres is included. The letters cover the period 1604-28. Each is preceded by a short résumé. A handy edition.

------. *La Dorotea*. Trans. into Italian, in part. See Croce, "La Dorotea de Lope de Vega..." (1940): Studies — Prose — Individual Prose Works.

------. *La Dorotea*. Madrid, Espasa-Calpe, 1941. Pp. 333. (Later eds.)

------. *La Dorotea*. (Facsimile, Madrid, 1632.) Madrid, Castalia, 1951.
Rev: Otis H. Green, HR, XXI(1953), 270.

------. *La Dorotea*. Barcelona, Fama, 1955. Pp. 275.

------. *La Dorotea*. Ed. José M. Blecua. Madrid, Rev. de Occidente, 1955. Pp. 625.
Rev: J. L. Cano, Clav, VII, No. 38 (1956), 76-77; J. Blanco Amor, La Torre, V(1957), 201-02; M. S. Carrasco Urgoiti, RHM, XXIII (1957), 334-35; A. S. Trueblood, HR, XXV(1957), 290-99 (a review article which states that while Blecua's edition marks a tremendous advance over earlier ones, it also displays imperfections due to inaccuracy and hastiness, particularly in the annotation; that the introduction combines a competent synthesis of recent criticism with some fresh comments); A. Alatorre, NRFH, XII(1958), 419-22 (a review which states that the editor deserves all credit for his extensive introduction to the work, and for his copious annotation, even if he has not always avoided errors and inaccuracies in the notes).

------. *La Dorotea*. Ed. Edwin S. Morby. Berkeley-Los Angeles, Univ. of California Press (Valencia, Castalia), 1958. Pp. 501.
Rev: Walter Heilman, Jr., Hisp, XLII(1959), 645 ("the most ambitious study yet completed on any of Lope de Vega's works ... by far the most definitive edition of *La Dorotea*"); E. Segura Covarsí, Arbor, XLIV, Nos. 165-66 (1959), 602-04 (commends the editor's annotations); A. S. Trueblood, NRFH, XIII(1959), 125-29 (states that this edition brings skillfully together the results of exhaustive research; that the introduction and notes, illuminating the text, add significantly to understanding every aspect of the work; indices and bibliography praised); Alice M. Pollin, RHM, XXVI(1960), 133-34 ("Obra de gran erudición, esmero y labor dedicada"); Robert Ricard, BH, LXII(1960), 212-13 (high praise); E. M. Wilson, BHS, XXXVII(1960), 252-54 ("a model for others to follow"); A. G. Reichenberger, HR, XXIX(1961), 149-51 (the edition is commended as a model of its kind); A. E. Sloman, RPh, XV(1961), 95-96 ("Rarely has a text been annotated with such erudition and such discretion.").
The enthusiastic reviews are sufficient to attest to the merits of the edition.

------. *Novelas a Marcia Leonarda*. Ed. Martín Riquer. Barcelona, Broquel, Horta, 1947. (Col. Broquel.)

------. *Novelly*. Ed. A. A. Smirnov and Yu. B. Kovneeva. Moscow, State Pub. House for Belles-Lettres, 1960.

------. *Pastores de Belén*. Ed. R. Olivares Figueroa. Barcelona, Edit. Juventud, 1941. Pp. 158.
An edition for children (Lope dedicated the work to Carlos Félix), reduced to one-third of the whole.

------. *El peregrino en su patria*. See *Las aventuras de Pánfilo* (above).

STUDIES

GENERAL, INCLUDING BIOGRAPHY

(Anon.) "Lope de Vega." Bol. de Información (Colegio Nac. de
   Veterinarios de España), Supl. Cient., No. 79 (1948), 107-22.

Alarcos, Emilio. "Los sermones de Paravicino." RFE, XXIV(1937),
   162-97.
   Lope's praise of Fray Hortensio Félix Paravicino (pp. 162-63
   and 178-79).

Aleixandre, Vicente. "José Ortega y Gasset en el jardín de Lope."
   In Los encuentros, Madrid, Guadarrama, 1958, pp. 47-56.
   A pleasant evocation of Lope's house in Madrid, although Ortega,
   not Lope, is the author's main concern. (See also Índice de
   Artes y Letras, XII, No. 115, 1958, 5.)

Allue y Morrell, Fernando. "La 'Raquel hermosa' de Lope de Vega."
   Clav, V, No. 28 (1954), 30-34.
   A study of Lope's use of this story in the Jerusalén conquistada
   and in Las paces de los reyes. The critic believes that these
   two works were either written or given final polish in Toledo,
   since they reflect the Toledo environment.

Alonso, Dámaso. "Todos contra Pellicer." RFE, XXIV(1937), 320-42.
   Lope's diatribe against Joseph Pellicer de Salas y Tovar (pp.
   339-40).

Almagro San Martín, Melchor de. "La casa de Lope de Vega." La
   Nación (Buenos Aires), Dec. 7, 1941, Sect. 2: "Artes-Letras,"
   pp. 4 and 20.
   After an excellent and authentic restoration by experts, the
   Madrid house, which had passed out of the hands of Lope's
   family forty years after his death, was opened shortly before
   the outbreak of the Civil War, closed during the War, and re-
   opened in 1941. Details as to measurements, furnishings, etc.,
   are given, and there follows a very convincing evocation of
   Lope's life in the house during the last twenty-five years of
   his life.

Amezúa. See González de Amezúa.

Anzoátegui, Ignacio N. "Niñez y desnudez de Lope de Vega." In
    Extremos del mundo, Madrid, Espasa-Calpe, 1942, pp. 23-30.
  An article already published in *La Nación* (Buenos Aires), May
    29, 1938.

Arauz, Álvaro. *Notas sobre Lope de Vega y Calderón*. Mexico,
    Atlántico, 1951. Pp. 171.
  Lope de Vega: pp. 21-48. Unsupported generalizations, tossed
    off at random, with more concern for their stylistic effect
    than for the substance of their content. The book was re-
    published as *Lope de Vega y Calderón de la Barca. Ensayos*,
    Mexico, Costa-Amic, 1959 (Col. Panoramas, 16).

Arco y Garay, Ricardo del. "Lope de Vega." In *Historia general de
    las literaturas hispánicas*, ed. Guillermo Díaz-Plaja, III,
    Barcelona, Barna, 1953, pp. 215-19.
  This is a section of a general history of Hispanic literature,
    and is very well done. The book also contains a section by
    F. C. Sainz de Robles on "El ciclo dramático de Lope de Vega."

Areny Batlle, Ramón, and A. Porqueras Mayo. "Lope de Vega en
    Lérida." *RL*, XII(1957), 56-68.
  Description of six Lope editions printed in Lérida during Lope's
    lifetime: *La Arcadia*, 1612; *Los pastores de Belén*, 1612, 1613,
    1617; *Rimas sacras*, 1615, 1626. Copies of all but the 1626
    Rimas sacras are in the library of D. Ramón Areny.

Armas Ayala, Alfonso. "La isla arcángel de Lope de Vega." *Cultura
    Universitaria* (Caracas), No. 40 (1953), 56-80.
  Under the headings, "ardor," "brasa," "agua," "río," "Castilla,"
    "mar," "nave" and "isla," Armas Ayala traces what he calls a
    voyage or *recorrido antológico* with copious quotations from
    Lope's works.

Astrana Marín, Luis. *Vida azarosa de Lope de Vega*. Segunda ed.
    corregida y aumentada. Barcelona, Plana, 1941. Pp. 344.
  The 1st edition was 1935.

------. *Lope de Vega. El monstruo de la naturaleza*. Madrid, Bébé,
    1944. Pp. 51.

Barberán, Cecilio. "La casa de Lope de Vega en Madrid." *Rev. de
    Educación Nac.*, Segunda Época, X, No. 95 (1950), 33-48.
  A description of Lope's house as it reflects his way of life.
    Four plates.

Bell, Aubrey F. G. *Castilian Literature*. Oxford, Clarendon Press,
    1938. Pp. xiv, 261.
  Rev: Alfred Coester, *Hisp*, XXI(1938), 227-28; I. L. McClelland,
    BHS, XV(1938), 158-60.

Numerous references *passim* to Lope. Chapter XIV, "Dramatic Instinct," characterizes Lope's contribution to the drama as "life and naturalness" (p. 190).

Benítez Claros, R. "Lope de Vega y la Congregación de esclavos del Caballero de Gracia." RBN, VI(1945), 333-38.
De article reproduces four photostatic pages of the libros de actas (1609-11) of the Congregación of which Lope was a member. Fragments of four letters from Amezúa's Epistolario, for 1615-17, are also given. Beyond the known fact that Lope joined the Congregación in 1609, the minutes reproduced throw no new light on Lope's activities.

Blecua, J. M. "Más sobre la muerte y entierro de Lope." RFE, XXVIII(1944), 470-72.
Re a letter by Francisco Ximénez de Urrea to Juan Francisco Andrés de Ustarroz, Sept. 1, 1635.

Boggs, Ralph S. Outline History of Spanish Literature. Boston, Heath, 1937. Pp. 154.
A very brief summary of Lope: pp. 54-56.

Bomli, P. W. La Femme dans l'Espagne du Siècle d'Or. The Hague, Nijhoff, 1950. Pp. viii, 390.
Rev: G. Larrieu, BH, LII(1950), 408-09 ("première étude d'ensemble sur la femme espagnole durant le siècle d'or"); Otis H. Green, HR, XX(1952), 255-57 (useful book, but author "has worked ... with unnecessary bibliographical limitations and with too narrow a view of what was to be done").

Buchanan, M. A. "Cervantes and Lope de Vega: Their Literary Relations. A Preliminary Survey." PQ, XXI(1942), 54-64.
The friendship which united these two authors seems not to have been strained until after 1602, the year in which Cervantes contributed a dedicatory sonnet to Lope's Dragontea. M. A. B. limits himself to matters of La comedia nueva. Owing largely to the frustrations of being unable to succeed as a popular playwright, Cervantes here seems to have lost some of his philosophic calm, and, while critical of Lope on the basis of classical precepts, is not himself always consistent in putting into practice his own theories. (Buchanan did not, in print, add to this "preliminary survey.")

Cabañas, Pablo. El mito de Orfeo en la literatura española. Madrid, CSIC, 1948. Pp. 408. (Doct. diss., Univ. of Madrid, 1947.)
Includes references to El marido más firme and El Orfeo en lengua castellana.

Campos, Jorge. "La sinceridad de Lope." Agora, Nos. 61-62 (1961), 10 and 11.

Caravaca, François. "Notes pour une psychologie amoureuse de Lope de Vega (1562-1635)," LanM, XLVIII(1954), 30-43.
Interesting, but adds nothing new.

Chandler, Richard E., and Kessel Schwartz. A New History of Spanish Literature. Baton Rouge, Louisiana State Univ. Press, 1961. Pp. xiii, 696.
Lope gets frequent and fleeting mention in one connection or another. He is discussed more fully as a dramatist on pages 82-87, and as a poet on pages 324-26. The treatment suffers from an obvious lack of completeness, but is adequate for the space the authors have permitted themselves.

Cisneros, Luis Jaime. "Amarilis: Otra posible huella." Mar del Sur: Revista Peruana de Cultura, No. 26 (1953), 74.

(Comediantes.) "A Current Bibliography of Foreign Publications Dealing with the Comedia." In BCom, from II, No. 2 (Nov., 1950) on.
Contains a systematic semi-annual bibliography of Lope publications outside of U. S. A. and Canada. The present compilers are Warren McCready and Robert Bishop. Lope in general.

Correa Calderón, E., and Fernando Lázaro. Lope de Vega y su época. I: Vida y obra del Fénix. Salamanca-Madrid, Anaya, 1961. Pp. 141. (Textos Anaya. Serie Preuniversitaria.)
"Contestación a la parte histórica o primera del Cuestionario de Literatura correspondiente al Curso Preuniversitario del año actual. Una sucinta bibliografía y unos fragmentos del Arte nuevo de hacer comedias ... dan cima (con el segundo volumen de esta serie, el texto y notas de El villano en su rincón) a esta interesante monografía adaptada fielmente al Cuestionario citado." The two-volume set was prepared as the text for students of the bachillerato in Spain.

------, and ------. Lope de Vega y su época. II: Estudio especial de "El villano en su rincón". Salamanca-Madrid, Anaya, 1961. Pp. 206. (Textos Anaya. Serie Preuniversitaria.)
The complete play, with many notes. With introduction, and a breve antología lírica. Prepared, with the preceding volume, for the Spanish bachillerato course.

Cossío, José María de. "Lope de Vega y el capitán Contreras." Correo Erudito, III(1943), 107-08.

David, Marcel. Contribution à l'étude du vocabulaire de Lope de Vega. Unpub. doct. diss., Univ. of Innsbruck, 1945.

Davies, R. Trevor. The Golden Century of Spain: 1501-1621. London, Macmillan, 1937. Pp. xi, 327. (Repub., 1954.)
Rev: A. M. Fox, QQ, LXII(1955), 131-33.
A brief section notes Lope's importance in the drama.

Diego, Gerardo. "El supremo poeta humano." *Agora*, Nos. 61-62 (1961), 31-32.

Eguía Ruiz, Constancio. *Cervantes, Calderón, Lope, Gracián: Nuevos temas crítico-biográficos*. Madrid, CSIC, 1951. Pp. 158. (*Cuad. de Lit.*, Anejo 8.)
    Lope de Vega: pp. 65-139. The Lope section was originally given as one of a series of lectures in Rome. There are many quotations from Lope's works.

Entrambasaguas, Joaquín de. *Vida de Lope de Vega*. Barcelona, Labor, 1936. Pp. 271. (Reprinted, 1942.)
    Rev: M. Romera-Navarro, *HR*, V(1937), 274-75 ("una verdadera biografía sin la tacha que tienen para mí casi todas las biografías de nuestros ingenios clásicos: falta de sentido de proporción entre su vida y carácter de un lado y, de otro, su producción literaria... El señor E. ha acertado en esta *Vida*. Es eso, una vida y un hombre ... estamos en contacto directo e íntimo con el hombre, metidos, no en la historia de los dramas que escribió, sino en el mayor y más espléndido de sus dramas: el drama de su vida.")

------. "El lopismo de Moratín." *RFE*, XXV(1941), 1-45.
    Against a traditional background of anti-Lope criticism, Leandro Fernández de Moratín displayed a lively interest in the *Fénix* and a keen perspective in evaluating his works. A synthesis of his critical judgment is probably best found in a letter to Juan Ceán Bermúdez: "Mi opinión es que nada hizo (Lope) absolutamente malo ni absolutamente bueno; que abusó de su inagotable facundia, y que no hay lector de buen gusto que no reniegue de él y que no le admire."

------. "Santa Teresa de Jesús y Lope de Vega." *Consigna*, IX(1941), 12-15.
    Lope's participation in the *fiestas*, which took place in 1614, to celebrate the canonization of Santa Teresa. Entrambasaguas also cites two plays and several sonnets of Lope's which were inspired by his great devotion to the Saint.

------. "Sobre un amor de Lope de Vega desconocido." *RFE*, XXV(1941), 103-08.
    Upon the discovery of new documents, Entrambasaguas retracts a theory he advanced in 1935, to the effect that there had been another chapter in the amorous life of the youthful Lope which had escaped the biographers. His original theory was based on a birth certificate found in the records of San Ginés, in Madrid, dated Jan. 2, 1581, which referred to Manuela, "hija de Lope de Vega y de doña María de Aragón." The subsequent discovery, by Joaquín Montaner, of new documents indicates that the father of Manuela was not the *Fénix*, but rather one Lope de Vega Portocarrero.

------. El curioso lector (pseud.). "Una visita a la casa de Lope de Vega." <u>Santo y Seña</u> (Madrid), No. 5 (Dec. 24, 1941), 17.

A pleasant tour of Lope's house and garden. Evocation of Lope's life and writings.

------. "Datos acerca de Lope de Vega en una relación de fiestas del siglo XVII." <u>RF</u>, LVI(1942), 266-81.

Re the published account of the celebration of 1614 of the canonization of Santa Teresa, which contains some pages in prose and a <u>romance</u> by Lope. There are references also to the presentation of plays (celebrating the life of the Saint) which may have been Lope's. (This article was also published in <u>Rev. Nac. de Educación</u>, No. 21, 1942; as a 16-page monograph, Madrid, Samarén, 1942; and in Entrambasaguas' <u>Estudios sobre Lope de Vega</u>, II, 1947.)

------. "Lope de Vega, Feijóo y Sarmiento." <u>Correo Erudito</u>, II, No. 18 (1942), 179-82.

As a sequel to his article on "El lopismo de Moratín," Entrambasaguas finds, unexpectedly, that Feijóo and Sarmiento both speak with praise of Lope. They recognize the literary importance of the dramatist, although they fail to understand the beauty of his creative art. Sarmiento particularly laments his condescension to the taste of the masses.

------. "Acerca del raptor de la hija de Lope de Vega." <u>Correo Erudito</u>, III, No. 19 (1943), 24-26.

------. "El mayor amigo de Lope de Vega." <u>El Español</u>, No. 57 (Nov. 27, 1943), 4.

Juan de Piña.

------. "Proyecto de una edición de las <u>Obras completas</u> de Lope de Vega." <u>RBN</u>, V(1944), 197-229. (Reprinted: <u>Anales de la Asociación Española para el Progreso de las Ciencias</u>, II, 1946, 809-35.)

Entrambasaguas complains that, up to the time of writing, Lope's <u>Obras completas</u> have not been "publicadas íntegramente, aunque ello parece increíble a estas alturas," and suggests that as a national homage to Lope it would have been natural and of prime importance to have gathered together all of Lope's works after "la no lejana celebración del tricentenario de la muerte del poeta." Entrambasaguas then speaks of "Intentos de ediciones generales, anteriores a este proyecto," and goes on to outline the "Carácter de la edición proyectada;" stating that the works should be printed in chronological order, with fidelity to orthography and punctuation, and that "La edición será crítica, en cuanto a la fijación de los textos mejores; pero sin notas ni comentario con respecto a su contenido, su valor literario, lingüístico, etc.," since if they were edited with critical comments, "ni se acabarían nunca, ni cabrían en un número de volúmenes razonable." The proposal would be to divide the Obras completas into I, Obras no dramáticas and II, Obras dramáticas; and the opinion is that, "con todas las reservas debidas," the non-dramatic works could be edited in six volumes, the dramatic works in twenty-five, the index, vocabulary and bibliography in one, giving a total of thirty-two volumes.

Entrambasaguas, it seems, had in mind to carry out the project himself: "...para quien como yo, lleva ya muchos años acopiando elementos con estos fines, la empresa queda, en verdad, limitada a una cuestión de tiempo y de labor correctora principalmente... Y si mi vida no diera para ello, aquí queda el plan a seguir para que otro, mejor y más afortunado lo lleve a cabo si lo juzga conveniente. Y a mí, quédeme como disculpa una vieja frase que tengo por lema en estos casos:
      Yo he hecho lo que he podido;
      Fortuna, lo que ha querido."

------. *Vivir y crear de Lope de Vega*. Vol. I. Madrid, CSIC, 1946. Pp. viii, 571.

Rev: H. Cidade, Rev. da Fac. de Letras, XIII(1947), 103-05; E. Segura Covarsí, Cuad. de Lit., II(1947), 162-65 ("the biography"); A. F. G. Bell, BA, XXXIII(1949), 277 (favourable); R. M. de Hornedo, Razón y Fe, CXLIX(1949), 192-94 (work of divulgación, hence regrettable lack of documentation; otherwise favourable); W. J. Entwistle, MLR, XLV(1950), 97-99.

This first volume (of three planned) has a sub-title "La vida del hombre." The order is chronological. Many references to literary works and letters. The Entrambasaguas book has very little value for the scholar since everything in the sixty-one chapters is a repetition of well-known facts in Lope's life, and it is not even of value for a serious student who may want to use this book in search of references for there is an absolute lack of the sources (editions, editors, years, pages, etc.) from which Entrambasaguas drew his quotations. This monograph is much inferior to the Vida by Rennert and Castro, which it resembles, except that the Rennert-Castro work is of high scholarly value. It is true that Entrambasaguas' avowed purpose is to reach "un público selecto, pero amplio," but he could, at the same time, have given to a truly "público selecto" the notes and references that would have satisfied its curiosity. Vols. II and III, to appear in the future, will deal with "La creación del poeta," his non-dramatic and his dramatic works.

------. *Estudios sobre Lope de Vega*. 3 vols. Madrid, CSIC, 1946, 1947, 1958. Pp. xiii, 585; 652; 664.

Rev: J. Simón Díaz, Razón y Fe, CXXXIV(1946), 260-61; W. L. Fichter, HR, XV(1947), 239-43 (says of Vol. I: "...not every statement or conclusion in 'Una guerra literaria...' is beyond dispute, yet the work is so thoroughly documented and the reasoning on the whole so cogent that scholars will doubtless find relatively little to disagree with;" E. Segura Covarsí, Cuad. de Lit., II(1947), 162-65; A. F. G. Bell, BA, XXIII (1949), 141; W. J. Entwistle, MLN, XLV(1950), 97-99; L.-G. Lefebvre, LR, IV(1950), 163-65; A. Rüegg, Erasmus, V(1952), 616-20; Edwin S. Morby, HR, XXIX(1961), 148-49 (summarizes the contents of Vol. III, which includes "Los famosos libelos contra unos cómicos" and other previously published articles, and praises the author's scholarship. Notes that the volume, although carefully done, does not make as significant a contribution as the first two of the series.).

This set brings together a number of studies by Entrambasaguas, which studies had already appeared, usually more than once, in other publications. In all cases, it is stated that they have been revised. Vol. I has a nota preliminar, a general article on "Lope de Vega, poeta nacional" (with special reference to Fuenteovejuna), "Localización de la sepultura de Lope de Vega," and the beginning of a long, important article on "Una guerra literaria del Siglo de Oro: Lope de Vega y los preceptistas aristotélicos" (Entrambasaguas' doctoral dissertation). Vol. II continues "Una guerra literaria...", with reference to La Filomena, the Orfeos, etc. Other studies in the volume are: "Censura coetánea de una poesía de Lope de Vega," "Una traducción latina de Lope de Vega," and "Datos acerca de Lope de Vega en una relación de fiestas del siglo XVII" (published in 1942, see above). Vol. III contains some twelve studies published originally over the previous 25 years. Most deal with Lope's lyric and circumstantial verse. As Morby stated in his review the volume on the whole includes less significant material than its two predecessors.

------. "Blair y Munárriz, mentores de la crítica lopiana." Rev. Bibliográfica y Documental, IV(1950), 5-30.

José Luis Munárriz translated in 1789 Hugo Blair's Lectures on Rhetoric and Belles Lettres (Edinburgh, 1783) under the title Lecciones sobre la Retórica y las Bellas Letras (Madrid, 4 vols.), with commentary and criticism about Spanish literature added to the original. It is the most representative and influential work of neoclassic critism (until the publication in 1826 of Gómez Hermosilla's Arte de hablar) for his time as for subsequent generations. Entrambasaguas extracts the criticism on Lope, divided into sections on "Lenguaje y estilo," "Novela pastoril," "Épica," with ample treatment of the Jerusalén conquistada, and "Teatro," concentrating on La Estrella de Sevilla, in the refundición by Cándido María Trigueros. The book by Blair-Munárriz is often pedantic, sometimes sympathetic and understanding in details, but mostly critical of Lope, their judgment being based on a dosis of Scottish common sense. The article is an important contribution to the history of Lope's appreciation in the neo-classic period. From the conclusion: "El peso de los juicios de Blair-Munárriz ... no ha de encarecerse. Hoy mismo no podemos decir que la crítica lopista se haya desprendido totalmente de muchos de estos tópicos...."

------. "Cervantes y Lope: El tiempo y el momento." AUC, CVIII, No. 80 (1950), 235-44.
After reviewing the vicissitudes of the Lope-Cervantes relationship, Entrambasaguas confronts the two authors (p. 241): "Cervantes ... no es un hombre de su siglo, en su momento. Es un hombre en el tiempo... El hombre en su siglo es Lope, el hombre del momento, reflejo de su época, conforme a su época, de acuerdo con ella...."

------. "Lope de Vega y Portugal." Rev. de Educación Nac., Segunda Época, X, No. 95 (1950), 7-11.
Notes on Lope's plays in Lisbon, on plays with Portuguese subject matter, on Portuguese authors mentioned by Lope and on Portuguese authors collaborating in Montalván's Fama póstuma.

------. El Madrid de Lope de Vega. Madrid, Inst. de Estudios Madrileños, 1952. Pp. 23. (Itinerarios de Madrid, I.) (2nd ed., 1959.)
Rev: R. M. de Hornedo, Razón y Fe, CXLVII(1953), 102; Fr. G. Placer, Estudios, X(1954), 194.
Evokes names and places intimately associated with Lope: where he lived, wrote, loved, hated, confessed, died and was buried. With a map and illustrations.

------. "La valoración de Lope de Vega en Feijóo y su época." Cuad. de la Cátedra de Feijóo, Oviedo, 1956. (Also pub. as a monograph, Oviedo, Edit. Universidad, 1957.)

Espino Gutiérrez, Gabriel. "El clasicismo y el romanticismo en la obra de Lope de Vega." BBMP, XXV(1949), 84-98.
Superficial considerations about Lope as a "romantic" poet in his theatre and as a "classical" poet in his lyric and epic poetry and in his novels.

Estrella Gutiérrez, Fermín. Historia de la literatura española con antología. Buenos Aires, Kapelusz, 1945. Pp. 758.
Chapter VI (pp. 250-317) is devoted to the Golden Age drama, and the Lope de Vega study is the longest one (pp. 261-73). "Él (Lope de Vega) y Cervantes son los dos valores más altos y representativos de las letras hispanas." Contributes nothing new.

Farinelli, Arturo. Lope de Vega en Alemania. Barcelona, Bosch, 1936. Pp. 324.
Rev: G. C., BH, XXXIX(1937), 176-77.

This is a translation into Spanish, by Enrique Massaguer, of *Grillparzer und Lope de Vega*, Berlin, 1894.

------. "Centenarios que pasan y la fama de Lope de Vega." *La Nación* (Buenos Aires), Apr. 4, 1937.

Fernández Galiano, Manuel. "Sobre la evolución de la leyenda de Ciro en nuestros siglos XVI y XVII." *Estudios Clásicos*, VI, No. 32 (1961), 93-98.
    In Lorenzo de Sepúlveda, Juan de Timoneda and Lope de Vega (particularly the play *Contra valor no hay desdicha*).

Fichter, William L. "The Present State of Lope de Vega Studies." *Hisp*, XX(1937), 327-52.
    At the close of the tercentenary of Lope's death, Professor Fichter, in this important article, proposed "to examine the present status of our knowledge of Lope's life and works ... to give a rapid survey of the situation, listing the more important recent contributions down through 1936, as well as indicating some of the many things that still need to be done...." (p. 327). A comprehensive survey and judicious appraisal. Our *terminus a quo*.

Figueiredo, F. de. "Camões e Lope." *RLC*, XVIII(1938), 160-71.

Flores, Ángel. *Vida de Lope de Vega*. Buenos Aires, Losada, (1948). Pp. 152.
    A Spanish translation, by Guillermo de Torre, of an English fictionalized "life" (*Lope de Vega, Monster of Nature*, New York, 1930), one of the type that Fichter (*Hisp*, XX, 1937, 327) described as belonging "to the familiar class of novelized biography, which combines incontestable fact with imagined and often fantastic and sensational elements." The prologue is a laudatory account of Lope the man and his work, and of Flores the author. The "life" is of no value to the student of Lope.

Fraile, Medardo. "Refranillo y recortes pensando en Lope." *Agora*, Nos. 61-62 (1961), 15-18.

Franco Rodríguez, Ángel. *El tema de América en los autores del Siglo de Oro español*. Unpub. doct. diss., Univ. of Madrid, 1954.

Fucilla, Joseph G. "Etapas en el desarrollo del mito de Ícaro, en el Renacimiento y en el Siglo de Oro." *Hispanó*, No. 8 (1960), 1-34.
    Pp. 22-27 concern Lope. Lope's treatments of the Icarus theme stem mainly from Luigi Tansillo, who linked the myth to his own thought, desire and amorous passion, in two sonnets ("Amor m'impenna l'ale..." and "Poi che spiegato ho l'ale...") and a madrigal ("Quel vago animaletto...").

Gaos, Vicente. "Lope de Vega: Siglo de Oro." Agora, Nos. 61-62 (1961), 15-18.

Gavaldá, Antonio C. Pensamientos de Lope de Vega. Barcelona, Sintes, 1957. Pp. 75. (Col. Literatos y Pensadores, 30.)
Selected thoughts, with annotation.

Gillet, Joseph E. "Lucrecia-necia." HR, XV(1947), 120-36.
In giving examples of the Lucrecia-necia rhyme, Gillet quotes from Lope's La cortesía de España, El dómine Lucas, Las ferias de Madrid, La malcasada, El perro del hortelano, El valor de las mujeres and Rimas humanas y divinas.

Glaser, Edward. "El lusitanismo de Lope de Vega." BRAE, XXXIV (1954), 387-411.
Although Lope generally shows true admiration and liking for the Portuguese, his private letters occasionally demonstrate a critical and unsympathetic attitude. Glaser's study of Lope's letters, and of some of his literary works, brings to light some inconsistencies not ordinarily recognized.

------. "Lope de Vega e Manuel Faria e Sousa: Achega para o estudo das relações culturais entre Portugal e Espanha." Colóquio, No. 8 (1960), 57-59.
Lope and the Portuguese writer felt a true mutual esteem, well beyond the exaggerated praise in fashion at the time. Lope referred to Faria e Sousa on several occasions, and praised his command of Spanish. Faria e Sousa, in turn, warmly defended Lope's art.

Gómez de la Serna, Ramón. Lope viviente. Buenos Aires, Espasa-Calpe, 1954. Pp. 147.
Rev: J. L. C., Ínsula, X, No. 112 (1955), 6 (calls it a "poetic biography," and praises it highly).
A biography which adds nothing new. Undertakes to defend Lope's love life. Makes interesting comparisons between Lope and the painter Velázquez. The chapter on Cervantes is irrelevant.

------. "Lope viviente." Cultura Universitaria (Caracas), No. 45 (1954), 49-67.
A defence of Lope's love life. Cf. the previous title.

González de Amezúa, Agustín. "Unas honras frustradas de Lope de Vega." In Opúsculos histórico-literarios, II, Madrid, CSIC, 1951, pp. 268-86. (Previously pub. in RH, LXXXI, 1933, 225-47.)
Rev (of complete vol.): Vásquez Dodero, Arbor, XXI(1952), 292-93.

------. "Un enigma decifrado: El raptor de la hija de Lope de Vega." In Opúsculos histórico-literarios, II, Madrid, CSIC, 1951, pp. 287-356. (Previously pub. in BRAE, XXI, 1934, 357-404 and 521-62.)

------. "La casa de Lope de Vega." In *Opúsculos histórico-literarios*, II, Madrid, CSIC, 1951, pp. 357-63. (Previously pub. as prologue to Muguruza Otaño's book, Madrid, 1941. See below.)

------. "A Portrait of Lope de Vega." *Atlante*, II(1954), 107-08.
Description of a portrait by Pedro de Guzmán, of Lope in his later years.

González Paredes, Ramón. "Una vida derramada." *Cultura Universitaria* (Caracas), No. 42 (1954), 61-75.
Inspired by reading Ángel Flores' *Vida de Lope de Vega*, the author gives us a sketch of the life and loves of the dramatist. It is unfortunate that this kind of article continues to appear, especially in university publications.

Goyri de Menéndez Pidal, María. "Con motivo del reajuste de unas fechas. La muerte de doña Isabel de Urbina." *NRFH*, III(1949), 378-85.
New documentary evidence indicates either Sept. 15 or 20, 1594, not May 20, 1595, as hitherto assumed. Reference to public auction of Isabel de Urbina's possessions, beginning Feb. 25, 1595 (cf. Salazar, *RFE*, XXV, 1941, 478-506, listed below). The Goyri de Menéndez Pidal article was republished in *De Lope de Vega y del Romancero*, Zaragoza, 1953, pp. 89-101 (see Studies — Poetry — Individual Poems, *romances*).

------. "La Celia de Lope de Vega." *NRFH*, IV(1950), 347-90.
The identification of the name of Celia with Micaela de Luján, addressed as "Camila Lucinda" or "Lucinda." The relationship with her began in 1593, not 1599 (cf. Américo Castro, *RFE*, V, 1918). However, Morley and Bruerton's article, "Lope de Vega, Celia y *Los comendadores de Córdoba*" (*NRFH*, VI, 1952) effectively refutes Doña María's argumentation. (See Studies — Drama — Individual Plays.) The Goyri de Menéndez Pidal article was republished in *De Lope de Vega y del Romancero*, Zaragoza, 1953, pp. 103-74 (see Studies — Poetry — Individual Poems, *romances*).

Gregor, Joseph. *Das spanische Welttheater*. Vienna, Reichner, 1937. Pp. 536.
Rev: W. C. A., *BHS*, XV(1938), 165-66.
A survey of Spanish history, literature, art and architecture under the Hapsburgs, with particular attention to the drama (Lope de Vega: pp. 425-42).

Guerrieri Crocetti, Camillo. "Lope de Vega e l'Italia." In *Pensiero e Poesia*, Genoa, 1938, pp. 61-86.

Hainsworth, George. "Notes supplémentaires sur Lope en France (XVIIe siècle)." *BH*, XLI(1939), 352-63.

Halstead, Frank G. *The Attitude of Lope de Vega Toward Astrology.*
Unpub. doct. diss., Univ. of Virginia, 1937. (*Abstracts of Diss.*, Univ. of Virginia, Charlottesville, 1937, pp. 19-21.)

------. "The Attitude of Lope de Vega toward Astrology and Astronomy." *HR*, VII(1939), 205-19.
A valuable and richly documented study.

Harrod, G. R. "Blanco White on Spanish Literature." *BHS*, XXIV (1947), 269-71.
The article deals with some notes in Blanco White's copy of Bouterwek's *History of Spanish Literature.* Blanco White did not think much of the Spanish drama of the Golden Age. He allowed Lope little merit, and thought his plays weak ("to have read one or two is to have read them all").

Hermenegildo, Alfredo. *Burgos en el romancero y en el teatro de los Siglos de Oro.* Madrid, Fundación Universitaria Española Dulce Nombre de Jesús y San Antonio, 1958. Pp. 183.
Rev: Juan de Castro y Delgado, *Razón y Fe*, CLIX(1959), 541 ("fuerte prueba de capacidad investigadora y analítica ... dominio de una metodología rigurosamente científica"); Fr. Ángel López, *Estudios*, XV(1959), 309-10; Maxime Chevalier, *BH*, LXII(1960), 459-60 (the title is not wholly adequate since the work also contains material from prose sources; copious material, but no clear conclusions); Norma Pérez Martín, *RUBA*, V(1960), 138-39 (many examples from Lope; the author reveals himself as an "alert critic" who is carefully selective); Stephen Reckert, *BHS*, XXXVII(1960), 64 (this "earnest catalogue of allusions to Burgos, many of them frankly marginal," would better have gone unpublished).
Reviews differ greatly in the estimate of this book! An anthological work. The passages quoted are subjected to no critical analysis.

Herrero, Miguel, and Manuel Cardenal. "Sobre los agüeros en la literatura española del Siglo de Oro." *RFE*, XXVI(1942), 15-41.
The interpretation and significance of omens in Golden Age literature, with a catalogue of different types of omens. Numerous references to Lope.

Herrero García, Miguel. "Nueva interpretación de la novela picaresca." *RFE*, XXIV(1937), 343-62.
Lope's mention of *la picardía* (pp. 344-45).

------. "Lope de Vega y Tomé de Burguillos." *Correo Erudito*, II, No. 18 (1942), 184.
The author suggests as quite likely, since a poet named Burguillos actually had lived in Toledo, that Lope knew of him and enjoyed using the alias of Burguillos for his humorous poetry.

------. "Lope estuvo enfermo en Alba de Tormes." Correo Erudito, II, No. 18 (1942), 190.
    Six lines are transcribed from a poem by Lope (1615), in which he alludes to illness, and cure brought about by a relic of Santa Teresa. Cf. Entrambasaguas, "Datos acerca de Lope de Vega en una relación de fiestas del siglo XVII," RF, LVI (1942), 266-81.

Hierro, José. "La primera patria de Lope." Agora, Nos. 61-62 (1961), 19-23.

Jiménez Martos, L. "Lope en televisión." Agora, Nos. 61-62 (1961), 24-25.

Jiménez Rueda, J. "Lope de Vega, ensayo de interpretación." In Estampas de los Siglos de Oro, Mexico, Univ. Autónima, 1957, pp. 73-82.
  Rev: A. B. N., Univ. de México, XII(1957-58), 30.
    A discurso académico prepared for the tercentenary of 1935, which makes no claim to profundity or originality.

Juliá Martínez, Eduardo. "La alegría de Lope y la tristeza de Cervantes." Cuad. de Lit., I(1947), 7-39.
    The hypersensitivity of both authors led them to capture life, one with fecund profusion, the other with profound analysis. A subjective article, interesting to read.

King, Willard F. Literary Academies and Prose Fiction in Seventeenth-Century Spain. Unpub. doct. diss., Brown Univ., 1957.
    See the PMLA article following. Private literary academies flourished in the period 1620-30 especially. Academies are frequently referred to in the literature of the time.

------. "The Academies and Seventeenth-Century Spanish Literature." PMLA, LXXV(1960), 367-76.

Krauss, Werner. "Lope de Vegas poetisches Weltbild in seinen Briefen." RF, LVI(1942), 282-99.
    This number of the periodical is dedicated to Karl Vossler. The article is evidently prompted by Amezúa's Epistolario. Krauss comments on the significance of the intimate, unguarded nature of the correspondence, which makes it interesting and trustworthy for biographical study.

Leonard, Irving A. "More Conjectures regarding the Identity of Lope de Vega's 'Amarilis indiana'." Hisp, XX(1937), 113-20.
    See also Studies — Poetry — Individual Poems (La Filomena — Ureta).

------. "Notes on Lope de Vega's Works in the Spanish Indies." HR, VI(1938), 277-93.
    Presents evidence of Lope's popularity among the reading public and the theatre-goers in the New World.

Levi, Ezio. *Lope de Vega e l'Italia.* Florence, Sansoni, 1935. Pp. xix, 174. (*Bib. Hispano-Italiana*, 4.)
Rev: G. C., *BH*, XXXIX(1937), 175-76.

------. "Roma e Lope de Vega." In *Atti del IV (1935) Congresso Nazionale di Studi Romani*, IV, Rome, Istituto di Studi Romani, 1938, pp. 263-69.

Lida de Malkiel, María Rosa. "Alejandro en Jerusalén." *RPh*, X (1956-57), 185-96.
 The episode of Alexander's worship in the temple at Jerusalem is reflected by Lope in *Jerusalén conquistada* and elsewhere, and constitutes a high point of his play *Las grandezas de Alejandro*, where it is treated with an impetuosity that shows Lope's youthful response to the youthful conqueror.

Lincoln, J. N. *Saint Ursula, the Infanta Isabel and Lope de Vega.* Ann Arbor, Univ. of Michigan Press, 1947. Pp. 17. (*Univ. of Michigan Contributions in Modern Philology*, 7.)
 Reference to a letter of Nov. 10, 1602, written to accompany some holy relics sent from Cologne to Magdalena de San Jerónimo of the retinue of Isabel Clara Eugenia, daughter of Philip II. There is also a description of the nuptials in Valencia between Isabel and the Archduke Albert of Austria, in which Lope participated. The relationship of the three persons of the title is very tenuous.

Lins, Juan. *Lope de Vega e o significado da sua obra.* Montevideo, Instituto de Cultura Uruguayo-Brasileño, 1943. Pp. 39.
 Delivered as a lecture.

Looten, C. "Rapports littéraires entre la Néerlande et l'Espagne." *RLC*, XVII(1937), 613-50.
 Refers briefly to Lope's influence.

Lorenz, Erika. "Wunder und Weltbild in der spanischen Barockliteratur." *RJ*, XI(1960), 397-407.
 The article contains references to Lope.

Macrí, Oreste. "L'Ariosto e la letteratura spagnola." *LM*, III(1952), 515-43.
 The portion that has to do with influences on Lope adds a few particulars to studies already made by Menéndez Pelayo, D'Amico, Parducci and Entrambasaguas.

Mandiola, Anita. "La Santísima Virgen en la obra de Lope de Vega." *Unitas* (Manila), XXVII(1954), 739-49.
 A study of Lope's presentation of the Virgin in his plays and poetry. Apparently Lope had a very definite idea of Her appearance ("*morena*") and an attitude of great emotion toward Her.

Mantero, Manuel. "Tres siglos entre dos posiciones." <u>Agora</u>, Nos. 61-62 (1961), 26-27.
Lope and Rubén Darío.

Marasso, Arturo. "Humanismo de Lope de Vega." In <u>Estudios de literatura castellana</u>, Buenos Aires, Kapelusz, 1955, pp. 187-214.
Briefly studies such themes as "La época de Lope," "Platonismo," "El vulgo y Lope," "El teatro de Lope y lo popular," "<u>Orfeo</u>," "Humanidad de Lope," etc.

Massa, Pedro. "Rapto de Antonia Clara: El más grande dolor de Lope de Vega." <u>Cervantes</u> (Havana), XVI(1941), 31-32 and 68.
The illicit union from which Antonia Clara sprang, that of Lope and doña Marta de Nevares, did not provide a model background for the daughter's behaviour. To this implication is added additional blame placed on Lope for the ultimate flight of Antonia Clara with don Cristóbal Tenorio y Azofeijo: his indiscretion in dictating <u>comedias</u> to her, from the contents of which she must have become aware of frequent lapses of virtue, and his acquiescence in permitting her to attend many social functions where her beauty attracted great attention.

Mazzara, Richard A. <u>Italian and Spanish Influences and Parallels in the Life and Works of Saint-Amant</u>. Unpub. doct. diss., Univ. of Kansas, 1959. (<u>DA</u>, XX, 1365.)
Includes indirect influence of Lope.

McClelland, I. L. <u>The Origins of the Romantic Movement in Spain</u>. Liverpool, Inst. of Hispanic Studies, 1937. Pp. xii, 402.
Rev: A. F. G. Bell, <u>BHS</u>, XIV(1937), 156-57; G. Cirot, <u>BH</u>, XXXIX (1937), 418-20; R. Hilton, <u>MLR</u>, XXXII(1937), 643-45; John T. Reid, <u>Hisp</u>, XX(1937), 294-95; Sterling A. Stoudemire, <u>RR</u>, XXVIII(1937), 360-61; N. B. Adams, <u>HR</u>, VI(1938), 80-82.
A comprehensive survey of the native Spanish "romanticism" in literary theory and literature of 18th-century Spain forming the connection between the Golden Age and the 19th century. The book contains numerous references to Lope. "For the first three-quarters of the (18th) century, the history of Spanish romantic thought is actually the history of more or less disconnected defences ... of the national tradition; for the most part they could be described more particularly as defences of Lope and Calderón"(p. 5).

McCready, Warren T. "Lope de Vega's Birth Date and Horoscope." <u>HR</u>, XXVIII(1960), 313-18.
An important and timely contribution, anticipating the quadricentennial sufficiently to set celebrations on the newly-established date, <u>December 12</u>, new style. Pérez de Montalván, long the unchallenged authority for the November 25 birthdate, confused two saints' names, for St. Lupus' day is Dec. 2, o.s. This also matches the astrological data found in Lope's writings.

Menéndez Pidal, Ramón. <u>De Cervantes y Lope de Vega</u>. Buenos Aires, Espasa-Calpe, 1940. Pp. 166. (<u>Col. Austral</u>, 120.) (Later eds.)
    Contains material of earlier years. Pp. 59-66: "El hogar de Lope de Vega" (pub. by Centro de Estudios Históricos, Fichero de Arte Antiguo, <u>La casa de Lope de Vega</u>, Madrid, 1935, pp. 7-17); pp. 67-138: "Lope de Vega: El arte nuevo y la nueva biografía" (<u>RFE</u>, XXII, 1935, pp. 337-98); and pp. 139-66: "Del honor en el teatro español" ("Conferencia dada en la Habana, en la Sociedad Hispano Cubana de Cultura, por marzo de 1937").

------. <u>El P. de las Casas y Vitoria con otros temas de los siglos XVI y XVII</u>. Madrid, Espasa-Calpe, 1958. Pp. 152. (<u>Col. Austral</u>, 1286.)
    Includes both "El lenguaje de Lope de Vega" (pp. 99-121), which pays a good deal of attention to <u>La corona trágica</u>, and "<u>El castigo sin venganza</u>: Un oscuro problema de honor" (pp. 123-52).

Meregalli, Franco. "L'ispanismo tedesco dal 1945." <u>QIb</u>, No. 16 (1956), 524-27, and No. 18 (1956), 103-09.
    Refers to studies on Lope de Vega and others.

Mesa, Carlos E. "La casa de Lope de Vega." <u>Univ. de Antioquia</u> (Medellín, Colombia), XXXIII(1957), 208-23.
    A delightful evocation of the life and times of Lope by means of a description of a visit to his house in Madrid.

Modern Humanities Research Association. <u>The Year's Work in Modern Language Studies</u>.
    Our period is covered by this excellent, running bibliographical-critical commentary, published in Cambridge, England.

Modern Language Association of America. "Annual Bibliography." In <u>PMLA</u>, LXXII, No. 2 (Apr., 1957) on.
    The annual "American Bibliography" (begun in 1919) ceased in Vol. LXXI, No. 2 (Apr., 1956), and since 1957 (material of 1956), the coverage has been <u>international</u>. Lope is well treated. No book reviews.

Molinaro, Julius A. R. <u>Angélica and Medoro: The Development of a Motif from the Renaissance to the Baroque</u>. Unpub. doct. diss., Univ. of Toronto, 1954. Pp. iii, 181.
    References to <u>La hermosura de Angélica</u> and other Lope works.

Montesinos, José F. <u>Estudios sobre Lope de Vega</u>. Mexico, El Colegio de México, 1951. Pp. 332.
  Rev: C. V. Aubrun, <u>BH</u>, LIII(1951), 445; M. M. C., <u>Clav</u>, III, No. 15 (1952), 74; R. Gullón, <u>Insula</u>, No. 78 (1952), 6-7; J. H. Silverman, <u>Hisp</u>, XXXV(1952), 256; E. Müller-Bochat, <u>RF</u>, LXVII (1956), 446-49.

A collection of the author's previously published studies (1921-35), with adiciones y enmiendas in the form of notes at the end of the volume. The original texts have not been altered. Some of the studies of this distinguished lopista have not been readily accessible. Those and most of the other valuable contributions (missing are the Observaciones of his editions of TAE) are now under one cover. An onomastic index makes the volume useful as a work of reference. The studies included are: "Algunas observaciones sobre la figura del donaire en el teatro de Lope de Vega" (Homenaje a Menéndez Pidal, I, Madrid, 1925); "Lope, figura del donaire" (Cruz y Raya, Nos. 23-24, 1935); "Contribuciones al estudio del teatro de Lope de Vega" (RFE, VIII, 1921, and IX, 1922); "Dos reminiscencias de La Celestina en comedias de Lope de Vega" (RFE, XIII, 1926); "Una cuestión de amor en comedias antiguas españolas" (RFE, XIII, 1926); "Las poesías líricas de Lope de Vega" (prólogo, Poesías líricas de Lope de Vega, Madrid, 1925-26, Clás. Cast., 68 and 75); "Contribuciones al estudio de la lírica de Lope de Vega" (RFE, XI, 1924, and XII, 1925); "Notas sobre algunas poesías de Lope de Vega" (RFE, XIII, 1926); "Para la bibliografía de las obras no dramáticas de Lope de Vega" (RFE, XIX, 1932); "Lope de Vega, poeta de circunstancias" (El Sol, May 17, 1935); "Lope y su tiempo" (El Sol, Nov. 21 and Dec. 15, 1935).

Montoto, Santiago. "Contribución al vocabulario de Lope de Vega. Colección de palabras y acepciones empleadas por el Fénix de los Ingenios españoles que no figuran el Diccionario de la Real Academia Española." BRAE, XXVI(1947), 281-95, 443-57; XXVIII(1948), 127-43, 301-18, 463-77; XXIX(1949), 135-49, 329-38. (Pub. as a monograph: Madrid, Aguirre, 1949. Pp. 114.)
Rev: R. M. Hornedo, Razón y Fe, CXLIV(1951), 532-33.
In this collection, according to Montoto, there shines forth the genius of Lope, his profound knowledge of the Castilian language and the wealth and richness of his vocabulary. Some 725 words are listed, including forgotten words and those of his own invention. The verse or sentence in which the word appears is given and the word itself is italicized. No commentary is furnished since the compiler believes that the words are self-explanatory in nearly every case. The study is a real contribution, and might be enriched immeasurably with commentary and comparison with similar uses (if any) by other authors.

Moragón y Maestre, Manuel. La mitología en la obra de Lope de Vega. Unpub. doct. diss., Univ. of Madrid, 1948.

Morínigo, Marcos A. "Indigenismos americanos en el léxico de Lope de Vega." RNC (Caracas), No. 84 (1951), 72-95.
An enriching contribution to Lope's "American" vocabulary.

Morley, S. Griswold. <u>The Pseudonyms and Literary Disguises of Lope de Vega</u>. Berkeley-Los Angeles, Univ. of California Press, 1951. (UCPMP, XXXIII, No. 5, pp. 421-84.)
  Rev: C. V. A., <u>BH</u>, LIII(1951), 338-39; W. L. Fichter, <u>HR</u>, XX(1952), 345-47; Gerald E. Wade, <u>Symposium</u>, VI(1952), 403.
  An objective, thorough study of all the names in Lope's writings that have ever been considered as representing Lope himself. Through comparison with the known facts of the writer's life, Morley has tested their autobiographic value. The results demonstrate that no personage can always be identified with Lope himself, and, therefore, no act or saying of such a person can be considered "as true of Lope unless it is substantiated by external evidence."

Muguruza Otaño, Pedro. <u>La casa de Lope de Vega</u>. Madrid, Artes Gráficas Faure, 1941. Pp. 48.
  Rev: Joaquín de Entrambasaguas, <u>RFE</u>, XXVI(1942), 524-26 (praises this <u>precioso folleto,</u> "una lección perfecta de investigación histórico-arquitectónica que muchos restauradores de monumentos debieran leer").
  Following a prologue by González de Amezúa, Muguruza, the architect in charge of the restoration of Lope's house, explains in detail the procedures involved in his task. His commentary is greatly enhanced by photographs and architectural sketches (58 illustrations) covering many significant stages of the work. The only printed negative reaction to the restoration of which the author was aware, that found in Astrana Marín's <u>Vida azarosa de Lope de Vega</u>, is included at the end of the book.

Müller-Bochat, Eberhard. <u>Lope de Vega und die italienische Dichtung</u>. Mainz, Akademie der Wissenschaften und der Literatur, 1956. Pp. 158. (<u>Abhandlungen der Geistes- und Sozialwissenschaftlichen Klasse</u>, Jahrgang 1956, No. 12, pp. 1019-1176.)
  Rev: A. E. Bean, <u>Bol. de Filologia</u> (Lisbon), XVI(1956-57), 59-60; M. Newels, <u>RF</u>, LXX(1958), 442-47 (fresh insights praised); A. S. Trueblood, <u>NRFH</u>, XII(1958), 220-26.
  Setting aside the usual division between dramatic and non-dramatic, this careful work sheds new light on the interconnection between different areas of Lope's production. It clarifies the nature and meaning of Lope's debt to Italian literature and literary theory and considers his place in Western dramatic and epic tradition. Its only weakness is a tendency to systematize Lope too categorically and too theoretically.

Navarro Tomás, Tomás. "Notas fonológicas sobre Lope de Vega." <u>Archivum</u>, IV(1956), 45-52.

Oñate, María del Pilar. <u>El feminismo en la literatura española</u>. Madrid, Espasa-Calpe, 1938. Pp. 256.
  References to Lope: <u>La Dorotea</u> (pp. 135-36), <u>Teatro</u> (pp. 143-56).

Parker, J. H. "Lope de Vega and Juan Pérez de Montalván: Their
    Literary Relations." In Hispanic Studies in Honour of I.
    González Llubera, Oxford, Dolphin, 1959, pp. 225-35.
  Rev: Marcel Bataillon, BHS, XXXVIII(1961), 216-24 ("nos ofrece un
    avance de sus investigaciones sobre las relaciones literarias
    de los dos escritores entre 1620 y 1636...").
  Lope's acquaintance with Pérez de Montalván grew out of his as-
    sociation with the younger man's father, a bookseller, and
    continued until Lope's death, which Montalván commemorated by
    means of the Fama póstuma, Madrid, 1636. For references to
    this "first biography," see Torre, "Nueva interpretación de
    Lope de Vega" (1946) and Entrambasaguas, "Lope de Vega y
    Portugal" (1950), both in Studies — General; and Alonso, "Lope
    y el Adone de Marino" (1951), in Studies — Poetry — General.

Pérez Gómez, Antonio. "Notas para la bibliografía de Lope de Vega y
    de los romances de don Álvaro de Luna." El Libro Español, I,
    No. 6 (1958), 293-99.

Pfandl, Ludwig. Historia de la literatura nacional española en la
    Edad de Oro. Trans. from the German by Jorge Rubió Balaguer.
    2nd ed. Barcelona, Gili, 1952. Pp. xv, 740.
  The sections dealing with Lope remain the same as in the text of
    the 1933 edition. What is new in this edition is the Suple-
    mento al Apéndice bibliográfico (pp. 713-40). The Lope section
    (pp. 733-35) contains a few items of 1950 and 1951, but nothing
    by American and Canadian scholars later than 1949.

Play Cargol, Joaquín. El Fénix de los ingenios. Gerona, Dalman
    Carles, 1957. Pp. 184. (Bib. Clás.)

Pound, Ezra. "La calidad de Lope de Vega." CHA, XXI, No. 59 (1954),
    141-64.
  A Spanish translation of an essay in the Spirit of Romance, pub-
    lished for the first time in 1910, when Pound was 25 years old.

Rennert, Hugo A. The Life of Lope de Vega. New York, Stechert,
    1937. Pp. xiii, 587. (Reprint of the edition of Glasgow,
    1904.)

Reyes, Alfonso. "Silueta de Lope de Vega." In Capítulos de litera-
    tura española (primera serie), Mexico, La Casa de España, 1939,
    pp. 73-97; and in Cuatro ingenios: Arcipreste de Hita, Lope de
    Vega, Quevedo, Gracián, Mexico-Buenos Aires, Espasa-Calpe, 1950,
    pp. 35-57 (this vol. reviewed by Allen W. Phillips, RHM, XVII,
    1951, 152-53). (A fragment of the essay appeared in Rev. de
    América, VIII, 1946, 333.)
  "Romántico, prerromántico, conserva todo el universo en sus
    apetitos y por eje de su personalidad escoge el amor. Gran
    transformador de la naturaleza en poesía, nos parece como
    vertiginosa rueda metafísica que arrojara sobre el mundo

estético la realidad práctica triturada y desmenuzada." The <u>Silueta</u>, in a first version, formed the prologue to <u>Teatro de Lope de Vega</u>, I, Madrid, Calleja, 1919, pp. 9-22; and was also published in <u>Homenaje a Lope de Vega Carpio en el tercer centenario de su muerte: 1635-1935</u>, Rio de Janeiro, Cámara Oficial Española de Comercio e Industria, 1935, pp. 49-64. In both <u>Capítulos</u> and <u>Cuatro ingenios</u>, the <u>Silueta</u> is followed by an essay on <u>El peregrino en su patria</u>. See Studies — Prose — Individual Prose Works.

Ricard, R. "Sacerdoce et littérature dans l'Espagne du siècle d'or. Le cas de Lope de Vega." <u>LR</u>, X(1956), 39-49.
A general biographical article. Speculations on the double life of Lope, priest and lover. Makes comparisons with Tirso and the Archpriest of Hita in this respect.

Riquer, M. de. "Un pasaje de Lope de Vega y un símil de Richart de Berbezilh." <u>RBN</u>, V(1944), 339-49.

Riva Agüero, José de la. <u>Lope de Vega</u>. Milan, Treves, 1937. Pp. 99.
Rev: Ross H. Ingersoll, <u>Hisp</u>, XXI(1938), 330-31.
The reviewer points out that "the text of this book was first given in the form of an address at ... the Peruvian Academy.... This address has since been published ... in an Italian translation by Fratelli Treves.... Riva Agüero evidently chose as his principal source the work of Luis Astrana Marín (<u>Vida azarosa de Lope de Vega</u>, Barcelona, 1935).... The book treats only two things which might be original. First, it offers a five-page attempt to prove that the <u>Epístola</u> written to Lope supposedly by the Peruvian lady Amarilis really was written by her.... Second, it offers a summary vision of the Spanish colony of Peru as Lope imagined it to be and as he presented his picture of it in his various works."

Rodríguez Casado, Vicente. "Lope de Vega en Indias." <u>Escorial</u>, XII (1943), 249-64.

Romero Flores, H. R. <u>Estudio psicológico sobre Lope de Vega</u>. Madrid, Sucesores de Rivadeneyra, 1936. Pp. 227.
Rev: Otis H. Green, <u>HR</u>, V(1937), 370.

------. "Lope de Vega, Goya, y Manzanares." <u>RIE</u>, XIV(1956), 147-57.

Sainz de Robles, Federico Carlos. <u>Jubileo y aleluyas de Lope de Vega. Ensayos de simpatía.</u> Madrid, Espasa-Calpe, 1936. Pp. 189.
Rev: A. R., <u>RHM</u>, III(1937), 227.

------. <u>El "otro" Lope de Vega</u>. (Ensayo de conocimientos "por el envés"). Buenos Aires, Espasa-Calpe, 1940. Pp. 194. (<u>Col. Austral</u>, 114.) (2nd. ed.: 1943.)

------. *Ensayo de un diccionario de la literatura.* Vol. II:
Autores españoles e hispanoamericanos. Madrid, Aguilar, 1949-
50. Pp. 1866.
    Lope de Vega, pp. 1747-75. Encomiastic sketch of Lope's life
and works. Still identifies the Marfisa of *La Dorotea* with
María de Aragón and gives the number of plays in the second
Peregrino as 333 instead of 448. Devotes much space to the
non-dramatic works (pp. 1759-1770). Bibliography (pp. 1770-75).

------. *Lope de Vega: Retrato, horóscopo, vida y transfiguración.*
Madrid, Aguilar, 1958. Pp. 321.
    Reëdition of the author's introductory study to his edition of
Lope de Vega, *Obras escogidas,* Madrid, Aguilar, 1946. (Published again as a monograph in 1962.)

Salazar, María de la Concepción. "Nuevos documentos sobre Lope de
Vega." *RFE,* XXV(1941), 478-506.
    Published here are the certificate of baptism of Isabel de Urbina,
Lope's first wife, and other documents referring principally to
Lope's stay in Alba de Tormes, including a rental contract,
dated Jan. 26, 1594, and the detailed account of an auction,
dated Aug., 1595, in which Lope disposed of his wife's possessions, some seven months after her death.

Salomon, Noël. *Recherches sur le thème paysan au temps de Lope de
Vega.* Unpub. doct. diss., Sorbonne, 1959.

Sánchez, José. *Academias literarias del Siglo de Oro español.*
Madrid, Gredos, 1961. Pp. 357.
    References to Lope, *passim.*

Sánchez Estevan, I. *Frey Lope Félix de Vega Carpio. Semblanza.*
Mexico, Edit. Nacional, 1957. Pp. 192.
    A reëdition of this work, originally published in Barcelona,
Sociedad General de Publicaciones, 1931.

Sánchez Marino, Rafael. "Nuevo documento de Lope de Vega." *Anales
Cervantinos,* III(1953), 380.
    A document of Lope's, asking that his son Félix del Carpio be
legitimized, raises an interesting problem of identification:
son of which "muger soltera"? Sánchez Marino leaves the solution to the *lopistas.*

------. *Alonso Pérez de Montalbán. Su importancia en el círculo
literario de Lope de Vega.* Unpub. doct. diss., Univ. of Madrid,
1955.

Serrano Medialdea, Antonio. "Un rey de armas en el derecho diplomático de Lope de Vega." *RL,* XVIII(1960), 129-33.

Serrano Poncela, Segundo. "Unamuno y los clásicos." La Torre, IX (1961), 505-35.
    Unamuno on Cervantes, Lope, Calderón, etc.

Simón Díaz, José. "Los estudios del primer protector de Lope." In Aportación documental para la erudición española, Segunda serie, Madrid, 1947, pp. 14-15.

------. "Una semblanza del raptor de la hija de Lope." RL, IX(1956), 161-63.
    Don Cristóbal Tenorio.

------. Bibliografía de la literatura hispánica. Vol. VI: Literatura castellana. Siglos de Oro, autores (continuación). Madrid, CSIC, 1961. Pp. 937.
    In the Índice onomástico de autores, p. 771, the author lists those item numbers that refer to Lope. The items total 139, and they comprise several categories: references to poems by Lope that appeared originally in various places, usually as dedicatory to other poets; references to poems by other poets in his memory after his death; aprobaciones of some of Lope's works by others; other odds and ends including references to articles on Lope's work, articles published before 1961.

Simón Díaz, José, and Juana de José Prades. Ensayo de una bibliografía de las obras y artículos sobre la vida y escritos de Lope de Vega Carpio. Madrid, Centro de Estudios sobre Lope de Vega, 1956. Pp. ix, 233.
    Rev: J. M. Martínez Cachero, Archivum, V(1956), 425-26; H. E. Woodbridge, BA, XXX(1956), 327; J. H. Parker, HR, XXV(1957), 66-69; E. Müller-Bochat, RF, LXX(1958), 440-42.
    The most serious attempt to present a Lope bibliography as complete as possible. In spite of some omissions, inconsistencies and other shortcomings, a most useful tool for lopistas.

------, and ------. Lope de Vega: Nuevos estudios (Adiciones al "Ensayo de una bibliografía de las obras y artículos sobre ... Lope de Vega Carpio"). Madrid, CSIC, 1961. Pp. 16. (Cuad. Bibliográficos, 4.)
    The booklet offers 221 items of Lopean bibliography, representing an addition, as the title indicates, to the volume listed above.

Spitzer, Leo. Romanische Literaturstudien, 1936-1956. Tübingen, Max Niemeyer, 1959. Pp. 944.
    Rev: Arnold G. Reichenberger, HR, XXIX(1961), 134-37.
    Contains: "A Central Theme and its Structural Equivalent in Lope's Fuenteovejuna," which had appeared in HR, XXIII(1955), 274-92; and "Lope de Vega's Al triunfo de Judit," which had appeared in MLN, LXIX(1954), 1-11.

Steiger, Arnald. "Madrid zur Zeit Lope de Vegas." Hesperia, VIII (1951), 27-46.

Studies in Philology. "Recent Literature of the Renaissance. A
    Bibliography and Index." In SP, XXXVI, No. 2, part 2 (1939) on.
    Earlier volumes had contained "Continental Influences: Selected
    Studies of Renaissance Literature in Foreign Countries" as part
    of "English Renaissance Bibliography." In the number for Apr.,
    1939, an annual bibliography (material for 1938) for Spanish
    was begun and has been continued. Lope is fully treated. The
    present compilers for Spanish are Robert Bishop and Warren
    McCready.

Tiemann, Hermann. Lope de Vega in Deutschland. Kritisches Gesamt-
    verzeichnis der auf deutschen Bibliotheken vorhandenen älteren
    Lope- Drucke und Handschriften, nebst Versuch einer Bibliogra-
    phie der deutschen Lope-Literatur, 1629-1935. Hamburg, Lütcke
    und Wulf, 1939. Pp. xv, 310.
  Rev: Franz Rauhut, RF, LIV(1940), 453-54; W. L. Fichter, HR, X
    (1942), 179-80 ("an indispensable tool for the student of
    Lope's dramatic productions, supplementing at many points the
    now outdated Bibliography of Rennert"); Alwin Kuhn, Literatur-
    blatt für germanische und romanische Philologie, LXIII(1942),
    184-87.
  Arranged chronologically, which has the advantage of showing
    trends in scholarship over the period presented. It has rich
    sources to draw upon — the German libraries and the Vienna
    Nationalbibliothek — and is a key contribution to Lopean
    bibliographical studies. The Kuhn review places it on a par
    with the Rennert Bibliography (1915) and the catalogue of
    Biblioteca Nacional (1935).

------. "Über Lope de Vegas Bild und Wirkung in Deutschland." RJ,
    I(1947-48), 233-75.
  Rev: A. Porqueras Mayo, RFE, XLII(1960), 496-97.
  The article summarizes the interest in, and work on, Lope in
    Germany from the 17th to the 20th centuries. Lope-studies are
    comparatively sparse. Tiemann attributes this partly to the
    fact that Lope has left no truly representative work and no
    truly "finalized" one because of his haste and his failure to
    go back and polish, and because of the mass and variety of his
    work. Mention is made, among others, of a German version of
    El peregrino en su patria in 1629, of a performance of El
    vellocino de oro, in Spanish, in 1633, and a German translation,
    from the Dutch, of El palacio confuso, in 1652.

Torre, Guillermo de. "Lope de Vega y su mundo." Asomante, II(1946),
    33-43.
  The article is divided into six sections: "Autocrítica. Inter-
    pretación del 'arte nuevo'" (pp. 33-36), with reference to
    Menéndez Pelayo's interpretation of the Arte nuevo as a
    "lamentable palinodia" and to Menéndez Pidal's opposite view
    of "la idea libertadora"; "El público de los corrales" (pp.
    36-37), referred to as "realmente amedrantador"; "¿Verdad o

estilización? (pp. 37-38), in which the author does not reach
a conclusion; "Espontaneidad y lima. Llanismo y culteranismo"
(pp. 38-40); "Lope de Vega y Góngora" (pp. 40-42); and "El común de-
nominador barroco" (pp. 42-43). This essay is an important contribution on various aspects of Lope's work and aesthetic ideas.

------. "Nueva interpretación de Lope de Vega." Rev. de América,
 VIII(1946), 328-33.
In the first part of the essay, "Bajo el signo de la hipérbole,"
Lope is presented as legend and tradition represented him, that
is, a myth, to which Pérez de Montalván's Fama póstuma contributed.
In the second part, Torre presents the image of Lope as the
extraordinary man that he was, but nevertheless a man, thanks
to the publication of his private correspondence.

------. "Prisma de Lope de Vega: Lo clásico, lo español, lo universal." Cuad. Americanos, XXXI(1947), 179-90.
The author laments the fact that although Lope has his specialists, neither his name nor his work is included in universal
literature. Lope is peculiar to his age and country. Twelve
works of Spanish literature considered worthy of belonging to
world literature are listed, among them La Dorotea. The
author neither defends Lope sufficiently nor proves his point.
This is one of the articles whose loss would not be any loss.

Torres Bodet, Jaime. "Balzac, Lope de Vega y Proust." La Gaceta
 (Mexico), V, No. 50 (1958), 1-2.
The author distinguishes between Lope and Balzac, both men of
action, by noting that action in Lope is alegría vital, while
in Balzac it leads inevitably to tragedy. A provocative
article, though the assertion that Lope's characters "live
(only) in the present" is open to serious question.

Valbuena Prat, Ángel. Historia de la literatura española. Vol. II.
 Barcelona, Gili, 1937. Pp. 1016. (Later eds.)
 Rev: E. Allison Peers, BHS, XV(1938), 111-14.
Two chapters (pp. 193-255) devoted entirely to Lope; many other
references to Lope passim. This Historia has become the
classic manual for the undergraduate student of Spanish literature, and the various chapters it devotes to the personality
of Lope de Vega and his comedias, autos, epic and lyric poetry
and prose are useful enough and generally accurate for the
stated purpose.

Valle, José-María del. Lope de Vega. Madrid, Hernando, 1947.

Van Dam, C. F. A. "Lope de Vega en het Nederlands." Nieuwe Taalgids,
 LIV(1961), 336-37.

Vázquez Cuesta, Pilar. "Nuevos datos sobre doña Marta de Nevares." RFE, XXXI(1947), 86-107.
   Gives data and genealogy of Marta de Nevares y Santoyo and her family. Mentions others with the names of Nevares and Santoyo.

Vian, Francesco. Introduzione alla letteratura spagnola del "Siglo de Oro." Milan, Società Editrice "Vita e Pensiero," 1946. Pp. 122.
   References to Lope in the section entitled "Problemi critico-spirituali del Siglo de Oro," pp. 50-122.

Voltés, Pedro M. Breves biografías íntimas de grandes poetas. Barcelona, Molina, 1951. Pp. 223.
   Of a popular nature; includes Lope de Vega.

Vossler, Karl. "Lope de Vega und wir." In Aus der romanische Welt, II, Leipzig, Koehler & Amelang, 1940, pp. 81-103.

------. Lope de Vega y su tiempo. Trans. Ramón de la Serna. 2nd ed. Madrid, Rev. de Occidente, 1940. Pp. 367.
   This is a reprinting of the Spanish edition of 1933. The original German version of 1932 was reprinted, with a few changes in the notes, in Munich, Biederstein Verlag, 1947. Pp. x, 374 (Lope de Vega und sein Zeitalter). Fichter (Hisp, XX, 1937, 327) considered this work to be the most satisfactory biographical account to have appeared between 1920 and 1935: "As an evaluation of Lope's life and works it is the best book that has yet appeared: a profound and brilliant exposition, obviously written con amore, and destined, it would seem, to remain for a long time unsurpassed."

------. Introducción a la literatura española del Siglo de Oro. Seis lecciones. Buenos Aires-Mexico, Espasa-Calpe, 1945. Pp. 151.
   Lope is frequently mentioned. In particular, lessons two "Las formas literarias" (pp. 35-55), three "El elemento religioso" (pp. 59-80) and five "Los motivos idílicos y la poesía de la naturaleza" (pp. 107-25) contain valuable remarks concerning Lope, which in many instances sum up thoughts Vossler has expressed in his scholarly essays about Lope de Vega's works.

------. "Lope und sein Eigentum." Rheinischer Merkur (Koblenz), III, No. 50 (1948), 5.

Wardropper, Bruce W. "An Early English Hispanist." BHS, XXIV(1947), 259-68.
   An appraisal of Henry Richard Vassall Fox, Baron Holland (1773-1840), biographer of Lope. Wardropper discusses Holland's Life of Lope, and his position with regard to problems of literature.

Winkler, Eugen G. "Lope de Vega." In <u>Gestalten und Probleme</u>, Leipzig, Karl Rauch, 1937. Reprinted in <u>Dichtungen, Gestalten und Probleme</u>, Reutlingen, Günther Neske Pfullingen, 1956, pp. 402-08.

Ximénez de Sandoval, Felipe. "Por los pecados del Fénix." <u>Escorial</u>, XX, No. 63 (1949), 633-67.
   Marcela, daughter of Lope and Micaela Luján, "no puede hacer más que ofrecer (su vida) al Niño-Dios, ultrajado por los horribles pecados del poeta.... Será esposa de Cristo" (p. 641). A sentimental biography of Sor Marcela de San Félix, based on unidentified quotations from Lope, on the few published poems by Sor Marcela (see p. 667), and on empathy.

Zabala, Arturo. "Rastros léxicos del valenciano en la obra de Lope de Vega." <u>Mediterráneo</u>, No. 5 (1944), 37-48.
   Studies, above all, <u>El bobo del colegio</u>.

------. <u>Valencia y Lope de Vega</u>. Unpub. doct. diss., Univ. of Madrid, 1944.

------. "Alusión de Lope de Vega a unos supuestos amores valencianos." In <u>Estudios dedicados a Menéndez Pidal</u>, VI(Madrid, 1956), 591-609.
   Concerning Fernando Pellicer.

Zamora Lucas, Florentino. <u>Lope de Vega, censor de libros. Colección de aprobaciones, censuras, elogios y prólogos del Fénix, que se hallan en los preliminares de algunos libros de su tiempo, con notas biográficas de sus autores.</u> Larache, Artes Gráficas Boscá, 1941. Pp. 185.
   The <u>Notas preliminares</u> (pp. 11-30) treat several aspects of Lope's connection with the Church and with the Inquisition as well as random sub-topics ranging from "Religiosidad de Lope" to Lope's feelings on "Amistad y cortesía," all of which are given but rapid and necessarily superficial treatment. Includes 56 documents, arranged chronologically, from 1607-1635. Zamora Lucas claims that some entries of his are not included in the <u>Apuntes</u> of Millé y Giménez.

Zamora Vicente, Alonso. "Lope de Vega." In <u>Diccionario de literatura española</u>, Madrid, Rev. de Occidente, 1949, pp. 733-37. (2nd ed.: 1953.)
  Rev: C. D. Ley, <u>BHS</u>, XXVII(1950), 56-58.
   Excellent introduction to Lope. Praises the total fusion of the traditional element with the personal lyric gift. Selected bibliography.

------. <u>Lope de Vega. Su vida y su obra</u>. Madrid, Gredos, 1961. Pp. 292. (<u>Bib. Románica Hispánica</u>, 7.)

For the general reader an adequate and well-written account. It lacks sufficient scholarly apparatus for the specialist, but is a volume worthy of praise.

Zertuche, Francisco M. "Trazo de Lope de Vega." <u>Vida Universitaria</u> (Univ. de Nuevo León, Monterrey, Mexico), III(1953), 3-4 and 7.
This sketch of the life and works of Lope offers nothing new, but is adequate as an introduction.

------. "Agravios entre Lope y Cervantes." <u>Vida Universitaria</u>, IV (1954), 3-4.
Gives the history of relations between Lope and Cervantes. Presents no new material, but is interesting.

DRAMA

A. GENERAL

Adam, Francis Osborne. <u>Some Aspects of Lope de Vega's Dramatic Technique as Observed in his Autograph Plays</u>. Unpub. doct. diss., Univ. of Illinois, 1936.
Rev: O. H. Green, <u>HR</u>, V(1937), 371.

Adams, Charles L. <u>Traditional and Novelesque Elements in the Development of Plot in the Dated Plays of Lope de Vega</u>. Unpub. doct. diss., Stanford Univ., 1954. Pp. 251. (<u>DA</u>, XIV, 1706.)
Adams shows that Lope made use of traditional and novelesque elements throughout his career, but especially in the period 1596-1615. He was more influenced by universal than by national motifs. These elements are basic in over half the plays, supporting in many and extraneous in a third, of 115 plays studied. A worthwhile contribution to our knowledge of Lope's plots and his habits of constructing plots.

------. "The Problem of the Motif-Index with Special Reference to Lope de Vega." <u>BCom</u>, VII, No. 1 (1955), 1-3.

Albarracín Teulón, Agustín. "La naturaleza humana en el teatro de Lope de Vega." <u>Archivo Iberoamericano de Historia de la Medicina</u>, III(1951), 475-517.

------. "La patología en el teatro de Lope de Vega." <u>Archivo Iberoamericano de Historia de la Medicina</u>, IV(1952), 407-535.

------. <u>La medicina en el teatro de Lope de Vega</u>. Madrid, CSIC, 1954. Pp. 382.
Rev: Kelvin M. Parker, <u>BA</u>, XXX(1956), 72 (the reviewer criticizes the study, saying that the author is interested in medicine and "perhaps in literature," and that the results are neither scientific nor literary).

This book gives evidence of a great amount of work and an extensive knowledge of medical terms and lore. Yet the author does not interpret his findings in such a manner as to add much to our knowledge and appreciation of Lope de Vega. The book is, however, a mine of references and quotations on the subjects discussed.

Alonso, Dámaso. "Tres procesos de dramatización." In De los siglos oscuros al de oro, Madrid, Gredos, 1958, pp. 144-47. (Bib. Románica Hispánica.)
Rev: Otis H. Green, HR, XXVIII(1960), 276-77.
In support of his assertion that a dramatist in adapting a plot to the stage may transfer it practically unmodified, expand it or compress it, the author briefly refers to Fuenteovejuna as an example of the first process, and to El caballero de Olmedo and Peribáñez as examples of the second.

Arco y Garay, Ricardo del. La sociedad española en las obras dramáticas de Lope de Vega. Madrid, Escelicer, 1942. Pp. 928.
Rev: S. G. Morley, HR, XII(1944), 352-53.
In this monumental undertaking, Arco y Garay has quoted some 5,000 passages from Lope's comedias. Rather than a study of texts, it is an immense catalogue of references made by Lope to certain topics. Occasional comparisons are drawn between Lope and other principal Golden Age literary figures. Although these are intentionally kept to a minimum, they are always relevant and interesting. The style of the commentaries is clear and lively and the classification of this vast amount of textual material should greatly facilitate the work of future investigators.

Arjona, J. H. "El disfraz varonil en Lope de Vega." BH, XXXIX(1937), 120-45.

------. "Dos errores de cronología lopesca." RR, XXVIII(1937), 311-17.
Valuable data regarding the dates of El vellocino de oro and La tragedia del rey don Sebastián y bautismo del príncipe de Marruecos.

------. "La introducción del gracioso en el teatro de Lope de Vega." HR, VII(1939), 1-21.
A detailed study of the gracioso. Offers also a valuable bibliography of earlier literature on the subject. A very important article.

------. "Defective Rhymes and Rhyming Techniques in Lope de Vega's Autograph Comedias." HR, XXIII(1955), 108-28.
Positivistic, interesting and effective criterion for attribution of authorship.

------. "False Andalusian Rhymes in Lope de Vega and their Bearing on the Authorship of Doubtful *Comedias*." HR, XXIV(1956), 290-305.
A study of Andalusian rhyme for criterion to establish authorship.

------. "Modern Psychology in Lope de Vega." BCom, VIII, No. 1 (1956), 5-6.
Reference to *El capellán de la Virgen* and *El castigo sin venganza*.

------. "Ten Plays Attributed to Lope de Vega." HR, XXVIII(1960), 319-40.
Nine of the plays (*Las audiencias del rey don Pedro*, *Las burlas y enredos de Benito*, *El cerco de Viena y socorro por Carlos V*, *La corona derribada y vara de Moisés*, *El esclavo fingido*, *El hijo por engaño y toma de Toledo*, *El premio riguroso y amistad bien pagada*, *La reina doña María* and *El sufrimiento de honor*) are considered doubtful in the M.-B. *Chronology*; but they accept the tenth, *La ingratitud vengada*, as authentic Lope. The principal test applied here is that of orthoëpy, together with a consideration of the number of autorhymes, words like *vide*, *vido*, *felice*, and so on. All ten fail these tests, to varying degrees.

Artman, Jim P. *The Soldier in the Dramatic Works of Lope de Vega*. Unpub. doct. diss., Univ. of California at Los Angeles, 1957.
Lope's fondness for heroic aspects of Spanish history naturally caused him to present a variety of soldiers. They have their distinctive traits, but share those of "valor, gallantry, discipline, and above all a devotion to the heroic traditions of Spain." (A paper of this title was read at the 1959 meeting of South Central Modern Language Association; cf. "Abstracts of Papers," *South Central Bulletin*, Feb., 1960, p. 20.)

Aubrun, Charles V. "Enfants terribles dans la *Comedia* (1600-1650)." RJ, VIII(1957), 312-20.
Lope is included among the dramatists cited to exemplify an unconscious obsession of the Golden Age with themes of parricide, incest and rebellion. The author finds psychological and sociological causes for this situation. Lope and his school tend to idealize it and impose a happy ending.

Avalle-Arce, Juan Bautista. "Dos notas a Lope de Vega." NRFH, VII (1953), 426-32.
1. The author gives two reasons, neither sufficient by itself but both plausible, for attributing the original version of *Las mocedades de Bernardo del Carpio* to Lope: (a) possible reference to Elena Osorio in "Félix Alba" and (b) mention of the *escudo* of Bernardo del Carpio, with its 19 castles, at a time when Lope was trying hard to establish his own nobility and described and used this crest many times.

2. The author convincingly demonstrates that the oft-repeated statement that Cubillo de Aragón's <u>Tragedia del duque de Berganza</u> dealt with the same story as the first two acts of Lope's <u>El duque de Viseo</u> is incorrect.

Barclay, T. B. <u>The Rôle of the Dance and Dance Lyrics in the Spanish "Comedia" to the Early Eighteenth Century</u>. Unpub. doct. diss., Univ. of Toronto, 1957. Pp. 342.
A careful and well-documented study of this theme.

------. "The Importance of the Dance in the Spanish <u>Comedia</u> before the Eighteenth Century." <u>BCom</u>, X, No. 2 (1958), 21-23.
Reference to Lope's <u>El maestro de danzar,</u> etc.

Barrett, Linton Lomas. <u>The Supernatural in the Spanish Non-Religious "Comedia" of the Golden Age</u>. Unpub. doct. diss., Univ. of North Carolina, 1938.

Bataillon, Marcel. "La Nouvelle chronologie de la <u>Comedia</u> lopesque: De la métrique à la histoire." <u>BH</u>, XLVIII(1946), 227-37.
Bataillon's article is not a book review of the M.-B. <u>Chronology</u>, but an essay in which he points out various aspects of the <u>Comedia</u> which need to be studied. The first part of the article does praise the <u>Chronology</u> as "un admirable instrument de travail," and confirms some of the <u>Chronology</u>'s tentative findings. In the second half of the article, Bataillon urges a careful study of the metrics of other dramatists, and a study of theme and character development; also, he asks that chronology be put "résolument ... au service de l'histoire avec l'étude des thèmes, des personnages, des situations, des scènes à effet, des morceaux de bravoure."

Baulier, Francis. "La Mise en scène dans deux pièces de Lope de Vega." <u>BH</u>, XLVII(1945), 57-70.
Baulier sets out to prove that Lope's powerful poetry (in <u>El grao de Valencia</u> and in <u>San Segundo de Ávila</u>), used to describe the place where the action took place, successfully, in the spectator's mind, made up for the absence of sets.

Bernard, Henri. "Lope de Vega et l'Extrême-Orient." <u>Monumenta Nipponica</u> (Tokyo), IV(1941), 278-83.
Arthur Lloyd, in his <u>Notes on Japanese Drama</u>, had suggested the influence of Lope on the Kabuki theatre, made by copies of his plays carried to the Far East by sailors and merchants. This theory remains pure conjecture. However, Lope did show interest in the Far East, as exemplified in <u>Los primeros mártires del Japón</u> and <u>El triunfo de la fe en los reinos del Japón</u>. The article has scant critical value and contains the misinformation that Lope died in Lisbon!

Boughner, Daniel C. *The Braggart in Renaissance Comedy*. Minneapolis, Univ. of Minnesota Press, 1954. Pp. ix, 328.
  Rev: K.-L. Selig, *RBPH*, XXXV(1957), 834-35.
    Chapter 9, "The Renaissance and the Golden Age in Spain," treats Lope de Vega, pp. 211-29. The author's evident lack of first-hand familiarity with the plays he discusses is regrettable. The rôle of the braggart in the *Comedia* needs a more critical treatment.

Bravo-Villasante, Carmen. *La mujer vestida de hombre en el teatro español*. *Siglos XVI-XVII*. Madrid, Rev. de Occidente, 1955. Pp. 238.
  Rev: María Alfaro, *Índice de Artes y Letras*, XI(1957), 28 ("la autora ha realizado un estudio muy completo..."); J. Campos, *Ínsula*, XII, No. 131 (1957), 8 ("trabajo interesante y cuidadoso"); G. E. Wade, *BCom*, IX, No. 2 (1957), 19-20 (Exploration of the literary sources of the device, mainly Italian, constitutes a significant contribution. The author traces its development and decline from Lope de Rueda on.); and, an outstanding review article: B. B. Ashcom, "Concerning 'la mujer en hábito de hombre' in the *Comedia*," *HR*, XXVIII(1960), 43-62.
    Lope de Vega, especially pp. 61-106. (See also *La mujer vestida de hombre en la literatura española*, unpub. doct. diss., Univ. of Madrid, 1957.)

Brenan, Gerald. "Lope de Vega and the New Comedy." In *The Literature of the Spanish People*, Cambridge, The University Press, 1951, pp. 199-221. (2nd ed.: 1953.)
  Rev (of vol.): E. A. Peers, *BHS*, XVIII(1951), 272-73; E. M. Wilson, *MLR*, XLVII(1952), 595-96.
    "The great defect of this volume is the treatment of the theatre. It does not much matter that Lope de Vega's names are given in the wrong order or that his father is described as a 'basket maker' (These errors are corrected in the 2nd ed.). Much more serious is the remark that Spanish drama 'is a literature of a rather light sort.' It is not true that in Lope's plays 'nothing is ever gone into deeply' (in 2nd ed. changed to '... a realist, who saw things as they were without going into them too deeply') or that in them 'no new light is ever thrown on human nature...' The account of Lope suffers from the fact that no single play is analysed in detail and generalizations like those just quoted apply only to his very poorest work." (Wilson, review, p. 596.)

Brown, Robert B. *Bibliografía de las comedias históricas, tradicionales y legendarias de Lope de Vega*. Mexico, Edit. Academia and Univ. of Iowa Press, 1958. Pp. 151.
  A very useful bibliography. Contains items not found in Simón Díaz — José Prades.

Bruerton, Courtney. "Lope's Belardo-Lucindo Plays." HR, V(1937), 309-15.

------. "The Date of Schaeffer's Tomo antiguo." HR, XV(1947), 346-64.
The sixth play of the volume is El caballero de Olmedo ascribed to Lope. On page 359 of his article, Bruerton gives a brief account of the play, which, he says, is "quite different" from Lope's. It is the play published by Juliá Martínez, Madrid, 1944.

------. "More on Lopean Chronology." BCom, V, No. 2 (1953), 30-31.
A timely reminder of Celestino López Martínez' Teatros y comediantes sevillanos del siglo XVI. Estudio documental (Seville, 1940), which adds important chronological details concerning Lope's plays, and which may have been missed by Lope scholars in North America because of the War.

Buchanan, Milton A. "Bibliographical Notes: IV." HR, V(1937), 186-88.
Deals with the question of the fidelity of literature (specifically the Comedia) to life.

Camón Aznar, José. "Citas de arte en el teatro de Lope de Vega." RIE, III(1945), 71-137 and 233-274.
This long and interesting essay is divided into two parts: references to architecture (pp. 71-137) and references to painting (pp. 233-53), sculpture (pp. 253-55) and the industrial arts (pp. 255-74). As Camón Aznar states, the article does not intend "estudiar la actitud estética de Lope de Vega, sino simplemente presentar unas citas de arte" (note on p. 71) which would serve as supplements to previous works, such as Ricardo del Arco's La sociedad española en las obras dramáticas de Lope de Vega (Madrid, 1942), and Miguel Herrero García's Contribución de la literatura a la historia del arte (Madrid, 1943).

Campiglia, Jeannette. Some Aspects of Nature in the "Comedia" of Lope de Vega. Unpub. doct. diss., Univ. of California at Los Angeles, 1959.
Lope uses nature in his capacities as poet, painter and technician. His handling of nature is based mainly on bucolicism, showing both classical and medieval influences. Most frequent are the pastoril motif, the Beatus ille, the menosprecio de corte y alabanza de aldea, "the recurring soledades ... and a kind of bucolic Franciscanism."

Cappelletti, Ángel J. "Notas sobre tres dramas y una epopeya de la libertad." Universidad (Univ. Nac. del Litoral, Santa Fe, Argentina), No. 36 (1957), 237-49.

    In this outstanding article which makes a distinction between a positive or absolute and a negative or relative liberty, the author uses <u>Fuenteovejuna</u> to illustrate how man attempts to liberate himself, in a relative sense, from social power.

Castillo, Homero. "Valor funcional del lugar en doce comedias de Lope de Vega." <u>Estudios</u> (Duquesne Univ.), No. 8 (1954), 15-21.
    The author studies twelve plays in which Lope describes Spanish cities or regions. He finds that in a few instances the place is an integral part of the play, and determines to a great extent the character of the protagonists, who are identified with the place. In other plays, the descriptions of places are lyrical interpolations that have no vital function. The article is somewhat confusing.

Castro, Américo. <u>De la edad conflictiva. I. El drama de la honra en España y en su literatura</u>. Madrid, Taurus, 1961. Pp. 221.

Castro Escudero, J. "Bailes y danzas en el teatro de Lope de Vega." <u>Les Langues Néo-Latines</u>, No. 150 (1959), 66-74.
    The author lists over 50 dances popular at the time, and insists upon a distinction between <u>baile</u> and <u>danza</u>. He stresses the great importance of dancing in Lope's day. Reference to <u>El maestro de danzar</u>. (The study is to be continued.)

Cauvin, Sister Mary Austin. <u>The "Comedia de privanza" in the Seventeenth Century</u>. Unpub. doct. diss., Univ. of Pennsylvania, 1957. Pp. 505. (<u>DA</u>, XVIII, 229.)
    Plays based on the theme of the <u>privado</u>, a result of the corresponding phenomenon at the court of Philip III, are grouped according to the type of <u>privado</u> who figures in them: historical <u>privados</u>, the <u>privado</u> who is his sovereign's rival in love, the <u>privado</u> in love with an <u>infanta</u>, the model <u>privado</u> and the criminally inclined one. Fifty works form the basis of the study, and there is much careful analysis to show the recurrence of themes, devices and situations.

Cioranescu, Alejandro. <u>El barroco o el descubrimiento del drama</u>. La Laguna, Univ. de La Laguna, 1957. Pp. 445.
  Rev: M. del P. Palomo, <u>RL</u>, XI(1957), 207-08 ("obra fundamental"); H. H., <u>CL</u>, X(1958), 179-81 ("rich and mature study," with, however, some faulty chronology and unjustified comparisons); C. Rizza, <u>SFr</u>, II(1958), 98-100 (a very important contribution); V. G. S., <u>RLMC</u>, Nos. 3-4 (1958), 308-09; A. Tovar, <u>PSA</u>, VIII (1958), 317-18 (a highly favourable notice; the book's greatest contribution is to place the Spanish baroque within a general European context).
  This major essay in analysis and interpretation, brilliant in conception, insight and execution, clears the air of much of the haziness surrounding the question of the baroque before proceeding inductively to an exploration of its essential

character. Chapters on fundamental cultural patterns and attitudes are followed by others of stylistic analysis, the latter in turn leading into an examination of an underlying conflict, the systematic exploration of which is the basis of the new drama. While Lope is never dwelt on for long, he is often brought forward in highly suggestive connections and the exposition is continually relevant to him.

Coe, Ada M. <u>Catálogo bibliográfico y crítico de las comedias anunciadas en los periódicos de Madrid desde 1661 hasta 1819.</u> Baltimore, Johns Hopkins Press, 1935. Pp. xii, 270.
  Rev: Paul Mérimée, <u>BH</u>, XL(1938), 218-23.

------ (ed.). <u>Carteleras madrileñas, 1677-1792, 1819.</u> Mexico (Wellesley, Mass., Hathaway House Bookshop), 1952. Pp. 256.
  Rev: A. G. Reichenberger, <u>Hisp</u>, XXXVI(1953), 389-90; Ramon Rozzell, <u>HR</u>, XXII(1954), 169-71.
  "By merely turning the pages ... one gets a telescopic view that is a revelation of changes ... in dramatic tastes. There is a constant mingling of the old and the new.... Lope and Calderón were still holding the boards in the closing days of 1819" (Rozzell, review, p. 169).

Correa, Gustavo. "El doble aspecto de la honra en el teatro del siglo XVII." <u>HR</u>, XXVI(1958), 99-107.
  Rev: P. G., <u>LR</u>, XIV(1960), 57-58.
  "Vertical" honour, an inherent possession, is an agent of social differentiation. It extends downward with diminishing force from its source, the king. "Horizontal" honour, a levelling and cohesive force, depends entirely on reputation, yet embodies the individual's self-esteem, linked with manliness in men, virtue in women. It has ritualistic overtones and extends to the common people. Honour situations in the theatre are an "artistic" equivalent of contemporary values.

Cossío, José María de. <u>Lope, personaje de sus comedias.</u> Madrid, RAE, 1948. Pp. 100.
  Rev: S. Griswold Morley, <u>HR</u>, XVIII(1950), 268-69 (Despite serious critical restrictions, the reviewer recognizes that Cossío "has made the first serious attempt to discover Lope behind Belardo.... Some day this subject must be investigated at much greater length...." Cossío "concentrates his attention almost exclusively upon the figure of Belardo," working "from an examination of 63 plays, of which five ... belong in the 'doubtful' class.").
  An interesting study, too general to be conclusive. But "suggestive and stimulating" for future investigation as Morley states.

Coyné, A. "Lope de Vega y sus ideas dramáticas." <u>Mercurio Peruano</u>, XXXVIII(1957), 475-509.

Within the context of conflicting theories of the drama —
classical precepts vs. "arte nuevo" — this interesting
article examines both Lope's poetics and his ambivalent
attitude toward his own work, drawing for the latter on Lope's
plays, poems, epistles, correspondence and other writings.

Crawford, J. P. W. Spanish Drama before Lope de Vega: A Revised
Edition. Philadelphia, Univ. of Pennsylvania Press, 1937.
Pp. 211.
Rev: John T. Reid, Hisp, XX(1937), 296; Aubrey F. G. Bell, BHS,
XV(1938), 49-52; Ralph E. House, HR, VI(1938), 270-71.
The standard text on the pre-Lope period, and the development of
pre-Lopean drama in Spain. Only a few and very brief references to Lope himself.

Crinò, Anna Maria. "Lope's Exertions for the Abolition of the
Unities in Dramatic Practice." MLN, LXXVI(1961), 259-61.
Lope corresponded with the Italian playwright Jacoppo Cicognini
about the hindrance offered to the plot of a play by the
observance of the unity of time.

Dale, George Irving. "Games and Social Pastimes in the Spanish Drama
of the Golden Age." HR, VIII(1940), 219-41.
Contains a few incidental references to Lope's theatre.

Díaz-Plaja, Guillermo (ed.). El teatro. Enciclopedia del arte
escénico. Barcelona, Noguer, 1958. Pp. 760.
Rev: J. L. C., Ínsula, XIV, No. 147 (1959), 6; José Montero Padilla,
BBMP, XXXV(1959), 393-96.
At once a broad historical survey, world-wide in scope and a
practical manual; this work does not treat given authors in
detail. Occasionally it offers useful background to Lope, as
in the section on costume (pp. 412-18 and 422-26).

Dunn, Peter N. "Some Uses of Sonnets in the Plays of Lope de Vega."
BHS, XXXIV(1957), 212-22.
By discriminating carefully between lyric and dramatic functions
of the sonnet, this highly perceptive article suggests a new
approach to the study of Lope's dramatic sonnets. The sonnet
is seen as an instrument of "dramatic exploration" which illuminates character, motivation, theme, and is in turn enriched
by its often subtle and ironical links to the total dramatic
context.

Entrambasaguas, Joaquín de. "Fernando el Católico, personaje de Lope
de Vega." RUBA, VI(1952), 215-57.
Entrambasaguas examines scenes from Lope's plays in which Ferdinand and Isabella both appear, or, as is more often the case,
Ferdinand alone. Except in those cases where it is necessary
to dim the character of Ferdinand in order not to overshadow
the hero proper, Lope presented him as an historical hero of
almost epic proportions.

------. "Un bofetón de Lope de Vega (comedia de amor y celos)."
 <u>Agora</u>, Nos. 61-62 (1961), 4-9.

Esteller, Juan. "Vigencia del teatro de Lope de Vega." <u>Acento Cultural</u>, Nos. 12-13 (1961), 115-18.

Fernández Cerra, Carmen Pilar. <u>El lirismo en los argumentos históricos de Lope de Vega</u>. Unpub. doct. diss., Johns Hopkins Univ., 1952.

Fichter, William L. "Recent Research on Lope de Vega's Sonnets" (1938). See Studies — Poetry — Individual Poems (<u>Sonnets</u>).

------. "New Aids for Dating the Undated Autographs of Lope de Vega's Plays." <u>HR</u>, IX(1941), 79-90.
 In this article, Fichter studies (1) pious invocations at the top of Lope's pages, either abbreviated or in full; (2) a eucharistic sketch showing two angels kneeling before a chalice containing the Host; and (3) the pious phrase "Loado sea el Santísimo Sacramento," included at the end of the manuscripts and sometimes at the end of an act. Fichter applies these observations to several autographs on which the date is missing.

------. "Orthoëpy as an Aid for Establishing a Canon of Lope de Vega's Authentic Plays." In <u>Estudios Hispánicos. Homenaje a Archer M. Huntington</u>, Wellesley, Mass., Spanish Dept., Wellesley College, 1952, pp. 143-53.
 Rev: A. Carballo Picazo, <u>RFE</u>, XXXVII(1953), 360; Otis H. Green, <u>HR</u>, XXI(1953), 231.
 "W. L. Fichter tests provisionally the authenticity of (eleven of) the plays considered by Morley-Bruerton as <u>possibly</u> by Lope, on the basis of the dramatist's use of syneresis, dieresis, synalepha and hiatus. While such evidence may strengthen the case for or against Lope, a play might still look like Lope's and yet be the work of a contemporary. Other objective criteria, he says, should be sought: e.g., <u>do</u> as against <u>donde</u>." (O. H. Green review.)

Figuereido, F. de. "Erudição. Lope de Vega: Alguns elementos portugueses na sua obra." In <u>Últimas aventuras</u>, Rio de Janeiro, 1940, pp. 255-325.
 Rev: Raúl Moglia, <u>RFH</u>, IV(1942), 185-88.
 Influence of Gil Vicente is found in Lope's <u>autos</u>. Also, several instances are cited in which Camões and Lope seem to have a common source in Petrarch. Examples likewise are given to show Lope's tendency to use the Portuguese language in his <u>comedias</u>.

Flecniakoska, J. L. <u>La Formation de l'auto religieux en Espagne avant Calderón (1550-1635)</u>. Montpellier, Paul Déhan, 1961. Pp. 531.

Gaos, Vicente. "La poética invisible de Lope de Vega." In *Temas y problemas de literatura española*, Madrid, Guadarrama, 1959, pp. 119-42. (Col. Guadarrama de Crítica y Ensayo, 20.)
"Invisible" means that the poética has yet to be formulated, and that the preceptists have to derive it from the study of the plays. "Invisible" also implies that the less discernible the technique, the better the work is likely to be. Comparisons are made with French theatre.

Garasa, Delfín Leocadio. "Ángeles y demonios en el teatro de Lope de Vega." *Bol. de la Acad. Argentina de Letras*, XXV(1960), 233-67.
Most of Lope's comedias de santos contain either angels or devils. Angels usually appear as God's spokesmen and are omniscient; nearly always acted by women. As for devils, Lope tends to present a single one, and he remembers that this is an angel, albeit a perverse one. The Devil assumes human form, and is allowed to tempt and influence people to a certain extent.

Gasparetti, Antonio. *Las novelas de Mateo Bandello como fuentes del teatro de Lope de Vega*. Salamanca, Univ. de Salamanca, 1939. Pp. 96.

Gavidia, Francisco. "La obra de Lope de Vega en la historia del teatro español." In *Discursos, estudios y conferencias*, San Salvador, Imp. Nacional, 1941, pp. 100-17.
Originally delivered as an address in observance of the tercentenary of Lope's death, this study proposes to single out the greatness of the Fénix and to use him as an example to stimulate the growth of dramatic art in Latin America. A very superficial glance at Spanish theatre, with frequent and at times surprising errata.

González de Amezúa, Agustín. *Una colección manuscrita y desconocida de comedias de Lope de Vega Carpio*. Madrid, Centro de Estudios sobre Lope de Vega, 1945. Pp. 139. (Later pub. in *Opúsculos histórico-literarios*, II, Madrid, CSIC, 1951, pp. 364-417.)
Rev: C. Prieto, *Arbor*, V(1946), 312-14 (points out several questions which must be satisfactorily answered, otherwise "las conclusiones perderían valor e incluso cabría plantear la autenticidad de las copias, ante el riesgo de encontrarnos con un caso análogo al de Pedraza con la Celestina"; W. L. Fichter, HR, XV (1947), 468-72.
"This little volume — wrote Fichter in his review — announced one of the most significant discoveries in the field of Spanish studies in recent years. It was surely beyond the fondest hope of the most devoted student of Lope de Vega that there could come to light at this late date as many as 32 manuscript copies of Lopean authographs..." (p. 468). The volume describes the amazing discovery of five volumes, four of which contain thirty-two manuscript copies made by the scribe Ignacio de

Gálvez in 1762 in the Sessa archives. The importance of this discovery is threefold: first, it provides the text of three lost comedias: El favor agradecido (only the first act was known), El amor desatinado and El príncipe inocente; second, it provides the place and exact date of composition of thirty-one of the plays, of which sixteen were undated, and in almost every case the date in the manuscript copy coincides with the one proposed by the M.-B., Chronology (1940); and third, it seems to be a very faithful manuscript copy of Lope's originals, which will be invaluable in the establishment of more correct texts of Lope's comedias.

Gouldson, Kathleen. "The Spanish Peasant in the Drama of Lope de Vega." BHS, XIX(1942), 5-25. (Later pub. in Spanish Golden Age Poetry and Drama, ed. E. Allison Peers, Liverpool, Inst. of Hispanic Studies, 1946, pp. 63-89.)
Rev: A. F. G. Bell, BHS, XXIII(1946), 222-24; C. V. Aubrun, BH, XLIX(1947), 233-34 (the review is important for Aubrun's ideas on the subject); P. E. Russell, MLR, XLII(1947), 522-23 (criticizes Gouldson's assumption that Lope's pictures of peasant life represent everyday reality); Alberto Sánchez, RFE, XXXI(1947), 286-89 (interesting for Sánchez' views on the rustic); Otis H. Green, HR, XVI(1948), 351-52 (dismisses the study as an "elementary cataloguing of types and character traits, festivals and customs, without reference to problems"); Th. Stroobants, LR, III(1949), 238-40.
According to the investigation, the number of plays dealing with peasants and peasant life increases considerably in Lope's later years. The author is tempted to attribute this growing preoccupation with rural customs to the five or six years (ca. 1590-95) spent by Lope in Alba de Tormes during his exile from court. Several characteristics of Lope's peasants are indicated and documented: contentment and loyalty, but readiness to protest, and, if necessary, to revolt against tyranny and injustice; humility and reverence for religion; sensitivity to all kinds of superstition, etc. Frequently, in conflicts between the peasantry and the nobility, Lope takes up the cudgel for the former. His peasants are considered to be far more natural than those of Calderón.

Grupp, William J. Dramatic Theory and Criticism in Spain during the Sixteenth, Seventeenth and Eighteenth Centuries. Unpub. doct. diss., Cornell Univ., 1949.

Hamelin, Jeanne. Le Théâtre chrétien. Paris, Fayard, 1957. Pp. 122. (Col. Je sais-Je crois. Encyclopédie du Catholique au XXème siècle.)
Rev: J. L. Micó Buchón, Razón y Fe, CLVIII(1958), 381-82.
Treats Lope briefly: reference to autos (pp. 47-60) and comedias (pp. 61-64). The treatment is neither penetrating nor thorough, and Lope is strangely referred to as "en quelque sorte chef de l'Église."

Hamilton, T. Earle. "Spoken Letter in the comedias of Alarcón, Tirso and Lope." PMLA, LXII(1947), 62-75.
Hamilton studies both prose and verse letters, the number of plays in which they appear and the frequency of their appearance within a play, the various verse forms used, and other data. Among his discoveries: Lope employed verse and prose almost equally; he used a greater variety of verse forms and a greater number of uncompleted letters than the other two dramatists. Valuable for those interested in method and preference in determining authorship.

Hayes, Francis C. "The Use of Proverbs as Titles and Motives in the Siglo de Oro Drama: Lope de Vega." HR, VI(1938), 305-23.
The article lists 41 proverbial titles of Lope's, and gives a detailed analysis of two of the plays, El cuerdo en su casa and El perro del hortelano.

------. "Lope de Vega and the Common Man." In South Atlantic Studies for Sturgis E. Leavitt, Washington, D. C., Scarecrow, 1953, pp. 71-79.
Hayes reviews for us the vast army of "common" men who appear in Lope's plays. In almost every contest between the hidalgo and the villano, he says, the villano comes out best. The dramatist enjoyed showing the contrast between good commoner and bad noble and satirizing the nobility, especially the nobility without income or property.

Heald, William F. A Comparison of Plot Patterns in the Plays of Shakespeare and Lope de Vega. Unpub. doct. diss., Univ. of North Carolina, 1954.

Herrero García, Miguel. "Génesis de la figura del donaire." RFE, XXV(1941), 46-78.
The general thesis is that the gracioso is composed of three essential elements: (a) criado confidente (to which this article is mainly devoted), (b) hombre de placer, and (c) el sentido prosaico, económico y positivista del vulgo — all of which are taken directly from the historic reality of sixteenth-century Spain and consolidated in the comic figure created by Lope. The relationship between master and servant in university life is stressed, in the criado-confidente aspect.

------. "Ideas estéticas del teatro clásico español." RIE, No. 5, (1944), 79-109.
The article deals with ideas about beauty expressed in the Spanish drama of the XVI and XVII centuries. Lope's concepts of beauty are quoted not only from his comedias but also from his other works.

------. "La nobleza española y su función política en el teatro de Lope de Vega." <u>Escorial</u>, Segunda Época, XIX, No. 58 (1949), 509-47; "Más sobre la nobleza española ... en el teatro de Lope de Vega." <u>Ibid</u>., XX, No. 59 (1949), 13-60; "Más, aún, sobre la nobleza...." <u>Ibid</u>., XX, No. 64 (1949), 929-44.
  Lope's views of nobility in a hierarchic society, as based on military prowess, transmitted by blood. The bulk of the articles consists of a collection of passages concerning the noble families and their genealogical origin, their names and their coats of arms. The author claims nothing more for his work than that it is a "mera exposición descriptiva." As an anthology, with linking text, it is a useful source of information on the praise of noble families in Lope's theatre.

Heseler, Maria. <u>Studien zur Figur des Gracioso bei Lope de Vega und Vorgängern</u>. Hildesheim, Borgmeyer, 1933. Pp. 132. (Diss., Univ. of Göttingen.)
 Rev: Eva Seifert, <u>ZRP</u>, LIX(1939), 124-25.

Hierro, José. "Algunos aspectos del teatro del Siglo de Oro." <u>Bolívar</u>, No. 45 (1955), 865-74.

Hilborn, Harry W. "Comparative <u>culto</u> vocabulary in Calderón and Lope." <u>HR</u>, XXVI(1958), 223-33.
 Rev: P. G., <u>LR</u>, XIV(1960), 59.
  A comparison of dated plays of Lope and Calderón for the period 1623-29 shows that the difference between the two is one of degree only. Lope, despite his mockery, clearly used the <u>culto</u> language. Calderón went somewhat further.

Houck, Helen Phipps. "Navarro Tomás on the Character Value of Voice in Literature." <u>Hisp</u>, XX(1937), 389-91.
  Refers to Lope's inconsistency with regard to the rôle of the voice in the <u>Comedia</u>.

------. "Revival of Cervantes' <u>Numancia</u>." <u>Hisp</u>, XXI(1938), 225-26.
  Cervantes' theatre contrasted briefly with Lope's.

Hunter, William A. "The American Indian Languages as Literary Vehicles." In <u>Renaissance Papers</u>, 1956, pp. 42-49.
  An account of the efforts of the first Spanish priests in Mexico to master the native tongues and to utilize them for literary purposes. Includes mention of translations into náhuatl by a certain Fray Bartolomé de Alva around 1640 of two plays by Lope and one by Calderón. The Lope plays are not identified.

Isar, Erbert E. "La cuestión del llamado senequismo español." <u>Hispanó</u>, No. 2 (1958), 11-30.
  The melodramatic violence and horrors in pre-Lopean drama and in certain plays by Lope are not the result of Senecan influence. They are symptomatic, rather, of a "traumatic" period of deep moral and esthetic apathy.

Jacquot, Jean. "Le Théâtre du monde de Shakespeare à Calderón."
    RLC, XXXI(1957), 341-72.
  Lope figures briefly in this richly documented study which goes
  back to the ancient sources of the concept of the world as a
  stage and God as dramatic artist. Lo fingido verdadero is
  seen as fusing the concept of life as combat with that of life
  as a dramatic action.

Jones, C. A. "Honor in Spanish Golden-Age Drama: Its Relation to
    Real Life and to Morals." BHS, XXXV(1958), 199-210.
  Rev: P. G., LR, XIV(1960), 57-58.
  Jones rejects the view that the practices shown on the Spanish
  stage mirrored those of real life, and disputes Castro's
  assertion that the concepts held by the dramatists were derived
  from the casuists of the 16th century. Lope and Calderón, he
  holds, did not look favourably on the idea of vengeance and
  used it often only as a motif. The article does not add
  significantly to what we know about honour.

José Prades, Juana de. "El teatro de Lope de Vega en los años
    románticos." RL, XIX(1960), 235-48.
  Several of Lope's plays, largely in refundiciones of varying
  quality, were performed in Madrid theatres from 1830-39. 1830,
  with 24 performances was the busiest, and Oct., 1830 and June,
  1831, were the two most active months. The Teatro de la Cruz
  was the busiest theatre, and the Teatro del Príncipe the second.

Jouisse, Christiane. Moreto transposant Lope de Vega. Paris, 1954.
    (Mémoire pour l'obtention du diplôme d'études supérieures.)
  Rev: C. Aubrun, BH, LVII(1955), 214-15.
  Jouisse makes interesting findings known concerning contrasts
  between Lope and Moreto as shown in the latter's refundiciones
  of the former's plays.

Juliá Martínez, Eduardo. Las mujeres valencianas en las comedias de
    Lope de Vega. (Madrid, Librería Tormos, 1941. Pp. 16.
    (Reprint from Libros Hispanos: Bol. Bibliográfico de la
    Librería Tormos.)
  A lecture given during the tercentenary of Lope's death. E. J.
  M. considers Lope's first visit to Valencia (1588) to be the
  most important in the literary formation of the dramatist. He
  notes a distinct difference in the apparent authenticity of
  female characters in plays related to Valencia between those
  playing principal and secondary rôles. The secondary figures
  are artificial and reflect no local Valencian characteristics.

Keller, John E. "A Tentative Classification for Themes in the
    Comedia. BCom, V, No. 2 (1953), 17-23.
  "The plays chosen as test plays" include La Estrella de Sevilla
  and Fuenteovejuna.

Kohler, Eugène. "L'Art dramatique de Lope de Vega." <u>Revue des Cours et Conférences</u>, June 15, 1936, pp. 385-95; July 15, 1936, pp. 587-98; July 30, 1936, pp. 701-15; Jan. 30, 1937, pp. 358-71; Feb. 28, 1937, pp. 522-32; Apr. 30, 1937, pp. 167-76; June 15, 1937, pp. 468-80; June 30, 1937, pp. 544-60; July 30, 1937, pp. 736-48.

------. "Lope de Vega et Giraldi Cintio." In <u>Mélanges 1945</u>. II. <u>Études Littéraires</u>, Paris, 1946, pp. 169-260. (<u>Pubs. de la Faculté des Lettres</u>, Univ. de Strasbourg.)
  Rev: Georges Cirot, <u>BH</u>, XLVIII(1946), 377; Charles V. Aubrun, <u>BH</u>, XLIX(1947), 230-31.
  The author traces some thematic influences of Cintio's <u>novelle</u> in <u>El piadoso veneciano</u>, <u>Servir a señor discreto</u>, <u>La cortesía de España</u> and <u>El villano en su rincón</u>. Kohler believes that Lope probably read G. C.'s tales around 1609 and from this year until 1611 he drew from what he retained in his memory for these four <u>comedias</u>.

LaGrone, Gregory G. <u>The Imitations of "Don Quixote" in the Spanish Drama</u>. Philadelphia, Univ. of Pennsylvania Press, 1937. Pp. vii, 145. (<u>Univ. of Pennsylvania Pubs. in Romanic Langs. and Lits.</u>, 27.)
  Rev: C. E. Anibal, <u>RR</u>, XXIX(1938), 83-84; F. Courtney Tarr, <u>HR</u>, VI(1938), 168-74.
  Pp. 16-19 deal with the literary relations between Cervantes and Lope, and the question of borrowings from the <u>Quijote</u> in <u>Los amantes sin amor</u> and <u>La necedad del discreto</u>. The author concludes: "The review of possible points of contact with Cervantes in Lope's plays leads only to the confirmation of the originality and independence of Lope."

Lancaster, Henry Carrington. <u>A History of French Dramatic Literature in the Seventeenth Century</u>. Part III: <u>The Period of Molière, 1652-1672</u>. 2 vols. Baltimore, Johns Hopkins Univ. Press, 1936.
  Rev: Louis Cons, <u>MLN</u>, LII(1937), 275-79; L. Rivaille, <u>RLC</u>, XVII (1937), 423-30.
  Contains references to French borrowings from Lope.

Leavitt, Sturgis E. "The Popular Appeal of Golden Age Drama in Spain." <u>Univ. of North Carolina Extension Bulletin</u>, XXVIII (1949), 7-15.

Ley, Charles David. "Lope de Vega y la tragedia." <u>Clav</u>, I, No. 4 (1950), 9-12.
  Superficial considerations of <u>El caballero de Olmedo</u> and <u>El castigo sin venganza</u> (and other subjects not pertinent). The article is of little value.

------. *El gracioso en el teatro de la península (Siglos XVI-XVII)*. Madrid, Rev. de Occidente, 1954. Pp. 263.
Rev: C. Bravo-Villasante, Clav, VI, No. 31 (1955), 73; A. Zamora Vicente, Ínsula, X(1955), 6-7; Margaret Wilson, BHS, XXXIII (1956), 171-72 (calls this an "antología del gracioso," with no notes, classifications or general conclusions); N. E. Zingoni, Rev. de Educación (Buenos Aires), I (1956), 226-28.

Ley studies antecedents of the gracioso in the classical theatre and shows how this figure became a fundamental element in the Spanish drama of the Golden Age. Four graciosos are particularly discussed: those of El niño diablo, Fuenteovejuna, El caballero de Olmedo and El castigo sin venganza. (The volume was a doct. diss., Univ. of Madrid, 1950.)

Lionetti, Harold E. *Ariosto's Influence on the Plays of Lope de Vega*. Unpub. doct. diss., Northwestern Univ., 1955. (DA, XV, 1855.)

"Ariosto's influence is reflected in 103 plays ... allusions to love triangle (Angélica, Medoro, Orlando) occur in 31 plays."

Lohmann Villena, Guillermo. *El arte dramático en Lima durante el Virreinato*. Madrid, Pubs. de la Escuela de Estudios Hispanoamericanos de la Univ. de Sevilla, 1945. Pp. xx, 648.
Rev: R. Benítez Claros, Bibliografía Nac., VI(1945), 373-75; François Chevalier, BH, XLVIII(1946), 56; Irving A. Leonard, HR, XIV(1946), 364-66; José Rojas Garcidueñas, NRFH, I(1947), 91.

Leonard's review praises the book in high terms: "So exhaustive are his investigations of the vice-regal theater of Lima that it is unlikely that any subsequent explorer in the same field will be able to add more than minor details here and there to the basic account that he has presented." "The permanence of this monograph as a contribution to the history of the theater in colonial Peru and Spanish America is abundantly assured." Lohmann does not deal in any detailed manner with Lope's comedias or autos which were presented in Lima, but he does mention Lope from time to time throughout the book. One conclusion to be drawn from the study is that Lope was certainly not a popular dramatist in Peru, and another is that the very few plays of his which were known in the Viceroyalty are not among his best, as can be seen in the list of "popular" ones on pp. 327-33.

López Estrada, Francisco. "Las armas y las letras: El Gran Capitán en el teatro de Lope de Vega." Anales de la Univ. Hispalense, XV(1954), 3-41.

López Navío, José. "I. El entremés de los romances, sátira contra Lope de Vega, fuente de inspiración de los primeros capítulos del Quijote (pp. 151-212). II. Cide Hamete Benengeli: Lope de

Vega (pp. 213-224). III. Los dos autores del Quijote: primer autor (Lope), segundo autor (Cervantes) (pp. 225-239)." Anales Cervantinos, VIII(1959-60), 151-239.
Parts II and III are the same as the next article by J. L. N. The Entremés, and indeed the whole Quijote, is considered to be a satire against Lope and the excesses of his theatre, in which he sought to revive the romances of chivalry. Don Quijote is Lope, and Sancho, the faithful follower, is Tirso. Lope, too, is Cide Hamete Benengeli. Cide, or Señor, reflects Lope's aspirations to hidalguía. Hamete is related to Lope's fondness for this Moorish name, and for Moorish names in general; and Benengeli suggests berenjeneros, as Toledans were sometimes called (reference to Lope's residence in Toledo). Likewise, Cervantes may well have found some original papers of Lope's, making Lope primer autor, and Cervantes segundo autor.

------. "Cide Hamete Benengeli = Lope de Vega." BBMP, XXXVI(1960), 249-76.
See preceding article.

Lorenz, Charlotte M. "Seventeenth-Century Plays in Madrid from 1808-1818." HR, VI(1938), 324-31.
The article discusses the relative popularity of Lope and other 17th-century dramatists during the period stated, in comparison with the forty years preceding and the thirty years following this period (cf. N. B. Adams, "Siglo de Oro Plays in Madrid, 1820-1850," HR, IV, 1936, 342-57).

Lundelius, Ruth. Physical Aspects of the Spanish Stage in the Time of Lope de Vega. Philadelphia, Dept. of Romance Languages, Univ. of Pennsylvania, 1961. Pp. 77. (Private ed., mimeographed.)
A splendid brief account of stagecraft in Lope's time.

Marín, Diego. "Técnica de la intriga secundaria en Lope de Vega." Hisp, XXXVIII(1955), 272-75.
A preview (chronologically) of the later, very significant studies of the topic.

------. La intriga secundaria en la técnica dramática de Lope de Vega. Doct. diss., Univ. of Toronto, 1956. Pp. 275. (Pub., 1958.)

------. "Carácter y función de la intriga secundaria en el teatro de Lope de Vega." Hispanó, I(1957), 41-51.
An advance publication of the introductory section of the author's monograph on the same subject. Connected with his doctoral dissertation.

------. *La intriga secundaria en el teatro de Lope de Vega*. Mexico, Ediciones De Andrea (Toronto, Univ. of Toronto Press), 1958. Pp. 197. (Col. *Studium*, 22.)

Rev: Jim P. Artman, BA, XXXIII(1959), 331; Carlos Ortigoza, Hisp, XLII(1959), 645-47 (finds that Marín is too subjective, and does not evaluate the plays enough); E. Segura Covarsí, Arbor, XLIV(1959), 608-10 ("un intento valioso para remozar los estudios de Lope, sobre todo en lo que se refiere a su técnica dramática"); E. R. S., Universidad (Univ. Nac. del Litoral), No. 39 (1959), 294-95 (stresses the thoroughness of the study, and its painstaking analysis..., showing how Lope remains fresh to succeeding generations); Olga P. Ferrer, MLJ, XLIV (1960), 55-56; Raquel Minian de Alfie, Filología, VI(1960), 129-31; R. Ma. Hornedo, Razón y Fe, No. 163 (1961), 324-25 ("Estudios, como el presente, son de la mayor utilidad para llegar a un más depurado conocimiento de la técnica dramática de Lope...."); Ramon Rozzell, HR, XXIX(1961), 151-53 (This "first systematic study of the unity of action in the Comedia" shows that historical, legendary and hagiographic plays, which possess a distinct sub-plot, are written to "ensalzar deleitando," while other types are produced purely for entertainment, and "at an increasing rate during Lope's career." The book is done "with painstaking care and keen perception."); R. O. V., BFE, No. 9 (1961), 24.

This cogent analysis of 146 representative plays, including all the dated plays and all the tragedies and *tragicomedias*, shows that when Lope sought to maintain fidelity to a written source, as in most historical and hagiographic plays, he provided a secondary plot independent of the main action. When he invented the action wholly or in part, the secondary plot became integrated into a more complex main action. The different procedures provide a truer key to Lope's methodical dramaturgy than does the comic-tragic distinction. A monograph of highest value.

McCrary, William C. *The Classical Tradition in Spanish Dramatic Theory of the Sixteenth and Seventeenth Centuries*. Unpub. doct. diss., Univ. of Wisconsin, 1958. Pp. 331. (DA, XIX, 2092.)

"The purpose of this dissertation is to examine the aesthetic assumptions of the classically oriented theorists together with those of Lope's followers in order to demonstrate the persistence of classical thought in the poetics of both schools." It is shown that the "modernist" critics reinterpreted the ancient authorities in order to justify the baroque theatre as a new approach to drama quite compatible with the ancient masters.

McCready, Warren T. "*Empresas* in Lope de Vega's Works." HR, XXV (1957), 79-104.

Empresas, military and amorous, appear in over forty plays, sometimes presented on a shield, sometimes merely described, sometimes presented as a tableau. They seldom contribute to the plot, but are occasionally helpful in dating plays.

------. "*Era el remedio olvidar* Once More." BCom, IX, No. 2 (1957), 17-18.
It is noted that this song, appearing in the works of several Golden Age dramatists, is found in several plays by or attributed to Lope.

------. *La heráldica en las obras de Lope de Vega y sus contemporáneos*. Doct. diss., Univ. of Chicago, 1961. Pp. 552. (Pub., 1962.)
A monograph of great significance.

Menéndez Pelayo, Marcelino. *Estudios sobre el teatro de Lope de Vega*. Ed. Enrique Sánchez Reyes. 6 vols. Santander, CSIC, 1949. Pp. 375, 346, 434, 423, 431, 493.
Rev: C. V. Aubrun, BH, LI(1949), 450-51; E. Allison Peers, BHS, XXVII(1950), 61-62; A. G. R., HR, XIX(1951), 277-78.
A convenient reissue of M. P.'s introduction to the plays published in the Academy edition, enhanced by an index of names and subject matter.

Metford, J. C. J. "An Early Liverpool Hispanist: John Rutter Chorley." BHS, XXV(1948), 247-59.
An account of the life and character of J. R. Chorley (ca. 1807-1867), scholar and collector, and author of a catalogue of Lope's plays. Metford describes the catalogue and its vicissitudes.

------. "Lope de Vega and Boccaccio's *Decameron*." BHS, XXIX(1952), 78-86.
Lope scholars of the past have indicated that eight of his *comedias*, written between 1595-1608, are based on stories in the *Decameron*. Metford discusses the techniques Lope used in adapting the stories for the Spanish theatre.

Michels, Ralph John. *Las unidades dramáticas en el teatro de Lope de Vega*. Unpub. doct. diss., Stanford Univ., 1938. (*Stanford Univ. Abstracts of Dissertations*, XIII, 1938, 58-59.)

Miranda, Leonor de. "De Lope a Calderón: Ética y estética en el teatro del Siglo de Oro." Cuad. de Lit., II(1947), 215-48.
The author defends Lope's spontaneity as producing work perennially alive. Although his work is not the result of meditation, it often indicates review and correction. A subjective article of interest, but of little value.

Möller, Wilhelm. *Die christliche Banditen-Comedia*. Hamburg, Ibero-Amerikanisches Institut, 1936. Pp. 78. (*Ibero-Amerikanische Studien*, 8.)

Rev: A. A. Parker, <u>MLR</u>, XXXIII(1938), 464-65.
Reference to <u>La fianza satisfecha</u> and <u>El prodigio de Etiopía</u>, attributed to Lope.

Monge, F. "<u>La Dorotea</u> de Lope de Vega" (1957). See Studies — Prose — Individual Prose Works (<u>La Dorotea</u>).
<u>La Dorotea</u>'s relationship to the <u>Comedia</u>.

Montoliu, Manuel de. <u>El alma de España y sus reflejos en la literatura del Siglo de Oro</u>. Barcelona, Edit. Cervantes, (1942). Pp. 752.
Pp. 210-20 discuss "Lo caballeresco en el teatro de Lope de Vega y otros autores dramáticos."

Montoto, Santiago. "Un auto de Lope de Vega rechazado." <u>BRAE</u>, XXV (1946), 429-33.
Montoto discusses a reference to Corpus Christi festivities in Seville, 1622, to be found in Hipólito de Vergara's <u>Del Santo Rey San Fernando y de la Santísima Virgen de los Reyes</u> (1629). Lope apparently wrote four <u>autos</u> for the occasion, one of which was about the Virgin. However, the <u>auto</u> in question was finally rejected, after having been rehearsed by Alonso de Olmedo's company. Montoto states that "Lope escribió un auto dedicado a la Virgen de los Reyes que, como otras muchas obras del Fénix, se ha perdido a lo que creo."

Moore, Jerome Aaron. <u>The "Romancero" in the Chronicle-Legend Plays of Lope de Vega</u>. Philadelphia, Univ. of Pennsylvania Press, 1940. Pp. vii, 162. (<u>Univ. of Pennsylvania Series in Romance Languages and Literatures</u>, 30.)
Rev: (anon.), <u>BHS</u>, XVIII(1941), 224 ("a solid contribution to the study of Lope de Vega which future editors will consult with profit"); (anon.), <u>Hisp</u>, XXIV(1941), 251-52; S. G. Morley, <u>HR</u>, IX(1941), 507-09 (favourable comment; slight criticism for not having defined "chronicle-legend play"); L. K. Delano, <u>MLJ</u>, XXVI(1942), 223-24 (this work "will take its place among the well-known authoritative critical studies of the great Spanish dramatist"); W. J. Entwistle, <u>MLR</u>, XXXVII(1942), 531.
The revision of a doctoral dissertation, Univ. of Pennsylvania, 1937. An important contribution to Lope scholarship. The monograph includes an index of the first lines of ballads from which Lope quoted.

Morby, Edwin S. "<u>Gli Ecatommiti</u>, <u>El favor agradecido</u> and <u>Las burlas y enredos de Benito</u>." <u>HR</u>, X(1942), 325-28.
A study of these two Spanish plays and their apparent common source reveals some fascinating problems which cannot be disregarded in any speculation about the uncertain authorship of <u>Las burlas y enredos de Benito</u>. Whereas <u>El favor agradecido</u> seems to have been inspired directly by Giraldi's <u>Ecatommiti</u>, <u>Las burlas</u> could possibly have been inspired by only <u>El favor</u>

<u>agradecido</u>, since it elaborates precisely those elements of the latter which seem to be Lope's. However, although a logical chronological order would seem to place <u>Las burlas</u> later than <u>El favor</u>, existing dates of the two works contradict this theory, leaving a still unresolved problem in literary creation.

------. "Some Observations on <u>tragedia</u> and <u>tragicomedia</u> in Lope." <u>HR</u>, XI(1943), 185-209.
   In this important essay on Lope's concept of tragedy, it is demonstrated that those plays which Lope himself called <u>tragedias</u> (and some of the <u>tragicomedias</u>) follow most of the critical norms of tragedy as they were defined by Renaissance theorists. Lope's shortcomings as a tragedian are not due to his misunderstanding of the genre, but to his manner of treatment of tragic themes.

Morínigo, Marcos A. <u>América en el teatro de Lope de Vega</u>. Buenos Aires, Inst. de Filología de la Univ. de Buenos Aires, 1946. Pp. 259. (<u>RFH</u>, Anejo 2.)
   Rev: S. Gili Gaya, <u>RFE</u>, XXX(1946), 177-79; E. Amaya Valencia, <u>Bol. del Inst. Caro y Cuervo</u>, III(1947), 326-28 (favourable); Courtney Bruerton, <u>NRFH</u>, I(1947), 181-83 ("...fruto de larga y paciente labor ... cita pasajes de ciento diecinueve comedias, dos autos y una novela de Lope." Criticizes the mixing of authentic and attributed plays and the lack of a detailed index. "De todos modos, aunque el libro, en su forma actual, no sea definitivo, es sin duda una valiosa contribución y un necesario instrumento para el estudio de Lope."); William L. Fichter, <u>RR</u>, XXXVIII(1947), 265-69 ("on the whole both complete and accurate"); E. Allison Peers, <u>BHS</u>, XXIV(1947), 208-09; Claude E. Anibal, <u>HR</u>, XVI(1948), 183-85 (Calls it an interesting and useful book, although neither definitive nor, in general, distinctively original. Points out several misinterpretations and the necessity of working on authentic plays.); William J. Entwistle, <u>MLR</u>, XLV(1950), 97-99.
   The reviews, cited above, express very well important <u>Lopistas</u>' appreciation and slight criticism of this monograph.

------. "El teatro como substituto de la novela en el Siglo de Oro." <u>RUBA</u>, II(1957), 41-61.
   This capable article views the <u>Comedia</u> as Lope created it as the lineal successor to the romance of chivalry. When the novel came under attack from the humanists and the Church toward 1600, the way was open for the <u>Comedia</u> to recapture the style and audience of the romance of chivalry.

Morley, S. Griswold. "Objective Criteria for Judging Authorship and Chronology in the <u>Comedia</u>." <u>HR</u>, V(1937), 281-85.
   "...the problem ... is to find purely objective criteria by which the product of one mind may be distinguished from that

of another, the creation of one period from those belonging to another" (p. 281). The criteria discussed are vocabulary, syntax, the internal structure of the verse, the use of strophes and dramatic technique.

------. "Lope de Vega's Prolificity and Speed." HR, X(1942), 67-68.
References to Juan de Piña's prologue to his Varias fortunas (1627) (cites a total of 1500 plays) and to Fray Francisco de Ribera's Morales Disputationes (1631) (cites a total of 1000); as additions to the Morley-Bruerton article "How Many Comedias did Lope de Vega Write?," Hisp, XIX(1936), 217-34.

------. "The Curious Phenomenon of Spanish Verse Drama." BH, L (1948), 445-62.
Section II of the five sections in the article deals with Lope. Morley believes that the agility and virtuosity of Spanish versification is not of a serious nature, and that preoccupation with the glittering surface detracts from the solidity of the framework and content.

------. "Arabic Nomenclature in the Characters of Lope de Vega's Plays." In Semitic and Oriental Studies: A Volume Presented to William Popper, Berkeley, Univ. of California Press, 1951, pp. 339-43. (Univ. of California Pubs. in Semitic Philology, 11.)
Alphabetical lists of some two hundred names applied to Moorish and Turkish men and women in Lope's authentic plays.

------. "Dos notitas sobre Lope de Vega." NRFH, XV(1961), 193-97.
"Osorio el de los cuartos" and "Lope y las unidades dramáticas." The first notita refers to La prueba de los amigos, Los Porceles de Murcia, Quien ama no haga fieros, plays of the years 1604 to 1620-22(?); the second, to the Arte nuevo and a number of plays.

Morley, S. Griswold, and Courtney Bruerton. "The Date of Two Plays by Lope de Vega." HR, VI(1938), 153-55.
The article deals with La imperial de Otón and El ejemplo de casadas y prueba de la paciencia.

------, and ------. The Chronology of Lope de Vega's "Comedias". With a Discussion of Doubtful Attributions, the Whole Based on a Study of His Strophic Versification. New York, The Modern Language Association of America, 1940. Pp. xiv, 428. (MLA Monograph Series, 11.)
Rev: W. J. Entwistle, MLR, XXXVI(1941), 418-20 (with no reservations, the work is praised lavishly); E. Allison Peers, BES, XVIII(1941), 158-60 (stresses the validity of the authors' method and conclusions); W. L. Fichter, RR, XXXIII(1942), 202-11 (this review is a most erudite and thoroughgoing analysis of the monograph. Highly praised. Fichter adds many important

comments, and his review could profitably serve as a companion work in the use of the Chronology); Josefina Romo Arregui, RFE, XXVI(1942), 505-21 (The reviewer objects to the pretension of using rigid scientific methods to study and classify the chronology of the literary creation of an author who, in the Arte nuevo, declared: "Encierro los preceptos con seis llaves." Insists that the study of Lope's metrical system is valid, but that the matter of chronology enters into the realm of conjecture, "con puntos muy débiles y citas lamentablemente equivocadas."); C. E. Anibal, HR, XI(1943), 338-53.
A classic and an absolutely indispensable tool for the Lope scholar. Without doubt, the most important study in our whole period under consideration. Time has proved the correctness of the monograph's interpretations and decisions. It is difficult to understand the Romo Arregui objections and her belief that there existed "puntos muy débiles y citas lamentablemente equivocadas." No book has been brought forth with greater care and sobriety, and there is no doubt but that (in the words of E. Allison Peers) "the regularity of Lope's development is as noteworthy as it was unconscious, and the exceptions are remarkably few." See Silverman, below (Ínsula, 1957) for the fortunes of the book during fifteen years.

------, and ------. "Addenda to the Chronology of Lope de Vega's Comedias." HR, XV(1947), 49-71.
The authors successfully defend their monograph of 1940 against all attacks, make additions and some corrections, bearing in mind scholarship of 1940-46, and point (with justified pride) to Amezúa's findings in the Gálvez manuscripts which corroborate several of their statements.

Morley, S. Griswold, and Richard W. Tyler. Los nombres de personajes en las comedias de Lope de Vega. Estudio de onomatología. 2 vols. Berkeley-Los Angeles, Univ. of California Press (Valencia, Castalia), 1961. Pp. vii, 1-294; 295-722. (UCPMP, 55.) (Bib. de Erudición y Crítica, 6, 7.)
Rev: B. W. Wardropper, MLN, LXXVI(1961), 934-38.
The authors' aim is to try to determine why Lope chose certain names for his characters. From 320 plays they list both the names of the characters and the names of the persons alluded to. There are several headings: I. Listas de nombres (Hombres, Mujeres, Apellidos y títulos); II. Repartos; III. Categorías o Tipos (Hombres — abad, actor, caballero, italiano, etc. to vizcaíno; Mujeres). With a useful Índice at the end of Vol. II. The Introducción to Vol. I makes helpful comment on certain generalizations that follow from the listings.

Navarro, Tomás. "Notas fonológicas sobre Lope de Vega." Archivum (Oviedo), IV(1954), 45-52.
A study based on three plays edited by Montesinos in TAE: Barlaán y Josafat, La corona merecida and El marqués de las Navas.

interesting findings, but, as Navarro says, to appreciate their significance one would have to have similar information about other authors of the period and about many more texts of Lope's.

Nemtzow, Sarah. "El estudiante en la Comedia del Siglo de Oro." MLF, XXXI(1946), 60-81.
  The article studies the general characteristics and presentation of the student character in the Comedia in general, and makes an analysis of the various types of students. Lope de Vega is represented by La doncella Teodor, La escolástica celosa, La boda entre dos maridos, El bobo del colegio, El dómine Lucas and El alcalde mayor.

Nicoll, A. World Drama from Aeschylus to Anouilh. London, Harrap, 1950. Pp. 1000.
  Pp. 208-39 contain interesting criticism of the Comedia from the point of view of world drama.

Noble, Beth Wilson. The Function of the Rustic in the Dramatic Technique of Lope de Vega. Unpub. doct. diss., Yale Univ., 1948. Pp. 416.
  This is not a study of the gracioso, but of rustic scenes and the rustic character in 96 plays. These are considered chronologically in three divisions: to 1604; 1604-18; and 1619-35. In the earlier plays, the "rustic" material often seems to be crude and extraneous, but becomes more essential to the plot and is better integrated in later plays.

Oliver, William Irvin. Spanish Theatre: A Study in Dramatic Discipline. Unpub. doct. diss., Cornell Univ., 1959. (DA, XX, 2434.)
  The thesis compares Spanish drama with that of the contemporary American (U.S.A.), and concludes that the latter could learn much from the former, not to mention finding actual plays that could be successfully performed (in U.S.A.). Oliver presents, also, "actable translations of plays by three of the greatest playwrights in Spanish literature...": Lope's The Lady Nit-Wit (La dama boba), Unamuno's Phaedra and García Lorca's Blood Wedding. (The Oliver translation of La dama boba was performed at the Univ. of California, Berkeley, in May, 1959.)

Olmedilla, C. "Lope y Calderón en México: 1641." Historia Mexicana, VII(1957-58), 237-38.
  A very short bibliographical notice about the translation into náhuatl by don Bartolomé Alva of El gran teatro del mundo (Calderón), and of El animal profeta y dichoso parricida and La madre de la mejor. The manuscripts are now in the Bancroft Library.

Oñate, María del Pilar. El feminismo... (1938). See Studies — General.

Ortigoza Vieyra, Carlos. *Los móviles internos de la "Comedia" española. Estudios sobre Lope, Alarcón, Tirso, Moreto, Rojas, Calderón*. Mexico, Univ. Nac. de México, 1954. Pp. iv, 239. (Doct. diss.)
  Rev: Arnold G. Reichenberger, HR, XXV(1957), 138-41 (While the author sets out to demonstrate the complexity and originality of the characters of the Comedia through a study of their motivation, he succeeds in demonstrating only "variation and originality within the framework" of Comedia convention. The reviewer pleads for analysis of the Comedia according to its own laws, which centre around honour and faith.); Thora Sorenson, Hisp, XL(1957), 248-49 (The work is highly praised for its approach, both historical and modern, to the six major dramatists of the Golden Age, its emphasis on the psychological complexity of the characters and on the universally human nature of their motivation.); J. H. Parker, CMLR, XIV(1958), 55 ("Some may feel that Ortigoza labours ... his thesis of motif and motivation. None will deny, however, that he has presented his subject in an inspiring and thought-provoking way.").
  See reviews above. Ortigoza, through careful analysis, concludes that characters are more complex than usually thought. An important interest of the "Comediantes," motifs and motives.

Parker, A. A. "Reflections on a New Definition of Baroque Drama." BHS, XXX(1953), 142-51.
  Parker is reflecting upon and criticizing the Roaten-Sánchez y Escribano *Wölfflin's Principles* (1952). Roaten and Sánchez y Escribano find four plots in Fuenteovejuna, but Parker argues for one main and one secondary plot, and insists that Lope's drama was a stage in the development of the unified play with a subplot. Parker demonstrates, rather convincingly, that Wölfflin's principles do not help in interpreting Spanish drama, but, on the contrary, seem to complicate the matter unnecessarily.

------. *The Approach to the Spanish Drama of the Golden Age*. London, The Hispanic and Luso-Brazilian Councils, 1957. Pp. 27. (Col. Diamante, 6.) (Reprinted in TDR, IV, 1959, 42-59.)
  This extremely valuable seminal study formulates five principles of dramatic construction which prove highly effective keys for analysing Lope as well as other Golden Age playwrights.

Parker, J. H. *Breve historia del teatro español*. Mexico, De Andrea, 1957. Pp. 213. (Manuales Studium, 6.)
  Rev: Almela y Vives, Arbor, XLIII(1958), 337-38 ("...como manual de iniciación. Y en este sentido merece sinceros elogios tanto por el plan previamente fijado como por el desarrollo del mismo."); C. Alvajar, CCLC, No. 33 (1958), 109-10 (A highly favourable review which characterizes the work as "concisa, bien documentada y de indudable utilidad didáctica"

even though objections are raised concerning certain minor features of the book.); H. W. Hilborn, CMLR, XIV(1958), 54 ("everywhere shows evidence of painstaking research and careful composition;" laments the slight treatment of the gracioso and the lack of distinction between critiques and studies in the bibliography); W. K. Jones, BA, XXXII(1958), 308 (an outstanding work; a trustworthy guide to authors, works, periods and bibliography); Carlos Ortigoza, Hisp, XLI(1958), 539 (favourable, but the reviewer has some reservations about an occasional outmoded critical appreciation and the inclusion of some bibliographical items of little value); Helena Percas, RHM, XXIV(1958), 230 (valuable reference work, broad basis of documentation, succinct critical studies, bibliography); E. R. Storni, Universidad (Univ. Nac. del Litoral, Santa Fe, Argentina), No. 37 (1958), 266-67; M. S. Carrasco Urgoiti, The Americas, XV(1958-59), 412-14 (favourable, but bibliographical treatment of fertile authors like Lope is considered scanty); Charles V. Aubrun, BH, LXI(1959), 460-61 (praises, with certain reservations, the clarity, objectivity, compactness and accuracy of this guide); A. E. Sloman, BHS, XXXVI(1959), 241; Ramon Rozzell, HR, XXVIII(1960), 92 (This "handy source of accurately compiled historical data and bibliography" is highly commended, the reviewer regretting only that the "overly modest author" has not relied more on his own judgment rather than on those he quotes.).

Lope de Vega, pp. 33-44. The nine pages devoted to Lope in this useful manual offer the non-specialized reader a very brief glimpse at his public and private life and his non-dramatic works, then take an overall look at his theatre and dwell more particularly on the three main "monarchy-honour-justice" plays. The bibliography is naturally comprehensive and general rather than specialized.

Pascal, Jeannine. Contrastes entre Tirso de Molina et Lope de Vega dans les comedias d'intrigue semblable. Paris, 1954. (Mémoire pour l'obtention du diplôme d'Études supérieures.)
Rev: C. V. Aubrun, BH, LVII(1955), 213.
This mémoire contrasts plays by the two authors which have similar plots, to establish differences of treatment of the same situation.

Pavia, Mario N. Magic and Witchcraft in the Literature of the "Siglo de Oro," Especially in the Drama. Unpub. doct. diss., Univ. of Chicago, 1947. (See next item.)

------. Drama of the "Siglo de Oro": A Study of Magic, Witchcraft and Other Occult Beliefs. New York, Hispanic Inst., 1959. Pp. 166.
Rev: J. G. Fucilla, Hisp, XLIII(1960), 280-81; P. Irwin Watson, BHS, XXXVII(1960), 260; Everett W. Hesse, MLN, LXXVI(1961), 938-39; A. M. Pollin, RHM, XXVII(1961), 171.

Peers, E. Allison, William C. Atkinson and William J. Entwistle. **A Handbook to the Study and Teaching of Spanish**. London, Methuen, 1938. Pp. xv, 344.

    Comments on Lope de Vega and the Comedia in the sections on Spanish literature, comparative literature and research in Spanish literature.

Pemán, José María. **Algunos valores fundamentales del teatro de Lope de Vega**. Buenos Aires, Cumbre, 1942. Pp. 61.

    First of a series of lectures given by Pemán in South America, 1941. This one was delivered in the Teatro Nacional de Comedia, Buenos Aires. The author develops the interesting thesis that Spanish drama of the Golden Age, particularly in the hands of Lope, had as a primary function the conservation of fundamental national values which were in danger of extinction. Thus, these values which were being lost in the political reality of the day could still be seen and known on the stage. The desire of the Fénix to contemplate with devotion his country and its history is in contrast to the critical orientation of contemporaries such as Quevedo and Cervantes.

Penedo, Fr. Manuel. "El Ayuntamiento de Madrid y Lope de Vega. Acuerdos sobre autos sacramentales y el P. Remón." **Rev. Bibliográfica y Documental**, IV(1950), 313-17.

Rev: J. Ma. Asensio, **Rev. Estudios**, VIII(1952), 441.

    Six documents, two of which refer to the two libramientos of 300 reales each given to Lope by the Madrid City Council in 1611 and 1612.

Pérez, Louis C. "Observations by Ezra Pound on the Dramatic Quality of Lope de Vega." **BCom**, VII, No. 2 (1955), 19-21. (See Pound, below.)

------. **Afirmaciones de Lope de Vega sobre preceptiva dramática a base de cien comedias**. Doct. diss., Univ. of Michigan, 1957. (**DA**, XVIII, 1438-39.)

    The same work as the following monograph by Pérez-Sánchez Escribano.

Pérez, Luis Celestino, and Federico Sánchez Escribano. **Afirmaciones de Lope de Vega sobre preceptiva dramática a base de cien comedias**. Madrid, CSIC, 1961. Pp. 218. (**RL**, Anejo 17.)

    The publication, without change, of Pérez' dissertation (preceding item). Contains sections on "Rasgos esenciales," "Naturaleza y arte," "Entretener-deleitar," "La moral-enseñar," "La imitación," "Pintura y poesía," "La verisimilitud," "Arte nuevo. Consideración retrospectiva." No criterion of selection of the 100 comedias is given, and too much stress is put on moral purpose of Lope's plays and on the relationship between painting and (dramatic) poetry. Good chapters are "Naturaleza y arte," "La imitación" and "La verisimilitud."

A good principle of criticism is proclaimed: that we cannot correctly assess the 17th-century theatre from the 20th-century point of view ("Tendrían que trasladarse al XVII y comprender el gozo de oír una frase o metáfora poética, ya que lo poético estaba por encima de lo real, sentimiento muy opuesto al gusto del siglo XX," p. 52).

Petrof, D. K. "El amor, sus principios y dialéctica en el teatro de Lope de Vega." Escorial, XVI(1944), 9-41.

Peyton, Myron A. "Lope de Vega and His Styles." RR, XLVIII(1957), 161-84.
Lope's plays display a variety of styles manipulated not only for their theatrical effectiveness but also according to the dictates of Lope's "active will." The lofty styles include the courtly and the baroque; the earthy styles include the aphoristic and the realistic, the latter not confined to the figura del donaire. Some acute observations and some overlapping of categories.

Pfandl, Ludwig. "Ueber das Maerchendrama bei Lope de Vega." In Münchner Romanistische Arbeiten, 9, ed. Max Hueber, Munich, 1942. Pp. 146.

Poesse, Walter. The Internal Line-Structure of Twenty-Seven Autograph Plays of Lope de Vega. Unpub. doct. diss., Univ. of California, Berkeley, 1940. Pp. 223. (See next item.)

------. The Internal Line-Structure of Thirty Autograph Plays of Lope de Vega. Bloomington, Indiana Univ. Press, 1949. Pp. 105. (Indiana Univ. Pubs., Humanities Series, 18.)
Rev: G. E. Wade, Hisp, XXXII(1949), 415; W. L. Fichter, HR, XVIII (1950), 269-73.
A thorough study of the orthoëpy of thirty of Lope de Vega's plays, based on autograph texts and following the pattern established by Morley in his "Ortología de cinco comedias autógrafas de Lope de Vega," Homenaje a Bonilla y San Martín, I, Madrid, 1927, 525-44. Morley's findings "are ... confirmed by this more comprehensive survey and ... given greater authority through the number of examples. In addition, Poesse adds new and important details at many points" (Fichter, review). The study is divided into two main parts: "The Individual Word" and "Groups of Words." It provides important "objective criteria" to determine Lopean authorship of doubtful plays. Thanks to its detailed indices, it proved very helpful, for example, in relating Lope's orthoëpic habits in the autograph manuscripts of Carlos V en Francia (Nov. 20, 1604) and Los Benavides (June 15, 1600) to those of the autographs studied by Poesse. No exceptions were found. It is noteworthy that, contrary to Lope's preference for certain metres at given periods of his life, no change seems to be discernible in his orthoëpic preferences.

Pound, Ezra. "The Quality of Lope de Vega." In *The Spirit of Romance*, revised, London, Peter Owen, 1952, pp. 179-213. (First pub. in 1910.)

Pound's appreciative estimate of Lope must, in all fairness, be judged on the basis that it is a case of a non-specialist writing for a cultured English-speaking public. Even on a more rigid basis, the estimate has more validity and substance than many chapters that have appeared in the mid-twentieth century. Pound should not be criticized severely for commenting on three plays which more recent scholarship (the author's revisions for the 1952 edition were made in 1929) deems doubtful Lope: La Estrella de Sevilla, Los novios de Hornachuelos and La nueva ira de Dios y gran Tamorlán de Persia. For a fuller account, see Louis Pérez, above, in BCom, VII(1955).

Powers, Perry J. *The Concept of the City State in the Drama of Lope de Vega*. Unpub. doct. diss., Johns Hopkins Univ., 1947.

The author treats La Estrella de Sevilla and seven plays by Lope (Fuenteovejuna, El alcalde de Zalamea, Peribáñez, Las paces de los reyes, El mejor mozo de España, La mayor virtud de un rey and El mejor alcalde el rey. He discusses the philosophy of the state by the Spaniards Francisco de Victoria, Francisco Suárez, Juan de Mariana and Pedro de Rivadeneira; the incidents described in the chronicles in which a city has risen against injustice; the praise of cities to be found in the Comedia and elsewhere; and finally the De civitate Dei of St. Augustine, the Italian city state and the Visigothic state. The point of his thesis seems to be that the citizens of a city act collectively, as a unit, and thus the city serves as a character, whose function is to uphold justice against the tyranny of the king or his representative. The king, as a representative of God, should be perfect in his justice and when he deviates, the city acts to reprove him. The author discusses very thoroughly the concept of justice and honour expected of a king or his representative, but, actually, only Fuenteovejuna truly illustrates the idea of his title. The work is repetitious, and in the discussion of the praise of cities and (to a lesser extent) of political writers, goes rather far afield.

Price, Eva R. "The Peasant Plays of Lope de Vega." MLF, XXII(1937), 214-19.

Deals with El mejor alcalde el rey, Fuenteovejuna, El alcalde de Zalamea, Los Tellos de Meneses and Peribáñez.

Pujals, Esteban. "Shakespeare y Lope de Vega." RL, I(1952), 25-45.

The article sketches the origins of the Spanish and English theatres, describes the conditions of the respective theatres when Lope and Shakespeare arrived on the scene. There follows an informative and unbiased discussion of the similarities and the essential differences between the two dramatists.

Reichenberger, Arnold G. "The Uniqueness of the Comedia." HR, XXVII(1959), 303-16.
    An excellent analysis.

------. "La comedia clásica española y el hombre del siglo XX." FMod, No. 4 (1961), 21-43.
    The purpose of this article is to show "los rasgos principales que permitan comprender el teatro español del siglo XVII."

Reid, Charles Gordon. The Problem of Social Inequality in Love and Marriage as Presented in the Theater of Lope de Vega. Unpub. doct. diss., Univ. of Virginia, 1941. (Univ. of Virginia Abstracts of Dissertations, Charlottesville, 1941, pp. 32-34.)
    Based on the analysis of the 397 plays of the two Academy editions, the findings of the author constitute a valid contribution to Lope studies. The documentation which, for limitations of space, does not pretend to be complete, gives nevertheless a clear and representative picture of the textual evidence. Reid's conclusion is that Lope was interested in promoting the case of love between people of different social classes. (The goal of love in the context of Lope's plays was the "enjoyment" of the beloved and not marriage. There is however a rather low occurrence of marriages between social unequals in Lope's theatre.)

Roaten, Darnell H. An Explanation of the Forms of Three Serious Spanish Baroque Dramas According to Wölfflin's "Principles of Art History." Unpub. doct. diss., Univ. of Michigan, 1951. (Microfilm Abstracts, XI, 687-88.)
    See the item following.

Roaten, Darnell H., and F. Sánchez y Escribano. Wölfflin's Principles in Spanish Drama: 1500-1700. New York, Hispanic Inst. in the United States, 1952. Pp. 200.
    Rev: J. E. Gillet, HR, XXI(1953), 350-51; E. W. Hesse, Hisp, XXXVI (1953), 126-27; A. A. Parker, BHS, XXX(1953), 142-51 (see above, under Parker).
    Fuenteovejuna, pp. 94-132. In Chapter VI, "Wölfflin's Principles Applied to the Spanish Baroque Theater," Fuenteovejuna is the first of the three Baroque plays selected. The authors consider it a political play with four main plots: Nobles vs. the People (chief plot); Life of the People; Both Nobles vs. the People and Life of the People; and Defence of the Monarchy (chief ideological motive). In a scene by scene dissection of the play, these four plots, separately and in convergence, are subjected to the five categories developed by Wölfflin for the plastic arts: Painterly, Recession of Space, Open Form, Absolute Unity and Relative Unclearness.

Romera-Navarro, Miguel. La preceptiva dramática de Lope de Vega. Madrid, Yunque, 1935. Pp. 302.
Rev: Rudolph Schevill, HR, V(1937), 94-96.

Rosendorfsky, Jaroslav. "Einige italienische Motive in Lope de Vega's Dramen." Sborník Prací Filosofické Fakulty Brněnske University (Brna, Czechoslovakia), Series D (Rada Literárněvědna), IX, No. 7 (1960), 130-48.
The article concerns especially Lope's debt to Boccaccio (El halcón de Federico, El anzuelo de Fenisa) and Bandello (El genovés liberal, El castigo sin venganza). Plot summaries are given in Czech and Russian.

Rovner, Philip. Lope de Vega on Kingship. Unpub. doct. diss., Univ. of Maryland, 1958. (DA, XX, 307.)
Lope's political precepts as found in more than 100 plays form an ars gubernandi. The precepts treat of the political person of the king or of the political institution of kingship. The first type are linked with pagan and Christian specula of princes, the second form a credo of government related to general political theory as it developed from the Middle Ages.

Rüegg, M. A. "Aspectos originales en el arte dramático de Lope de Vega." Clav, VII, No. 37 (1956), 1-7.

Ruffner, Sidney J. The American Theme in Selected Dramas of the Golden Age. Unpub. doct. diss., Univ. of Southern California, 1953.

Salazar y Bermúdez, María de los Dolores. "Querella motivada por la venta de unas comedias de Lope de Vega." RBN, III(1942), 208-16.
Four of Lope's plays, written for and sold to Alonso de Riquelme, autor de comedias, are the subject of the litigation. Riquelme discovered in 1616 that these plays were being performed throughout the country by other actors. Upon his complaint, legal action was started against Antonio de Granados, also an autor de comedias, his wife and the other cómicos involved. In a document dated Jan. 7, 1617, upon agreement of the accused not to present these plays any more, under penalty of heavy financial indemnification for so doing, Riquelme withdraws his suit.

Sánchez Castañer, Francisco. La pecadora penitente en el teatro español. Sus fuentes y evolución. Unpub. doct. diss., Univ. of Madrid, 1941.

Sánchez Escribano, Federico. "Gracián ante la Comedia española del Siglo XVII." RL, XIX, Nos. 37-38 (1961), 113-15.
Although Gracián preferred the classic theatre (particularly Guarino's El pastor fido), he praises Lope and does not reject the national theatre as some have supposed.

Sanzoles, Fray Modesto de. "La alegoría como constante estilística de Lope de Vega en los autos sacramentales." RL, XVI(1959), 90-133.
   After analysing several of Lope's autos (of which he considers La siega the outstanding one), the author concludes that Lope, who was not at his best in handling the abstract, never dominated the allegory in its fullest sense. He excelled where vitality and imagination would allow him to do so, but fell short of the heights of the symbolic and conceptual that were to be scaled by Calderón.

Sch., G. "Notas sobre Lope de Vega en el teatro ruso." La Littérature Internationale, No. 6 (1942), 80-84.

Schevill, Rudolph. "Erasmus and the Fate of the Liberalistic Movement Prior to the Counter Reformation." HR, V(1937), 103-23.
   Pp. 119-20 deal with the Comedia, in which field "the creation of a stereotyped pattern of social conduct and thought is most apparent.... In hundreds of comedias a dominating conformist character in plot and idea can be verified.... With the destruction of Erasmian inquiry, dogmatic authority replaced question and speculation." Few specific references to Lope.

Schulte-Herbrüggen, Heinz. Studien zu Lope de Vegas Gotendramen. Unpub. doct. diss., Univ. of Würzburg, 1943.

------. "El arte dramático de Lope de Vega. Estudios críticos." AUC, CVIII, No. 80 (1950), 5-94.
   Actually this is only a study of El postrer godo de España and La vida y muerte del rey Bamba. The author dates the former before 1600, probably 1599 (p. 8), and the latter shortly before 1604 (p. 41) and probably 1602 (p. 90). He cites Hämel's metrical study of 1922, but is unfamiliar with Morley and Bruerton (1940), who date El postrer godo 1599-1603 (perhaps 1599-1600) quite like Schulte-Herbrüggen, but place El rey Bamba before Sept., 1598. This is important because the author wants to show that a change took place in Lope's art around 1600, and he intends to prove it by showing an improvement in skill between these plays. He has only shown in a detailed and somewhat repetitious study the virtues and faults of each of the two plays, but no change. The author studies the sources and their handling by Lope and evaluates each play, mostly by applying the categories of Aristotelian dramatic theory, but not without considering the un-Aristotelian tastes of Lope's audience. A chapter on style and metric, which does not yield very much, concludes the article, the title of which promises much more than it delivers. Schulte-Herbrüggen does not know Schevill's study of Lope's dramatic technique which accompanies his edition of La dama boba (1918).

Sears, Helen L. *The Concepts of Fortune and Fate in the "Comedia" of Lope de Vega.* Unpub. doct. diss., Univ. of California at Los Angeles, 1949. Pp. 505.

------. "The Concepts of Fortune and Fate in the *Comedia* of Lope de Vega." *BCom*, II, No. 1 (1950), 1-3. (An abstract of the above-listed diss.)
   A contradictory attitude emerges. Blind Fortune and Fortune as identified with, or as a handmaiden to, divine Providence both appear in Lope's plays. "Divine determinism" seems to prevail, but, somehow, allowance for free will is made.

Seymour, Consuelo W. *Popular Elements and the Idea of Justice in the "Comedias" of Lope de Vega.* Unpub. doct. diss., Stanford Univ., 1953. (*DA*, XIII, 813-14.)

Shergold, N. D. *The Staging of Secular Drama in Spain, 1550-1700.* Unpub. doct. diss., Cambridge Univ., 1954.

Shervill, Robert N. *The Old Testament Drama of the "Siglo de Oro."* Unpub. doct. diss., Univ. of North Carolina, 1958. (*DA*, XIX, 2093.)
   This drama would seem to have consisted of some 27 full-length *comedias*. Two of them are no longer extant. The majority of the authors follow the same dramatic technique and reflect the same strength and weaknesses as in their secular pieces. The thesis discusses the staging of these plays, their use of subplots, humour and Church doctrine, and the manner in which male and female characters are presented in them.

Silverman, Joseph H. *Lope de Vega's "figura del donaire." Definition and Description.* Unpub. doct. diss., Univ. of Southern California, 1955.

------. "La cronología del teatro de Lope." *Ínsula*, XII, No. 126 (1957), 5.
   An account of the fortunes of the M.-B. *Chronology* during the first fifteen years of its life. Silverman ends with an appeal for a Spanish translation.

Sloman, Albert E. "The Phonology of Moorish Jargon in the Works of Early Spanish Dramatists and Lope de Vega." *MLR*, XLIV (1949), 207-17.
   Lope differs from the early Spanish dramatists' imitation of Moorish jargon in (a) his limited use of *xexeo*; (b) his regular employment of features initiated, but only sporadically used, by earlier writers; (c) his elimination of extraneous elements. A thorough, well-documented study.

Sorkin, Max. *Paul Scarron's Adaptations of the "Comedia."* New York, Private, 1938. Pp. 115.
   This study, which has little reference to Lope, was presented as a doctoral dissertation at New York Univ., 1936.

Templin, Ernest H. *Money in the Plays of Lope de Vega.* Berkeley-Los Angeles, Univ. of California Press, 1952. Pp. 36. (UCPMP, XXXVIII, 1.)
   Materialism is not lacking in the *Comedia*, although it seldom plays a determining rôle. In Lope's plays there are numerous references to money, or some equivalent thereof, in such categories as financing wars, ransoms, inheritances, dowries, services, rewards and thefts. Lope being a dramatist, not an economist, his entire opus contributes little to a realistic appraisal of the economic conditions of Spain in his day.

Tiemann, Hermann. "Die Bedeutung der 'Spanish Plots' für das englische Drama der Frührestauration." *RJ*, XII(1961), 278-311.
   Contains slight reference to Lope.

Toll, K. "Die spanische *Comedia* im Unterricht der höheren Schule." *NS*, XLVI(1938), 418-24.

Tyler, Richard W. "On the Dates of Certain of Lope de Vega's *Comedias*." *MLN*, LXV(1950), 375-79.
   1. *La burgalesa de Lerma* (Oct. 16-Nov. 30, 1613); 2. *La cortesía de España* (reference to *Don Quijote*, I: 1605-12, probably 1610); 3. *El Hamete de Toledo* (1609-12, probably 1610); 4. *El hidalgo Bencerraje* (a Belardo-Lucinda play: 1599-1606); 5. *El mejor mozo de España* (reference to the expulsion of the *moriscos* under Philip III: 1610-11); 6. *El rústico del cielo* (allusion to the Queen's pregnancy: before Apr. 8, 1605, date of birth of Philip IV).

------. "Suggested Dates for More of Lope de Vega's *Comedias*." *MLN*, LXVII(1952), 170-73.
   Reasonable conjectures based on internal evidence suggest that the span of years proposed by the M.-B. *Chronology* may be narrowed for *La boda entre dos maridos*, *San Isidro labrador de Madrid* and *La viuda valenciana*. An autobiographical interpretation of four lines (ll. 2334-37) in *Peribáñez* suggests 1608, the *ad quem* date of the 1605-08 span proposed by Bruerton, *HR*, XVII(1949).

------. "Further Suggestions for Lope de Vega Chronology." *BCom*, IV, No. 2 (1952), 2-3.
   Inferences drawn from internal evidence support the dates of three plays proposed by Morley and Bruerton, and amend the dates which they give for two other plays: *El casamiento en la muerte*, *La discreta enamorada*, *Los españoles en Flandes*, *El labrador venturoso*, *La nueva victoria del marqués de Santa Cruz*.

Ulsamer, Federico. "Hans Schlegel y la difusión del teatro español en Alemania." *Cuad. del Inst. del Teatro* (Barcelona), 1957, 79-85.

Valbuena Prat, Ángel. "En torno a dos temas de Lope." <u>Clav</u>, I, No. 4 (1950), 26-28.
    I. <u>El teatro mitológico</u>. "Lope sigue más bien en la línea, un poco rezagada, de lo pastoril, y aun en la técnica de sus precursores." This part refers to <u>El Amor enamorado</u>, and very briefly to <u>Adonis y Venus</u> and <u>El marido más firme</u>. II. <u>"La Estrella de Sevilla": su atribución y mérito</u>. Reviews the problem of authorship without taking a clear stand. Valbuena Prat calls attention to Marañón's opinion that the play may allude to the Antonio Pérez-Philip II relationship (cf. <u>Antonio Pérez</u>, II, 1948, 937-42).

------. <u>Literatura dramática española</u>. Barcelona, Labor, 1950. Pp. 336. (<u>Col. Labor</u>, 258-59.) (Reprint of 1930 ed.) Lope de Vega, pp. 112-54.

------. "Lope, en la vida y en el drama." In <u>Historia del teatro español</u>, Barcelona, Noguer, 1956, pp. 79-103.

------. "<u>El Auto del nacimiento</u> en la escuela de Lope de Vega." In <u>Estudios dedicados a Menéndez Pidal</u>, VII (Madrid, 1957), 401-13.

Vásquez Dodero, José Luis. "La mujer española vista por los escritores." <u>Mundo Hispánico</u>, No. 37 (1951), 17-18.
    Includes passages from five of Lope's <u>comedias</u>. Lope, unlike the other writers quoted, does not specify that it is <u>la mujer española</u> whom he praises; it may be assumed, of course, that he has Spanish women in mind.

Villarejo, Oscar M. <u>Lope de Vega and the Elizabethan and Jacobean Drama</u>. Unpub. doct. diss., Columbia Univ., 1953. (<u>DA</u>, XIII, 816-17.)

Vockrodt, Ebba. <u>Der König D. Pedro I de Castilla in der spanischen "Comedia" der Blütezeit unter besonderer Berücksichtigung des Verältnisses der dichterischen Darstellung zur Geschichte</u>. Unpub. doct. diss., Univ. of Göttingen, 1948.

Vossler, Karl. "Los motivos de la soledad en el teatro." See Studies — Poetry — General: Vossler, <u>La poesía de la soledad...</u> (1946).

Wade, Gerald E. "The Literary Sources of <u>El castigo del Penséque</u> of <u>Tirso de Molina</u>." In <u>South Atlantic Studies for Sturgis E. Leavitt</u>, Washington, D.C., Scarecrow Press, 1953, pp. 81-96.
    In the section of this study that deals with Tirso's indebtedness to Lope, Wade concludes, after a careful examination, that Tirso borrowed from both <u>La ocasión perdida</u> and (for the letter episode) <u>El secretario de sí mismo</u>, as was first suggested by A. L. Stiefel.

------. "The Interpretation of the Comedia." BCom, XI, No. 1 (1959), 1-6.
A thought-provoking and intelligent presentation.

Wardropper, Bruce W. "The Search for a Dramatic Formula for the Auto sacramental." PMLA, LXV(1950), 1196-1211.
On Lope (p. 1208): "When he chose an essentially lyric theme ... the play was often successful. But he made few changes in the sacramental tradition as he found it. His sacramental drama was sterile because it was too dependent on the technique of the Comedia." The author proves his point by discussing a few autos.

------. "Honor in the Sacramental Plays of Valdivielso and Lope de Vega." MLN, LXVI(1951), 81-88.
Two attitudes toward honor meet in Lope: acceptance in his secular theatre, opposition in his novelas. A problem arose in his autos sacramentales. There honor is seen as un-Christian; yet, as a man the Spaniard had to avenge his dishonour, and Lope cannot completely abandon the idea that there is some good in honor. The author blames this futile attempt to reconcile the worldly and spiritual for Lope's inferiority in this genre. Valdivielso, on the other hand, was able to forego compromises, being first a priest and then a dramatist. He finds no place in his autos for worldly honor.

------. Introducción al teatro religioso del Siglo de Oro (La evolución del auto sacramental: 1500-1648). Madrid, Rev. de Occidente, 1953. Pp. 330.
Rev: Marcel Bataillon, BH, LVI(1954), 431-35 (generally complimentary, although the reviewer warns against some risky assumptions. He suggests more emphasis on the close relationship between the profane and religious theatre and the influence of the former on the latter); Courtney Bruerton, NRFH, VIII(1954), 328-30 ("Por su cuidadosa disposición de gran número de detalles significativos, por sus breves citas y resúmenes de los argumentos, por la sensatez de sus juicios,... es un modelo de proporción y claridad de exposición, y su lectura es muy amena."); Salvador Dinamarca, RHM, XXI(1955), 346-47 (commends Wardropper's "objetividad y mesura," mentions the excellent treatment of Valdivielso, and says the author has continued in an admirable manner the "trayectoria iniciada por Alexander A. Parker"); H. Lausberg, Archiv, CXCII(1955), 248 (favourable review. Lausberg commends especially the chapter on Valdivielso.).
Pages 265-82 treat of Lope de Vega, and three autos are analysed in detail: La adúltera perdonada, Los dos ingenios y esclavos del Santísimo Sacramento and La venta de la zarzuela. Wardropper concludes that Lope thought of drama in terms of action, while the auto sacramental deals with ideas. His autos are best when his imagination was controlled by some existing

literary work which he was transforming *a lo divino*, as in *La venta de la zarzuela*. He put theology at the service of poetry, rather than the reverse, as did Calderón. And, finally, his most important contribution was a plastic or pictorial scene at the end to be contemplated and to be carried away by the spectators, which he substituted for the traditional *villancico*.

------. "Cervantes' Theory of the Drama." *MP*, LII(1955), 217-21.
   This article relates obliquely to Lope. Wardropper shows that Cervantes was rather uncertain, his head arguing for the classical precepts while his heart was with Lope and his *Comedia nueva*.

------. "Poetry and Drama in Calderón's *El médico de su honra*." *RR*, XLIX(1958), 3-11.
   Rev: P. G., *LR*, XIV(1960), 59-60.
   While Calderón's play is used for illustration, the premise of this important article is made expressly applicable to Lope. It is that their theatre is essentially dramatic poetry, not poetic drama. It follows that the plays are to be studied as lyric poetry, one approach being through their imagery. Calderón's play is seen as one "complex, extended metaphor," an *idea representable*. While the assertion seems too uncompromising, the demonstration is skillful and persuasive and the article is a challenging stimulus to renew criticism of the *Comedia* with the new analytical tools so competently handled by British scholars.

Weaver, William Rowe. *An Introductory Study of Stage Devices in the "Siglo de Oro" Drama*. Unpub. doct. diss., Univ. of North Carolina, 1937.

Werner, Ernst. "Der Spassmacher (*Gracioso*) in den Dramen des Cervantes und in Lope de Vegas Jugendstücken." In *Gymnasium und Wissenschaft*. Festgabe zur Hundertjahrfeier des Maximiliansgymnasiums in München. Als Manuskript gedruckt. Herausgegeben von A. Schwerd, (1949), pp. 196-230.
   The major part of the study is dedicated to Cervantes (pp. 198-219). Considering the 26 *Jugendstücke* studied in A. Hämel's *Studien zu Lope de Vegas Jugenddramen* (Halle, 1925) and comparing the comic figures appearing with those found in Cervantes' dramatic production as published in 1615, the author confirms that Lope was indeed the first to create a real *gracioso* ("echten gracioso") in *La francesilla* (1595) in the servant Tristán. The other two genuine *graciosos* are Galindo in *Los comendadores de Córdoba* and Roberto in *El galán escarmentado*. Accepting the date of 1595 as established by Arjona (*HR*, V, 1937, 73-76, and VII, 1939, 1-21), he solves the problem of date for the other two plays by arguing that they possibly were composed after *La francesilla* (p. 228).

Morley and Bruerton, whose Chronology the author did not know, possibly due to post-war conditions in Germany, agree with these dates. The intensive study of Cervantes' comic figures actually serves the purpose to prove or to disprove Lope's claim to have first introduced the gracioso in La francesilla. Werner emphasizes Cervantes' fundamental dislike for the comic figure since he was a convinced adherent to the old theatrical theory. "Eigentliche gracioso-Rollen" occur only in La entretenida and La gran sultana, two late plays. And even here "erreicht Cervantes noch nicht jene Stufe der Vollendung wie sein Zeitgenosse Lope de Vega" and feels that only in Madrigal of La gran sultana a certain level of achievement is reached (p. 219).

The comparison of the early plays of Lope with those of Cervantes shows "dass Lope tatsächlich als erster den gracioso zielbewusst im Drama verwendete" (p. 228). In addition, Werner's study is valuable for the study of the many comic figures which are not yet real graciosos, in both Cervantes and Lope, based on a carefully worked out catalogue of traits of the real gracioso, among which parallelism of his action with those of his master is the real touchstone.

Whatley, Frances. The Life of the "dama" in Lope de Vega. Unpub. doct. diss., Univ. of Illinois, 1947. Pp. 272.

Miss Whatley has limited her study to 38 autograph plays. There has been no attempt to verify or correlate the data with those from other sources. She covers just about every aspect of life associated with the dama: her home, social life, clothing and cosmetics and her education. She discusses the unmarried dama, including the rôle of the guardian, her courtship and reasons for marriage; and the married dama, including her relationship with her husband and her family. Most of the dissertation consists of quotations preceded and followed by a line or more of commentary. It contains an index verborum. As a rapid-fire picture of the life of the dama in Lope's autographs, it is excellent, but may not give a complete picture of the dama since 38 is but a small proportion of Lope's nearly 500 plays. In view of the conventionalism of the Comedia and the fact that Miss Whatley does not compare Lope's dama with references to real life, it cannot be considered a true picture of the lot of women in the Golden Age.

Wilder, Thornton. "Lope, Pinedo, Some Child Actors and a Lion." RPh, VII(1953), 19-25.

In 1597 and 1598, the death of the King's sister, the closing of the theatres, and the death of Philip II himself, all brought hard times to the theatrical world. In the spring of 1599, with a royal double wedding and the promise of the reopening of the theatres, things looked brighter. Pinedo and his wife, who had been in the company of Porras and for whom Lope had written, started their own company. Lope wrote mad scenes and frantic laments for Pinedo and mujer varonil parts for Pinedo's wife, Juana de Villalba. The company also had one or two child actors and a lion or lion skin. All this helps in dating plays. Wilder, using four different methods, establishes a list of 19 plays written for this company between 1599 and 1606. All agree with the dates assigned by Morley and Bruerton, except Las paces de los reyes (1605). All are characterized by one or more of the following characteristics: child actors, increasing in age and importance over the years; lions, which never do anything except lie at the feet of the protagonists; decreasing importance of the mujer varonil. A very interesting and shrewd study.

Wilson, William E. "Contemporary Manners in the Plays of Lope de Vega." BHS, XVII(1940), 3-23, 88-102.
A good study of costumbres.

B. INDIVIDUAL PLAYS

El acero de Madrid

Morley, S. Griswold. "El acero de Madrid." HR, XIII(1945), 166-69.
The first part of the article deals with the medicinal properties of steel-water as a cure for opilación, and quotes from early Spanish scientific writers as well as literary writers such as Pérez de Montalván and Castillo Solórzano about its popularity and the time to take it. The second part deals with Lope's probable purpose in naming his steel-water "de Madrid," and states that "in Madrid (that rich and corrupt capital, that danger to provincials, that hot-bed of trickery...) girls used it to get rid of unwanted lovers and to catch those favored.... In short, Madrid steel-water was something different. It had special properties not known in Toledo or Salamanca or Seville. Lope does not say this in so many words, but the many passages in this play emphasizing the rare qualities of Madrid show what he had in mind" (p. 169). The article lacks development and his supposition that women in other cities of Spain behaved differently than those of Madrid with regard to unwanted lovers versus favoured ones is not supported by the many damas in the comedias of the Golden Age which take place outside Madrid.

Adonis y Venus

Fucilla, J. G. "A Classical Theme..." (1945). See Studies — Poetry — Individual Poems (Romances).

Valbuena Prat, A. "En torno a dos temas..." (1950). See Studies — Drama — General.

La adúltera perdonada (auto)

Wardropper, B. W. *Introducción al teatro religioso...* (1953). See Studies — Drama — General.

El alcalde de Zalamea

Price, E. R. "The Peasant Plays..." (1937). See Studies — Drama — General.

Powers, P. J. *The Concept of the City State...* (1947). See Studies — Drama — General.

Petriconi, H. "El tema de Lucrecia y Virginia." <u>Clav</u>, II, No. 8 (1951), 1-5.
  The legend of Rodrigo and La Cava is an early example in Spain of what the author calls the Lucrecia-Virginia theme: to make use of seduction or rape as grounds for political revolt or rebellion. Lope's <u>Alcalde de Zalamea</u> is contrasted with Calderón's version, emphasizing the differences in the treatment of the theme. Invaluable are the precise definitions for such terms as <u>seducción</u>, <u>burla</u>, <u>violación</u>, <u>inocencia</u>, <u>deshonra</u>, <u>honra</u>, <u>honor</u>.

Sloman, Albert E. *The Dramatic Craftsmanship of Calderón: His Use of Earlier Plays.* Oxford, Dolphin, 1958. Pp. 327.
  El alcalde de Zalamea, pp. 217-49.

El alcalde mayor

Nemtzow, S. "El estudiante en la Comedia..." (1946). See Studies — Drama — General.

Al pasar del arroyo

Torner, E. M. "Índice de analogías..." (1946). See Studies — Poetry — General.

Los amantes sin amor

LaGrone, G. G. *The Imitations of "Don Quixote"...* (1937). See Studies — Drama — General.

Amar, servir y esperar

Arjona, J. H. "The Case of Lope de Vega's <u>Amar, servir y esperar</u>." <u>RR</u>, XL(1953), 257-62.
  By comparison of the play with Castillo Solórzano's <u>El socorro en el peligro</u>, Arjona shows convincingly that in this case Lope was the borrower. It is one of the rare instances, he says, of Lope's copying so closely from a contemporary. A fruitful investigation.

Amar sin saber a quién

Buchanan, Milton A. "Two Passages in Lope de Vega's *Amar sin saber a quién*." HR, XV(1947), 465.
    One passage (ll. 298-301) refers to the Hieronymite monastery of La Sisla, and St. Jerome's beating himself on the chest with a stone. The other (ll. 126-29) concerns *la locura de las setas*, a "mushroom" madness inducing hallucinations. These notes correct corresponding ones in the Buchanan and Franzén-Swedelius edition of the play (New York, 1920).

Bravo-Villasante, Carmen. "Un debate amoroso: *Amar sin saber a quién*." RL, VII(1955), 193-99.
    An interesting study of an interesting psychological case.

El amor desatinado

González de Amezúa, A. *Una colección manuscrita...* (1945). See Studies — Drama — General.

El Amor enamorado

Valbuena Prat, A. "En torno a dos temas..." (1950). See Studies — Drama — General.

El animal profeta

Echegaray, Bonifacio de. "La leyenda de San Julián el hospitalario en romances castellanos." BH, LIII(1951), 13-33.
    El animal profeta y dichoso parricida San Julián (of doubtful authenticity: attributed to Lope in several *sueltas* and to Mira in three MS. copies) contains incidents of plot not found in the various legends of St. Julian, the Catalan *goigs* (*gozos*), the two versions of the ballad *Lucinda y Carlos*, nor in a ballad which C. Morán Bardón heard in Palencia la Negrilla. This ballad does contain ten lines — not consecutive — found in the one used in the play. (cf. Morán's *Poesía popular salmantina*, Salamanca, 1924.)

McCready, Warren T. "A Volume of Rare *sueltas*." BCom, VI, No. 1 (1954), 4-8.
    An interesting description of a volume of twelve *sueltas* which McCready had recently added to his rich private library. One play is Lope de Vega's *El animal profeta*.

Olmedilla, C. "Lope y Calderón en México: 1641" (1957-58). See Studies — Drama — General.

El anzuelo de Fenisa

Arjona, J. H. "Un dato sobre la fecha de El anzuelo de Fenisa." MLN, LIII(1938), 190-92.

Rosendorfsky, J. "Einige italienische Motive..." (1960). See Studies — Drama — General.

Alonso, José Luis. "Elección y montaje de El anzuelo de Fenisa." Acento Cultural, Nos. 12-13 (1961), 119-21.

Schroeder, Juan Germán. "Refundición de El anzuelo de Fenisa." Acento Cultural, Nos. 12-13 (1961), 121-23.

Melgar, L. T. "El anzuelo de Fenisa (Teatro Nacional María Guerrero)." Acento Cultural, Nos. 12-13 (1961), 124-26.

Nagy, Edward. "Lope de Vega en el teatro madrileño." Hisp, XLIV (1961), 555-56.
    An account of Germán Schroeder's refundición of El anzuelo de Fenisa, played at the Teatro María Guerrero on March 9, 1961.

El arenal de Sevilla

Arjona, J. H. "Apunte cronológico sobre El arenal de Sevilla de Lope de Vega." HR, V(1937), 344-46.

Dale, George Irving. "Periodismo in El arenal de Sevilla and the Date of the Play's Composition." HR, VIII(1940), 18-23.
    A discussion of references to contemporary events in the play.

Las audiencias del rey D. Pedro

Arjona, J. H. "Ten Plays Attributed to Lope de Vega" (1960). See Studies — Drama — General.

El auto de la Virgen

Pérez Gómez, Antonio. "Un auto de Lope censurado por el cabildo sevillano." BH, IX(1950), 93-94.
    Lope's Auto de la Virgen could not be performed in Seville in 1620 or 1621 because Lope worked into it erroneous information, obtained from a Sevillian priest, concerning the history of the Virgen Santísima de los Reyes. In the auto Lope maintained that St. Louis of France had sent the Virgin as a gift to San Fernando. However, tradition ascribed the origin of the statue to a miracle. Pérez Gómez' source of information is Hipólito de Vergara, Del Santo Rey D. Fernando y de la Santísima Virgen de los Reyes (Osuna, 1629).

Barlaán y Josafat

Spitzer, Leo. "Un Passage de Lope de Vega, l'espagnol segullo et l'étymologie du français talus." MLN, LII(1937), 79-82.
Reference to Barlaán y Josafat, I, 562 (ed. Montesinos, TAE, VIII, 1935, p. 275).

Navarro, T. "Notas fonológicas..." (1954). See Studies — Drama — General.

El bastardo Mudarra

Hanan, Julia Bette. The Ballad Sources of "Los siete infantes de Lara" and "El bastardo Mudarra." Unpub. doct. diss., Univ. of Washington, 1937. (Univ. of Washington Abstracts of Theses and Faculty Bibliography, Seattle, II, 1937, 287-91.)

Van Dam, C. F. A. "Un pasaje obscuro de una comedia de Lope de Vega enmendado y aclarado." RJ, VI(1954), 342-43.
Van Dam clarifies a passage in El bastardo Mudarra, Act I, by the substitution of Amiclas for Amidas. The original autograph had the former, but the Academy edition gives Amidas. This is another instance of an error in the Academy edition, says Van Dam, which Menéndez Pelayo said "se conforma escrupulosamente."

La batalla del honor

Morby, Edwin S. "Note sur La batalla del honor." BH, XLII(1940), 236.
On Lope's indebtedness to Boccaccio.

La bella Aurora

Martin, H. M. "Notes on the Cephalus-Procris Myth as Dramatized by Lope de Vega and Calderón." MLN, LXVI(1951), 238-41.
Lope, in La bella Aurora, and Calderón, in Celos, aun del aire, matan, made use of this myth. Both relied mainly on the Metamorphoses. Martin briefly points out the major differences between the two in plot and characterization and also the alterations introduced by Ovid.

El blasón de los Chaves

Bruerton, C. "Thornton Wilder and Lope's Peregrino Lists" (1951). See Studies — Drama — Peregrino Lists.

El bobo del colegio

Zabala, A. "Rastros léxicos del valenciano..." (1944). See Studies — General.

Nemtzow, S. "El estudiante en la Comedia..." (1946). See Studies—
    Drama — General.

La boda entre dos maridos

Nemtzow, S. "El estudiante en la Comedia..." (1946). See Studies—
    Drama — General.

Tyler, R. W. "Suggested Dates..." (1952). See Studies — Drama —
    General.

Las bodas entre el Alma y el Amor divino (auto)

Cirot, Georges. "L'Allégorie des tireurs à l'arc." BH, XLIV(1942),
    171-74.
    In Lope's verse Prólogo to this auto (included in El peregrino
    en su patria, 1604), Cirot finds a precedent for the theme of
    the archers which is only slightly modified in the loa of
    Calderón's La vida es sueño.

El Brasil restituido

Viqueira, José Maria. "Notas sobre El lusitanismo de Lope de Vega
    y su comedia 'El Brasil restituido'." Brasília, VI(1951),
    184-97.
    Comments on reactions to his edition of the play (Coimbra, 1950).

Valbuena Prat, Ángel. "En torno al hispanismo del Brasil." Clav,
    IV, No. 19 (1953), 46-49.
    Includes brief reference to El Brasil restituido.

Frieiro, Eduardo. "Lope de Vega e o Brasil caboclo." Kriterion
    (Belo Horizonte), VII(1954), 354-63. (Also pub. in O alegre
    Arcipreste e outros temas de literatura espanhola, Belo
    Horizonte, Nicolai, 1959, pp. 141-53.)
    A discussion of El Brasil restituido, cited as an example of
    Lope's nationalism, making him "o mais genuíno intérprete da
    alma espanhola tradicional e do espírito do seu tempo."

La burgalesa de Lerma

Tyler, R. W. "On the Dates..." (1950). See Studies — Drama —
    General.

Las burlas y enredos de Benito

Morby, E. S. "Gli Ecatommiti..." (1942). See Studies — Drama —
    General.

Arjona, J. H. "Ten Plays Attributed to Lope de Vega" (1960). See
    Studies — Drama — General.

El caballero de Olmedo

Gómez de la Serna, Ramón. "El caballero de Olmedo." Rev. Cubana, XIV(1940), 38-59.
   Rev: R. M., RFH, IV(1942), 96.
   "Ensayo de simpatía."

Bruerton, C. "The Date of Schaeffer's Tomo antiguo" (1947). See Studies — Drama — General.

Ley, C. D. "Lope de Vega y la tragedia" (1950). See Studies — Drama — General.

Rozzell, Ramon. "Facistol." MLN, LXVI(1951), 155-60.
   Explains the meaning of a passage in El caballero de Olmedo: "¿Quién fueron / los crueles sacristanes / del facistol de tu espalda?" (ll. 541-43).

Anderson-Imbert, Enrique. "Lope dramatiza un cantar." Asomante VIII(1952), 17-22.
   An admiring appraisal of Lope's utilization of a popular cantar in his dramatization of El caballero de Olmedo. The article was republished in Los grandes libros de Occidente, Mexico, De Andrea, 1957, pp. 63-74; and in Crítica interna, Madrid, Taurus, 1961, pp. 11-18.

Blecua, J. M. "Nota al Caballero de Olmedo." NRFH, VIII(1954), 190.
   A villancico from Lope's play is to be found in the Flor de romances y glosas y canciones y villancicos (Zaragoza, 1578), re-edited in Valencia in 1954 by A. Rodríguez Moñino.

Ley, C. D. El gracioso en el teatro de la península... (1954). See Studies — Drama — General.

Lenormand, Jacques. "Théâtre d'été." NRF, No. 56 (1957), 323-26.
   Camus' adaptation and staging of El caballero de Olmedo in the Château du roi René at Angers is called "one of the most wonderful open-air spectacles imaginable" and the best type of theatre for appealing to what is best in the audience.

Alonso, D. "Tres procesos de dramatización" (1958). See Studies — Drama — General.

McPheeters, D. W. "Camus' translations of plays by Lope and Calderón." Symposium, XII(1958), 52-64.
   Drawn by his Spanish blood to the Spanish classical theatre, Camus translated El caballero de Olmedo for a summer festival at Angers (June, 1957). The outdoor performance was highly acclaimed. The forceful dramaturgy and direct non-cerebral impact of Lope and Calderón help explain their popularity in France today.

Yates, Donald A. "The Poetry of the Fantastic in El caballero de Olmedo." Hisp, XLIII(1960), 503-07.

Soons, C. Alan. "Towards an Interpretation of El caballero de Olmedo." RF, LXXIII(1961), 160-68.
   In an attempt to add to the meaningfulness of El caballero de Olmedo, Soons seeks out certain poetic "signs" in the play, and he elucidates his conviction that "the feature which stands out with greatest relief is the fact that every major character is spoken of in relation to clothing, cosmetics or adornment...." Soons considers also the significance of the fact that the time of the play is the season of the feast of the Invention of the Cross.

El caballero del milagro

Promies, Wolfgang. "Mimik und Gebärde in Lope de Vegas El caballero del milagro." Maske und Kothurn, III(1957), 116-27.
   Addressed to theatrically-minded readers not conversant with the Spanish drama, the article sets up a double distinction: first, between a tendency to gesticulation and mimicry supposedly inborn in the Spaniard, and the aristocratic concept of compostura; second, between spontaneous natural gestures and studied artificial ones. Action and characters are then analysed in terms of these distinctions, which prove somewhat less illuminating than expected and do not save the author from such inaccuracies as supposing Lope an actor of bit parts and calling D. Juan and D. Quixote pícaros.

La campana de Aragón

Osma, José M. de. "Tres etapas en la dramatización de una leyenda: La campana de Huesca." Hisp, XXIV(1941), 180-92.

Ubieto Arteta, Antonio. "La campana de Huesca." RFE, XXV(1951), 29-61.

Simón Díaz, José. "El tema literario de La campana de Huesca." RL, VII(1955), 30-49.

   All three articles include references to Lope's La campana de Aragón.

El capellán de la Virgen

Bousfield, W. A. "Lope de Vega on Early Conditioning." American Psychologist, X(1955), 828.

Arjona, J. H. "Modern Psychology in Lope de Vega" (1956). See Studies — Drama — General.

El cardenal de Belén

Torner, E. M. "Índice de analogías..." (1946). See Studies — Poetry — General.

Carlos el perseguido

See El perseguido, below.

El casamiento en la muerte

Tyler, R. W. "Further Suggestions..." (1952). See Studies — Drama — General.

Castelvines y Monteses

Moore, Olin H. *The Legend of Romeo and Juliet*. Columbus, Ohio State Univ. Press, 1950. Pp. xii, 167. (Ohio State Univ. Contributions in Lang. and Lit., 13.)
    The play is referred to on pp. 123-26. The author refuses to assume any "lost" Italian source for Lope's Castelvines y Monteses. He compares the names of Lope's characters with Shakespeare's (p. 124). There is no evaluation of the play.

El castigo del discreto

Romo, Josefina. "Una mala interpretación de un texto de Lope." *Correo Erudito*, III, No. 19 (1943), 19-20.
    This article is almost a verbatim copy of the section of its author's review of the M.-B., Chronology (RFE, XXVI, 1942, 505-21), in which she objects to the date assigned to El castigo del discreto.

El castigo sin venganza

Consiglio, Carlo. "La fuente italiana de El castigo sin venganza, de Lope." *Mediterráneo*, XII(1945), 250-55.
    The author politely refutes van Dam's contention in his edition of the play that Lope was inspired by the Spanish version of the French short-story teller Belleforest (who also included Bandello's narration) rather than directly by Bandello. The author points out that "se trata de pormenores insignificantes, mientras que son mucho más interesantes las divergencias entre el texto de Bandello (y de su refundidor Belleforest) y las innovaciones que Lope introduce para acrecentar el dramatismo del relato." The author then goes on to single out the main differences between the Bandello treatment and the Lope treatment of the theme concluding that there is more similarity between Dante's and Lope's development of the blind force of love acting as an implacable destiny: "...hay como una fuerza fatal que domina actos y palabras, que anula a los personajes.

El drama se hace tragedia inexorable y el destino manda sobre los corazones y sobre las mentes. Este segundo acto del drama lopiano no hace ya pensar en Bandello, sino en algo mucho más elevado: en Dante, en el V Canto del Infierno, y en la desgraciada pasión de Pablo y Francisca." Thus, Consiglio concludes that Lope raises his motivating force above the low passions of the historical event and the Bandello narrative of lust and vengeance to a lofty conflict between "el sentimiento del amor y el del honor."

Meier, Harri. *Ensaios de Filologia Romãnica*. Lisbon, Rev. de Portugal, 1948.

Among the ensaios is one entitled "A honra no drama romãnico dos séculos XVI e XVII," within which is a section (pp. 243-46) devoted to Lope's *El castigo sin venganza*. Meier concludes that it does not have in its tragic ending the shocking harshness of the inhuman conventionalism for which it has been censured, nor does he agree with van Dam that the title ought to be instead *La venganza sin castigo*.. He points out that although the Duke, as God's representative on earth and as paterfamilias, with authority over his family, could justifiably exact legal punishment for the wrong done him, he returns the matter to God's hands (o Céu).

Ley, C. D. "Lope de Vega y la tragedia" (1950). See Studies — Drama — General.

Alonso, Amado. "Lope de Vega y sus fuentes." *Thesaurus*, VIII(1952), 1-24.

This actually is a study of only one of Lope's fuentes. To Amado Alonso, Lope's fuentes are merely blocks of marble in which the sculptor visualizes his statue. Bandello's *Novella XLIV* is the block from which Lope brought forth his work of art. He gives a résumé of Bandello's tale, but "por su misma naturaleza dramática," it is impossible to "resumir" *El castigo sin venganza*, which must be read whole. Instead, Alonso proposes to analyse (a) the nationalization of a foreign theme; and (b) the inexorable enchainment, the truly Shakespearean motivation "de los acontecimientos psíquicos y externos," found only in the greatest creations of the theatre.

Ley, C. D. *El gracioso en el teatro de la península...* (1954). See Studies — Drama — General.

Arjona, J. H. "Modern Psychology in Lope de Vega" (1956). See Studies — Drama — General.

Menéndez Pidal, R. *El P. de las Casas...* (1958). See Studies — General.

May, T. E. "Lope de Vega's El castigo sin venganza: The Idolatry of the Duke of Ferrara." BHS, XXXVII(1960), 154-82.
   The idolatry consists of the Duke's worship of "a god made in his own image." Later, May draws an analogy between Federico's death after a false accusation, abandonment by his father and an unfair trial, and that of Christ. He wonders whether Lope meant to have this seen, but cannot otherwise reconcile the play with the beliefs of Lope's day, as he believes necessary.

Rosendorfsky, J. "Einige italienische Motive..." (1960). See Studies — Drama — General.

El cerco de Santa Fe

Templin, E. H. "Carolingian Heroes and Ballad Lines in Non-Carolingian Dramatic Literature." HR, VII(1939), 35-47.
   Contains a reference to Lope's El cerco de Santa Fe.

El cerco de Viena y socorro por Carlos V

Arjona, J. H. "Ten Plays Attributed to Lope de Vega" (1960). See Studies — Drama — General.

Los comendadores de Córdoba

Werner, E. "Der Spassmacher..." (1949). See Studies — Drama — General.

Morley, S. G., and Courtney Bruerton. "Lope de Vega, Celia y Los comendadores de Córdoba." NRFH, VI(1952), 57-68.
   This is an answer to María Goyri de Menéndez Pidal's article, "La Celia de Lope de Vega," NRFH, IV(1950), whose thesis was that around the years 1591-95 Lope fell in love with a woman whom he poetically called Celia; that Celia was none other than Lucinda (Micaela de Luján). M.-B. adduce evidence to sustain the opinion expressed by Castro in 1918, that 1599-1608 was the period of Lope's ardor for Micaela; that Celia was perhaps the name that Lope used to group together poetically women of fleeting relationships. Therefore, the a quo date 1599, assigned to several plays, is still valid and the date 1593 is unacceptable for Los comendadores de Córdoba, which is not earlier than 1596.

Contra valor no hay desdicha

Fernández Galiano, M. "Sobre la evolución de la leyenda de Ciro..." (1961). See Studies — General.

El cordobés valeroso, Pedro Carbonero

See Pedro Carbonero, below.

La corona de Hungría

Kozma, Béla, and A. Zoltán Murányi. "Lope de Vega magyar tárgyú drámájának (Corona de Hungría) sorsa. Hova tünt el a Nemzeti Színházból Stefan Zweig, által Magyarországnak ajándékozott kézirat?" Élet és Irodalom, III, No. 34 (1959), 4.
  An inquiry concerning the fate of a lost photo-copy of the autograph, which Stefan Zweig apparently presented to the National Theatre, Budapest, in 1935.

La corona derribada y vara de Moisés

Arjona, J. H. "Ten Plays Attributed to Lope de Vega" (1960). See Studies — Drama — General.

La corona merecida

Navarro, T. "Notas fonológicas..." (1954). See Studies — Drama — General.

La cortesía de España

Kohler, E. "Lope de Vega et Giraldi Cintio" (1946). See Studies — General.

Gillet, J. E. "Lucrecia-necia" (1947). See Studies — General.

Tyler, R. W. "On the Dates..." (1950). See Studies — Drama — General.

La creación del mundo

Stanger, Jennie Abulafia. "El drama español basado en el Viejo Testamento." Judaica, VII(1940), 139-48.
  A superficial discussion of La creación del mundo.

El cuerdo en su casa

Hayes, F. C. "The Use of Proverbs..." (1938). See Studies — Drama — General.

Wilson, William E. "Bigoteras and the Date of Lope's El cuerdo en su casa." BCom, VII, No. 2 (1955), 29-31.

El cuerdo loco

Hoge, Henry W. "Notes on the Sources..." (1950). See Studies — Drama — Individual Plays (El príncipe despeñado).

La dama boba

Oliver, W. I. Spanish Theatre... (1959). See Studies — Drama — General.

Alonso, D. "Lope en vena de filósofo" (1950). See Studies — Poetry — General.

Fucilla, Joseph G. "Finea in Lope's La dama boba in the Light of Modern Psychology." BCom, VII, No. 2 (1955), 22-23.

Wardropper, Bruce W. "Lope's La dama boba and Baroque Comedy." BCom, XIII, No. 2 (1961), 1-3.

¿De cuándo acá nos vino?

San Román, Francisco de B. "El autógrafo de la comedia de Lope ¿De cuándo acá nos vino?" RFE, XXIV(1937), 220-23.
  Identifies the handwriting of Act II as that of Pedro de Valdés, who supposedly copied it from the original by Lope. Also discusses the date.

La difunta pleiteada

Goyri de Menéndez Pidal, María. De Lope de Vega y del Romancero (1953). See Studies — Poetry — Individual Poems (Romances).

La discreta enamorada

Tyler, R. W. "Further Suggestions..." (1952). See Studies — Drama — General.

Peyton, M. A. "La discreta enamorada as an Example of Dimensional Development in the Comedia." Hisp, XL(1957), 154-62.
  Comparison of the play with its Boccaccian sources shows, in Lope's characters, increased personal complexity and self-awareness and conflicts between individual purpose and the forces of society, the latter being viewed as personajes themselves. Boccaccio's "efficient" characters exist solely to function in their plot; they reflect a simple medieval order in contrast to Lope's baroque complexity. The difference, we are told, results simply from "changes brought by time itself."

El divino africano

Micó Buchón, José Luis. "El divino africano: Tragicomedia agustiniana de Lope de Vega." Humanidades (Santander), VI(1954), 105-17.
  Lope shows in many of his works a special devotion to this saint, whose life is similar in some ways to his own. Micó Buchón finds that the first two acts of the play are based faithfully

on St. Augustine's <u>Confessions</u>. He finds the third act the poorest, with too much crowded into it. The play was written for the sixteenth centennial of the saint's death.

El dómine Lucas

Nemtzow, S. "El estudiante en la <u>Comedia</u>..." (1946). See Studies — Drama — General.

Gillet, J. E. "<u>Lucrecia-necia</u>" (1947). See Studies — General.

La doncella Teodor

Nemtzow, S. "El estudiante en la <u>Comedia</u>..." (1946). See Studies — Drama — General.

Don Lope de Cardona

Bork, A. W. "Lope's <u>Don Lope de Cardona</u>: A Defense of the Duke of Sessa." <u>HR</u>, IX(1941), 348-58.
  Passages in Act III of this <u>comedia</u> which are rather unrelated to the rest of the action indicate to Bork that Lope wrote the play as a defence of the Duke of Sessa at the time of the latter's banishment from Madrid in 1611. In this last act, Don Lope de Cardona is, according to Bork, the Duke of Sessa speaking for himself through Lope's pen. Bork presented a master's thesis on the play at Univ. of Arizona in 1939.

Dos estrellas trocadas o los ramilletes de Madrid

Crosby, James O. "Quevedo, Lope, and the Royal Wedding of 1615." <u>MLQ</u>, XVII(1956), 104-10.
  Reference to Lope's description of festivities in the third act of <u>Dos estrellas trocadas</u>.

Los dos ingenios y esclavos del Santísimo Sacramento (<u>auto</u>)

Wardropper, B. W. <u>Introducción al teatro religioso</u>... (1953). See Studies — Drama — General.

El duque de Viseo

Avalle-Arce, J. B. "Dos notas a Lope de Vega" (1953). See Studies — Drama — General.

El ejemplo de casadas y prueba de la paciencia

Arjona, J. H. "La fecha de <u>Ejemplo de casadas y prueba de la paciencia</u> de Lope de Vega." <u>MLN</u>, LII(1937), 249-52.
  The date decided on is April 22, 1612.

Morley and Bruerton. "The Date of Two Plays..." (1938). See
  Studies — Drama — General.

Kohler, Eugène. "La Date de composition de El ejemplo de casadas
  de Lope et la valeur chronologique du gracioso." BH, XLVII
  (1945), 79-91.
   In the first part of the article, Kohler states his belief that
   the loa and the play were written as a unit, and dates the two
   as 1601. In the second part, he states his belief in the
   chronological value of the gracioso, noticing certain plays
   with and without the figura del donaire. In conclusion, he
   repeats that the play must have been written in 1601, and not
   in 1612, as previously believed.

------. "À propos de la date de composition de El ejemplo de casadas de Lope." BH, XLVIII(1946), 264-69.
   Kohler is very happy to see that his date (1601) is confirmed
   by the M.-B., Chronology, as opposed to Arjona's previous 1612.
   Kohler believes that the play, with loa and baile, was written
   to celebrate a marriage in the Moncada family, on April 22,
   1601.

El esclavo fingido

Arjona, J. H. "Ten Plays Attributed to Lope de Vega" (1960). See
  Studies — Drama — General.

La escolástica celosa

Nemtzow, S. "El estudiante en la Comedia..." (1946). See Studies —
  Drama — General.

Los españoles en Flandes

Tyler, R. W. "Further Suggestions..." (1952). See Studies —
  Drama — General.

La Estrella de Sevilla

Johnson, Harvey L. "A Recent French Adaptation of La Estrella de
  Sevilla." RR, XXXVI(1945), 222-34.
   Albert Ollivier's Étoile de Séville (adapted from the translation
   in Eugène Baret's Oeuvres dramatiques de Lope de Vega, Paris,
   1874) was very successfully presented in various French and
   North African cities during the German occupation in the second
   World War. The adaptation was published in Esprit, Revue
   Internationale, 1941. Ollivier accepts "without question the
   attribution of authorship to Spain's prolific dramatist."

Powers, P. J. The Concept of the City State... (1947). See Studies —
  Drama — General.

Entrambasaguas, J. de. "Blair y Munárriz..." (1950). See Studies — General.

Valbuena Prat, A. "En torno a dos temas de Lope" (1950). See Studies — Drama — General.

Pound, E. "The Quality of Lope de Vega" (1952). See Studies — Drama — General.

Keller, John E. "A Tentative Classification for Themes in the Comedia" (1953). See Studies — Drama — General.

Serís, Homero. "Un soneto del autor de La Estrella de Sevilla." NRFH, VII(1953), 433-38.
On the question of authorship of the play, Serís makes known his discovery of a sonnet by Pedro de Cárdenas, identified by A. F. G. Bell as "Cardenio" and the author of the play.

Brooks, J. L. "La Estrella de Sevilla: 'admirable y famosa tragedia'." BHS, XXXII(1955), 8-20.
Comments on Menéndez Pelayo's words.

Alonso, Dámaso. "Lope, don Pedro de Cárdenas y los Cardenios." RFE, XL(1956), 67-90.
In conclusively disproving Bell's assertion that "the Cardenio of Cervantes, Montalvo, Lope and Salas Barbadillo is one and the same person," namely don Pedro de Cárdenas, "author of La Estrella de Sevilla," Alonso considers, among others, the numerous Cardenios in Lope, notes their autobiographical overtones and raises but rejects the possibility that Lope is the author of the play. "Bajo el Cardenio de La Estrella de Sevilla puede ocultarse cualquier poeta que escribiera en España a principios del siglo XVII ... lo reduciré así: creo que ese poeta o es de Sevilla o había vivido en Sevilla bastante tiempo...."

Dulsey, Bernard. "La Estrella de Sevilla, ¿adónde va?" Hispanó, No. 2 (1957), 8-10.
She does not, according to this writer, go to a convent, as numerous previous critics have affirmed.

El favor agradecido

Morby, E. S. "Gli Ecatommiti..." (1942). See Studies — Drama — General.

González de Amezúa, A. Una colección manuscrita... (1945). See Studies — Drama — General.

Las ferias de Madrid

Gillet, J. E. "Lucrecia-necia" (1947). See Studies — General.

Bruerton, Courtney. "Las ferias de Madrid de Lope de Vega." BH, LVII(1955), 56-69.
An analysis of the Biblioteca de Palacio MS., and a comparison with the Cotarelo edition.

La fianza satisfecha

Möller, W. Die christliche Banditen-Comedia (1936; review: 1938). See Studies — Drama — General.

Lo fingido verdadero

Jacquot, J. "Le Théâtre du monde..." (1957). See Studies — Drama — General.

La fortuna adversa del infante D. Fernando de Portugal

Sloman, Albert E. The Sources of Calderón's "El príncipe constante," with a Critical Edition of its Immediate Source, "La fortuna adversa del infante D. Fernando de Portugal" (a Play Attributed to Lope de Vega). Oxford, Blackwell, 1950. Pp. 228.

La francesilla

Arjona, J. H. "La fecha de La francesilla." HR, V(1937), 73-76.

Herrero García, M. "Génesis de la figura del donaire" (1941). See Studies — Drama — General.

Werner, E. "Der Spassmacher..." (1949). See Studies — Drama — General.

Fuenteovejuna

Price, E. R. "The Peasant Plays..." (1937). See Studies — Drama — General.

Calle Iturrino, Esteban. Lope de Vega y clave de "Fuenteovejuna." Bilbao, Imp. Dochao, 1938. Pp. 126.

Macdonald, Inez I. "An Interpretation of Fuenteovejuna." Babel (Cambridge, England), I(1940), 51-62.

Mallarino, Víctor. "El alcalde de Zalamea y Fuenteovejuna frente al derecho penal." Rev. de las Indias, XIV(1942), 358-67; XVI (1942-43), 77-82; XVII(1943), 138-43; XIX(1943-44), 299-329.
Calderón and Lope.

Casalduero, Joaquín. "Fuenteovejuna." RFH, V(1943), 21-44. Trans. by Ruth Whittredge as "Fuenteovejuna: Form and Meaning," TDR, IV(1959), 83-107.
    The author takes issue with Menéndez Pelayo's attempt to read democracy into the play. The conflict is not political in nature; and the nature of Baroque society — a lower level ruled by an upper, with Church and Monarchy supreme — would not allow such an interpretation. There are really two endings: the happy one for Laurencia and Frondoso after the judge gives up his tortures, and the royal pardon for the village. After "the King-God ... crushes the Commander-Satan," the second ending parallels "the happy ending of Christian tragedy, the joy of the third day, of the Resurrection which follows Death and is its complement."

Entrambasaguas, J. de. Estudios sobre Lope de Vega, I (1946). See Studies — General.

Powers, P. J. The Concept of the City State... (1947). See Studies — Drama — General.

Cardenal Iracheta, Manuel. "Fuenteovejuna." Clav, II, No. 11 (1951), 20-26.
    Since Anibal's "The Historical Elements of Lope de Vega's Fuente Ovejuna" (PMLA, 1934) was not mentioned in this examination of the historical sources, it is to be presumed that the author wrote without knowledge of that article. Anibal would have provided Cardenal Iracheta with an excellent point of departure and a frame of reference for refutation. Several points of disagreement merit the attention of historians. Anibal accepted the well-established integrity, veracity and authenticity of F. de Palencia (e.g., Zurita: "el historiador más veraz de España"). C. I. declares "apenas si hay punto de verdad en el relato de Palencia." Anibal subjects Rades to a rigid test and, for the most part, accepts his Chronica, which to C. I. is "también fabulosa." For the real facts he goes to R. de Arellano (BRAH, 1901), whose investigation Anibal deems valuable but not impeccable. The latter believes that Fernán Gómez de Guzmán and Fernán Ramírez de Guzmán were one and the same person, who met his death in 1476; not C. I.: "se dice, según Carriazo (his ed. of Crónica de los Reyes Católicos) que el 31 de mayo de 1487 aún vivía el Comendador Mayor de Calatrava, don Fernando Ramírez de Guzmán."

Roaten, Darnell. "Wölfflin's Principles Applied to Lope's Fuenteovejuna." BCom, IV, No. 1 (1952), 1-4.
    A summary of a portion of Wölfflin's Principles in Spanish Drama, 1500-1700, published subsequently in 1952.

Roaten and Sánchez y Escribano. Wölfflin's Principles... (1952). See Studies — Drama — General.

Keller, John E. "A Tentative Classification for Themes in the *Comedia*" (1953). See Studies — Drama — General.

Parker, A. A. "Reflections on a New Definition..." (1953). See Studies — Drama — General.

Sloman, Albert E. "The Structure of Calderón's *La vida es sueño*." *MLR*, XLVIII(1953), 293-300.
    Only pp. 299-300 (one paragraph) of this article deal with Lope's *Fuenteovejuna*, but this elicited a reply from G. W. Ribbans in *BHS*, 1954 (see below). Sloman believes that the Ciudad Real episode is used only as a backdrop or bridge between scenes of the main plot of the play, and that the former is by no means essential to the play, which could stand with this secondary action removed.

Ley, C. D. *El gracioso en el teatro de la península...* (1954). See Studies — Drama — General.

Ribbans, G. W. "The Meaning and Structure of Lope's *Fuenteovejuna*." *BHS*, XXXI(1954), 150-70.
    This is an excellent analysis of the play as a whole. The author shows that *Fuenteovejuna* is outstanding for its clear vision of society as a coherent and interdependent whole, which can be upset from either the top or the bottom, with chaos resulting. He calls the play a masterly treatment of a problem of relations between the governor and the governed. The sub-plot he also believes to be an integral part of the theme and essential to the play, contrary to the opinion expressed by Sloman (*MLR*, 1953 — see above).

Spitzer, Leo. "A Central Theme and its Structural Equivalent in Lope's *Fuenteovejuna*." *HR*, XXIII(1955), 274-92.
    A fundamental article, which studies the concept of harmony as a structural element for the organic development and unity of the play. (This article was reprinted in Spitzer, *Romanische Literaturstudien*, 1959. See Studies — General.)

Wardropper, Bruce W. "*Fuente Ovejuna*: *El gusto* and *lo justo*." *SP*, LIII(1956), 159-71.
    The article examines the relationship of "*justo*" — "*gusto*" as key concepts for the play, which deals with the relations of individuals and is a treatment of (Platonic) love.

Alba, Marie-Louise. "Lope de Vega triomphe à Montauban." *NL*, July 11, 1957.
    The outdoor production of *Fuenteovejuna* by Jean Deschamps of the Comédie Française shows off to full advantage the "cathedral-like" structure and natural morality of this exacting yet popular epic piece. There are no superfluous characters and the grandiose *mise-en-scène* and musical score of Maurice Ohana round out the well-integrated effect.

Cappelletti, A. J. "Notas sobre tres dramas..." (1957). See
    Studies — Drama — General.

Alonso, D. "Tres procesos de dramatización" (1958). See Studies —
    Drama — General.

Dulsey, Bernard. "La literatura española en el ballet soviético."
    Hisp, XLIV(1961), 557.
    A brief account of the way in which the Russians changed Fuenteovejuna into a ballet entitled Laurencia.

McCrary, William C. "Fuenteovejuna: Its Platonic Vision and Execution." SP, LVIII(1961), 179-92.
    Building on the studies of Spitzer and others, McCrary argues
        that Fuenteovejuna is a "reconstitution of history according
        to the canons of a normative Platonic vision."

Soons, C. Alan. "Two Historical Comedias and the Question of
    Manierismo." RF, LXXIII(1961), 339-46.
    Soons discusses Lope's Fuenteovejuna and Tirso's Antona García,
        plays which deal with events of the time of Ferdinand and Isabella. In Lope's play there is a selection of "certain
        historical incidents as a basis for invention: to show the
        perversity of natural man transcended and the harmony of the
        great body of society restored." Tirso, however, had a
        different attitude in his drama, for whereas "Fuenteovejuna is
        a truly 'invented' play, (since) the conflict it introduces is
        profound and archetypal...", Tirso's play represents certain
        aspects of manierismo. "This contrast opens the question of
        manierismo in the Seventeenth Century drama and, it is hoped,
        permits criteria to be assembled for the illumination of that
        vast body of comedias which lack serious or quasi-philosophical
        themes."

El galán escarmentado

Werner, E. "Der Spassmacher..." (1949). See Studies — Drama —
    General.

El genovés liberal

Rosendorfsky, J. "Einige italienische Motive..." (1960). See
    Studies — Drama — General.

El gran duque de Moscovia

van Praag, J. A. "Más noticias sobre la fuente de El gran duque de
    Moscovia de Lope de Vega." BH, XXXIX(1937), 356-66.

Vernet, J. "Las fuentes de El gran duque de Moscovia." Cuad. de
    Lit., V(1949), 17-36.

The author believes that Lope modified the tradition of the printed sources, concerning the story of Demetrius, pretender to the throne of the Tsar, on the basis of oral reports received from members of a Spanish embassy returning from Persia to Spain via Moscow in 1608. The author publishes (pp. 25-36) in Spanish translation the French version of the "Relación del viaje realizado por el monje Agustín" (an Armenian monk), found in the Journal Asiatique, I(1837), 209-45, 401-21. The embassy started from Rome, where the Duke of Sessa, father of Lope's benefactor, was ambassador (according to the Duke's diplomatic correspondence).

Las grandezas de Alejandro

Lida de Malkiel, M. R. "Alejandro en Jerusalén" (1956-57). See Studies — General.

El grao de Valencia

Baulier, F. "La Mise en scène dans deux pièces de Lope de Vega" (1945). See Studies — Drama — General.

El halcón de Federico

Rosendorfsky, J. "Einige italienische Motive..." (1960). See Studies — Drama — General.

El Hamete de Toledo

Tyler, R. W. "On the Dates..." (1950). See Studies — Drama — General.

La hermosa Ester

Fishlock, A. D. H. "Lope de Vega's La hermosa Ester and Pinto Delgado's Poema de la reyna Ester: A Comparative Study." BHS, XXXII(1955), 81-97.
 This is an important study comparing the handling of the theme by Lope and by a marrano. It is not only a study to show Lope's influence, but also to acquaint scholars with the work of Pinto Delgado. (See the author's dissertation, London, 1952, on the Poems of Pinto Delgado.)

Glaser, Edward. "Lope de Vega: La hermosa Ester." Sefarad, XX (1960), 110-35.
 Lope has made the story of Esther "a drama of deliverance and not of revenge," and has not only shown the elevation of the humble at the expense of the proud, as he often did, but has presented Esther in terms of Mary. This is seen in the last line of Act I, "Lo que mujer dañó, mujer lo sana," suggesting St. Bonaventure's contrast of Eve and Mary; and in Esther's being likened to a fountainhead of salvation (Acad., III, 343).

La hermosa fea

Thomas, H. "A Forgotten Translation of Lope de Vega." *MLR*, XXXV (1940), 378-80.
   The article deals with an Italian translation of the play, by an unknown author.

El hidalgo Bencerraje

Tyler, R. W. "On the Dates..." (1950). See Studies — Drama — General.

El hijo por engaño

Arjona, J. H. "Ten Plays Attributed to Lope de Vega" (1960). See Studies — Drama — General.

La ilustre fregona

Sloman, Albert E. "The Spanish Source of *The Fair Maid of the Inn*." In *Hispanic Studies in Honour of I. González Llubera*, Oxford, 1959, pp. 331-41.
   Rev: Marcel Bataillon, *BHS*, XXXVIII(1961), 216-24 (see p. 223).
   The article states that the play, attributed to Fletcher, Massinger and Rowley, is based on *La ilustre fregona* attributed to Lope, which in turn was inspired by Cervantes' novel.

La imperial de Otón

Morley and Bruerton. "The Date of Two Plays..." (1938). See Studies — Drama — General.

Strzalkowa, Maria. *Studia Polsko-Hiszpanskie*. Cracow, Nakladem Uniwersystetu Jagiellonskiego, 1960. Pp. 189. (*Rozprawi i Studia*, 26.)
   The volume includes studies on the literary fortunes of Calderón and Lope in Poland, and an analysis of Lope's *La imperial de Otón*.

La ingratitud vengada

Arjona, J. H. "Ten Plays Attributed to Lope de Vega" (1960). See Studies — Drama — General.

Juan de Dios y Antón Martín

Tyler, Richard W. "The Date of Lope's *Juan de Dios y Antón Martín*." *HR*, XVII(1949), 250-51.
   Internal evidence points toward a time after Aug. 20, 1611, versification to not later than 1612. Morley and Bruerton's *terminus ad quem* is 1610.

Los jueces de Castilla

Henríquez Ureña, Pedro. "Los jueces de Castilla." RFH, VI(1944), 285-86.
  The article argues in favour of Lope's authorship of this play, often attributed to Moreto.

El labrador venturoso

Tyler, R. W. "Further Suggestions..." (1952). See Studies — Drama — General.

El lacayo fingido

Arjona, J. H. "Did Lope de Vega write El lacayo fingido?" SP, LI (1954), 42-53.
  Arjona here demonstrates the need for objective criteria in determining authorship. Nobody has seriously questioned Lope's authorship of this play, listed by him in the first Peregrino list, and published in 1613 and again in 1617 in a volume of plays by Góngora and Lope. Yet an analysis of its rhyme and orthoëpy leads to the conclusion that this is not the same play that Lope wrote and listed as his.

Loa famosa de las calidades de las mujeres

Entrambasaguas, Joaquín de. "Acerca de la atribución de una Loa a Lope de Vega." RBN, V(1944), 339-49.

La madre de la mejor

Olmedillo, C. "Lope y Calderón en México: 1641" (1957-58). See Studies — Drama — General.

El maestro de danzar

Barclay, T. B. "The Importance of the Dance..." (1958). See Studies — Drama — General.

Castro Escudero, J. "Bailes y danzas..." (1959). See Studies — Drama — General.

La mal casada

Gillet, J. E. "Lucrecia-necia" (1947). See Studies — General.

El marido más firme

Cabañas, P. El mito de Orfeo... (1948). See Studies — General.

Valbuena Prat, A. "En torno a dos temas..." (1950). See Studies — Drama — General.

El marqués de las Navas

Navarro, T. "Notas fonológicas..." (1954). See Studies — Drama — General.

El mayor imposible

Bohning, William H. "Lope's El mayor imposible and Boisrobert's La Folle gageure." HR, XII(1944), 248-57.
The article states that the French comedy is a very free translation, scene by scene, of the Spanish play, and that Boisrobert's claim to having made important changes is exaggerated.

El mayor prodigio

Fichter, W. L. "Is El mayor prodigio by Lope de Vega?" RR, XXX (1939), 345-51.
Fichter proves that the attribution of the play to Lope is doubtful.

La mayor virtud de un rey

Powers, P. J. The Concept of the City State... (1947). See Studies — Drama — General.

El mejor alcalde el rey

Price, E. "The Peasant Plays..." (1937). See Studies — Drama — General.

Powers, P. J. The Concept of the City State... (1947). See Studies — Drama — General.

Leavitt, Sturgis E. "A Maligned Character in Lope's El mejor alcalde el rey." BCom, VI, No. 2 (1954), 1-3.
Leavitt accomplishes successfully what needed to be undertaken: the defence of Feliciana and the reassessment of her function and character.

Sloman, Albert E. "Lope's El mejor alcalde el rey: Addendum to a Note by Sturgis E. Leavitt." BCom, VII, No. 2 (1955), 17-19.

El mejor mozo de España

Powers, P. J. The Concept of the City State... (1947). See Studies — Drama — General.

Tyler, R. W. "On the Dates..." (1950). See Studies — Drama — General.

Entrambasaguas, Joaquín de. "Pedro Vergel, 'El mejor mozo de España,' a quien Lope de Vega dedicó esta comedia." Rev. de la Biblioteca, Archivo y Museo, XX(1951), 75-98.

Las mocedades de Bernardo del Carpio

Avalle-Arce, J. B. "Dos notas a Lope de Vega" (1953). See Studies — Drama — General.

El molino

Parramón y Doll, A. M. "Lérida en el teatro de Lope. La comedia El molino." Ilerda (Lérida), XIV-XV(1956-57), 167-324.

La moza de cántaro

Wagner, Charles Philip. "Lope de Vega's Fifteen Hundred comedias and the Date of La moza de cántaro." HR, IX(1941), 91-102.
This article is an attempt to show that the phrase mil y quinientas, as used by Lope at the end of La moza de cántaro, is without value for dating the play. Several examples are adduced to indicate that Lope used the phrase merely to express a large, indefinite number. Internal evidence, corroborated by findings on versification, suggests the Christmas season of 1625-26 as the time not only of composition but also of performance in the presence of Felipe and Isabel.

Wilson, William E. "A Note on La moza de cántaro." HR, X(1942), 71-72.
Correction is offered to the explanation which the Holt edition (1913) gives for the verse: "volver la silla à el dosel" (III, x). Wilson cites two passages from Tirso's Próspera fortuna de D. Álvaro y adversa de Ruy López Dávalos to show that the verse in question refers to the ancient custom of venerating the chair occupied by the king during a visit in the home of a subject.

González Echegaray, Carlos. "Soror Juana y Frey Lope: Dos sonetos." BBMP, XXIV(1948), 281-89.
The author compares and contrasts a sonnet of Sor Juana Inés de la Cruz and one of Lope that appears in La moza de cántaro (ll. 1089-1102), which, the author is certain, Sor Juana had read.

Avalle-Arce, Juan Bautista. "Gutierre de Cetina, Gálvez de Montalvo y Lope de Vega." NRFH, V(1951), 411-14.
Identifies four lines of a song, beginning "¿De qué sirve, ojos serenos," in La moza de cántaro. Avalle-Arce shows that the redondilla is the same as the first strophe of a poem found in Pastor de Félida (Madrid, 1582) by Montalvo, whom Lope praised on two occasions. Montalvo was inspired by Cetina's famous madrigal Ojos, claros, serenos.

La necedad del discreto

LaGrone, G. G. *The Imitations of "Don Quixote"...* (1937). See Studies — Drama — General.

La niña de plata

Françon, M. "Sur le sonnet du sonnet." <u>MLN</u>, LXVII(1952), 46-47.
   The article contains a reference to Voiture's admission of imitating (in his <u>Rondeau du rondeau</u>) Lope's famous sonnet (of <u>La niña de plata</u>) and its ancestor by Diego de Mendoza, "Pedís, reina, un soneto."

Fucilla, Joseph G. "Sonetti sul Sonetto in Italia." In <u>Studi Letterari. Miscellanea in Onore di Emilio Santini</u>, Palermo, Univ. Manfredi, 1956, pp. 227-37.
   On versions of Diego de Mendoza's "Pedís, reina..." and Lope's "Un soneto me manda hacer Violante...", from <u>La niña de plata</u>.

Ryan, Hewson A. "A Note on Lope de Vega's <u>Soneto de repente</u>." <u>MLN</u>, LXII(1957), 121-24.
   An apparent allusion in a satirical poem to Lope's "Un soneto me manda hacer Violante" suggests that it was composed before 1604 and very probably before 1598 — well before the probable 1610-12 date of <u>La niña de plata</u>, in which it appears.

El niño diablo

Ley, C. D. *El gracioso en el teatro de la península...* (1954). See Studies — Drama — General.

El niño inocente de la Guardia

Glaser, Edward. "Lope de Vega's <u>El niño inocente de la Guardia</u>." <u>BHS</u>, XXXII(1955), 140-53.
   This is a keen analysis of the play, and a precise and imaginative source study in the light of <u>Judenbild</u> of the Middle Ages.

Los novios de Hornachuelos

Pound, E. "The Quality of Lope de Vega" (1952). See Studies — Drama — General.

Serrano Medialdea, Antonio. "Un rey de armas en el derecho diplomático de Lope de Vega." <u>RL</u>, XVIII(1960), 129-33.
   The <u>rey de armas</u> was a kind of envoy, originally with true diplomatic status. Lope portrays his <u>rey de armas</u> in <u>Los novios de Hornachuelos</u>, we are told; despite what seems to be fairly general present-day agreement, that the play belongs to Vélez de Guevara. The <u>rey de armas</u> appears only briefly, but may have had a larger part, if, as Hartzenbusch believed, there are gaps throughout the play.

La nueva ira de Dios y gran Tamorlán de Persia

Pound, E. "The Quality of Lope de Vega" (1952). See Studies — Drama — General.

La nueva victoria de Alemania de don Gonzalo de Córdoba

Nicolini, Fausto. "Una vittima storica di Alessandro Manzoni: Don Gonzalo Fernández de Córdoba. Saggio biografico." In Arte e storia nei "Promessi Sposi," Milan, Longanesi, 1958, pp. 83-263. (Originally published: Naples, Pironti, 1946.)
  In considering the historicity of Manzoni's presentation of the victor of Fleurus (1622), the author draws on Lope's presentation of him and of the battle in La nueva victoria... (1622) and upon other Lopean passages. He finds the historical accuracy of Lope's play such that he reproduces the pertinent scenes in an appendix along with a translation into Italian (new in this edition).

La nueva victoria del Marqués de Santa Cruz

Tyler, R. W. "Further Suggestions..." (1952). See Studies — Drama — General.

El nuevo mundo descubierto por Cristóbal Colón

Campos, Jorge. "Lope de Vega y el descubrimiento colombino." Rev. de Indias, IX(1949), 731-54. (Also pub. in Miscelánea americanista. Tomo I: Homenaje a D. Antonio Ballesteros Beretta, Madrid, CSIC, 1951, pp. 269-92.)
  This is a study of the play from the point of view of the americanista. It is actually a source study. The source is Lope de Gómara's Historia general de las Indias. "Lope se sirvió de un solo texto, añadiendo o elaborando según su propia impresión anterior o recurriendo en algún caso a un texto distinto." The purpose of the play is the "glorificación del héroe hispano, en la figura de Colón;" "exaltación de la fe católica;" "puesta en escena de los primeros colonizadores con sus puntas de crítica a la ambición."

Reims, Jeannine W. "Lope de Vega." Théâtre Populaire, No. 4 (1953), 30-44.
  This essay on Lope accompanies his El nuevo mundo published in French in this issue of the magazine. The very general discussion stresses the poetic quality of the Lopean theatre.

Flint, Weston. The Figure of Christopher Columbus in French, Italian and Spanish Drama. Unpub. doct. diss., Univ. of North Carolina, 1957.

Minian de Alfie, Raquel. "Lope y Ricardo del Turia (A propósito de una probable influencia)." Filología, VI(1960), 111-14.
Re El nuevo mundo descubierto por Cristóbal de Colón and La belígera española by Ricardo del Turia.

Flint, Weston. "Colón en el teatro español." EAm, XXII(1961), 165-86.
There is reference to Lope's El nuevo mundo on pp. 169-71. "Lope de Vega, el primer dramaturgo que hizo a Colón protagonista de una obra de teatro..." (p. 169).

La ocasión perdida

Wade, G. E. "The Literary Sources..." (1953). See Studies — Drama — General.

Bershas, Henry N. "An Autobiographical Allusion in Lope." HR, XXIX (1961), 238-40.
The author states his conviction that the gracioso Hernandillo is a mouthpiece for Lope in the expression of certain sentiments having to do with the dramatist's claim to gentility ("a coat of arms with nineteen castles...").

Las paces de los reyes y judía de Toledo

Powers, P. J. The Concept of the City State... (1947). See Studies — Drama — General.

Gómez de Salazar, J. "Alphonse VIII et Doña Fermosa." Évidences (Paris), No. 22 (1951).

Wilder, T. "Lope, Pinedo, Some Child Actors..." (1953). See Studies — Drama — General.

Allue y Morrell, F. "La 'Raquel Hermosa'..." (1954). See Studies — General.

MacCurdy, Raymond R. "The Bathing Nude in Golden Age Drama." RomN, I(1959), 36-39.
It is the sight of Raquel's bathing nude "which kindles in Alfonso VIII a consuming passion that causes him to lose all thought of wife and state."

El palacio confuso

Tiemann, H. "Über Lope de Vegas Bild..." (1947-48). See Studies — General.

Pedro Carbonero

Menéndez Pidal, Gonzalo. "Sobre Pedro Carbonero." BH, VIII(1949), 53-54.

The name <u>Pedro Carbonero</u> occurs as a well-known figure in <u>Estebanillo González</u> (Chapt. IV) and in Fernández de Oviedo's <u>Historia general y natural de Indias</u> (XXXIII, iv). He was famous for his "valor temerario," his "audacia y fortuna."

Bataillon, Marcel. "<u>Pedro Carbonero con su cuadrilla</u>...." <u>RPh</u>, VII(1953), 26-34.
    Bataillon disagrees with Menéndez Pelayo on the matter of the historical character of the play, and says that Pedro Carbonero did not belong to the traditions relating to Granada, but was an outlaw whose exploits were known to Lope and Cortés and probably to the people as a whole.

------. "La tradition recuellie par Lope de Vega dans <u>Pedro Carbonero</u>." <u>BH</u>, LV(1953), 375-77.
    More on the legend of Pedro Carbonero. Cortés, Bernal Díaz del Castillo and Gómara all mention this legend.

<u>Peribáñez y el comendador de Ocaña</u>

Price, E. R. "The Peasant Plays..." (1937). See Studies — Drama — General.

Poncet, Carolina. "Consideraciones sobre el episodio de Belardo en la tragicomedia <u>Peribáñez</u>." <u>Rev. Cubana</u>, XIV(1940), 78-99.
  Rev: R. M., <u>RFH</u>, IV(1942), 97.
    Poncet bases her discussion on Belardo's words "a la iglesia me acogí," arriving at the dates 1609-14 for the play. The review listed above points out that there has been much controversy over this line's being used as a basis for dating the <u>comedia</u>. At least in some instances, Srta. Poncet does not seem familiar with all the available data.

Powers, P. J. <u>The Concept of the City State...</u> (1947). See Studies — Drama — General.

Wagner, Charles P. "The Date of <u>Peribáñez</u>." <u>HR</u>, XV(1947), 72-83.
    Wagner favours the date Aug., 1605; he refers to the Belardo speech; he points out that all of the plays of the <u>Cuarta parte</u>, in which <u>Peribáñez</u> was first published, are dated by Morley and Bruerton between 1594 and 1610; also, that Lope was living in Toledo in Aug., 1605. Wagner dismisses the verse "a la iglesia me acogí" as a statement which cannot be reconciled, for purposes of dating, with the other data. Wagner argues convincingly.

Bruerton, Courtney. "More on the Date of <u>Peribáñez</u>." <u>HR</u>, XVII (1949), 35-46.
    Bruerton argues for a date of composition between 1605 and 1608, based on versification. He says that the flippant statement of the character Belardo about his age and church connection refers to the Belardo, <u>sacristán</u>, not to Lope under the disguise of Belardo.

Toledano, J. "Notas para una interpretación del Peribáñez."
  Escorial, Segunda Época, XX, No. 63 (1949), 737-44.
  Peribáñez is much more than an honour play. Peribáñez's and
  Casilda's actions depend on the Comendador, who is not "un
  libertino sin escrúpulos," but "simplemente un enamorado,
  esclavo de una pasión superior a su voluntad." The author
  contradicts Menéndez Pelayo's opinion of the Comendador as a
  despicable character, viewing him — correctly — as a victim
  of sincere passion and proving his point with ample quotations
  from the play.

Wilson, E. M. "Images et structure dans Peribáñez." BH, LI(1949),
  125-59.
  Imagery, style and vocabulary are interpreted as a function of
  the basic theme of the play: the normally harmonious relationship between nobles and villanos, based on the recognition of
  a fundamental equality of man (respect for each man's honra,
  regardless of his social status), is disrupted by the Comendador's destructive passion. The peasants' speech reflects
  their concrete world, even if idealized, the nobles' speech,
  the love language of literary convention. This is one of the
  few successful style studies in the field of the Comedia.

Bruerton, C. "La quinta de Florencia, fuente de Peribáñez" (1950).
  See Studies — Drama — Individual Plays (La quinta de
  Florencia).

Jobit, Pierre. "De Lope de Vega a Jean Anouilh." Clav, III, No. 16
  (1952), 1-4.
  The noble, yet human — "con su realismo crudo" — characterization of Peribáñez, Casilda and the Comendador in their portrayal
  of the theme of la doble constancia receives praise from this
  French critic. He compares Lope's execution with two different
  characterizations and reverse treatments of the theme found in
  Marivaux's Double inconstance and Anouilh's Répétition, which
  Jobit had recently seen performed in Paris.

Tyler, R. W. "Suggested Dates..." (1952). See Studies — Drama —
  General.

Loveluck, Juan. "La fecha de Peribáñez y el comendador de Ocaña."
  Atenea, Año XXX, CX, No. 336 (1953), 419-24.
  "Mi opinión es que Peribáñez fue escrita hacia 1614, aunque bien
  pudo serlo en 1613." The article is part of the prologue of a
  planned edition for Zig-Zag.

Silverman, Joseph. "Peribáñez y Vellido Dolfos." BH, LV(1953),
  378-80.
  The article corrects what Silverman believes to be a misunderstanding by E. M. Wilson (BH, 1949 — see above) of a passage
  in the play.

Sánchez, Roberto G. "El contenido irónico-teatral en el Peribáñez de Lope de Vega." Clav, V, No. 29 (1954), 17-25.
  This is an excellent analysis of the structure and meaning of the play. Sánchez believes that Peribáñez represents the campesino world, and the Comendador the aristocratic world; in Spain they are not opposites, but complementary elements of the social scene. The "irony" is in the peasant playing at being an "aristocrat," with the chorus of peasants in the background commenting on the burla. Since Peribáñez and the Comendador both recognize the reality of the two worlds, they can play with it without destroying it. Sánchez shows a sensitive and intelligent understanding of the play, and helps to correct the exaggeration of the lyrical value and the social importance of the play of which some critics have been guilty.

Alonso, D. "Tres procesos de dramatización" (1958). See Studies — Drama — General.

Correa, Gustavo. "El doble aspecto de la honra en Peribáñez y el comendador de Ocaña." HR, XXVI(1958), 188-99.
  Rev: P. G., LR, XIV(1960), 57-58.
  An examination of the structure of the play based on the author's categories of "vertical" and "horizontal" honour. In essence, the Comendador's acts bestow "vertical" honour on Peribáñez while taking away his "horizontal" honour. Symbolic external objects — cloaks, etc. — represent the interaction of the two aspects of honour, as does a subtle play of social values and stylistic levels.

Boorman, John T. "'Divina ley' and 'derecho humano' in Peribáñez." BCom, XII, No. 2 (1960), 12-14.
  Peribáñez uses both phrases in talking with Casilda at their wedding. Later the Comendador offends both laws by trying to seduce Casilda. Peribáñez avenges the affront to derecho humano by killing D. Fadrique, who settles matters with divina ley by repenting.

Ferguson, Charles A. "Personaje, imagen y tema en Peribáñez." Rev. de la Fac. de Humanidades (San Luis de Potosí), II(1960), 313-32.

Salomon, Noël. "Simple Remarque à propos du problème de la date de Peribáñez y el comendador de Ocaña." BH, LXIII(1961), 251-58.
  Pursuing the much-discussed question of the date of the play, Salomon argues that the name Luján is evidence of not an ab quo but of an ad quem of 1608.

El perro del hortelano

Hayes, F. C. "The Use of Proverbs..." (1938). See Studies — Drama — General.

Gillet, J. E. "Lucrecia-necia" (1947). See Studies — General.

Barrault, J. "Le Chien du jardinier." *Cahiers de la Compagnie Madeleine Renaud — Jean-Louis Barrault*, No. 14 (1955).

El perseguido

Baulier, F. "A propósito de El perseguido de Lope." RFE, XXV(1941), 523-27.
    A short, anonymous poem of the 13th century, La Châtelaine de Vergy, is suggested as the probable source of El perseguido, dated 1590. Thematic elements and minor details are quite similar, although the dénouement of Lope's comedia is far less tragic than that of the poem. Elements in El perseguido which are not found in the French poem seem to be inspired in part by an Italian prose treatment of the same theme by Bandello.

El piadoso aragonés

Reichenberger, Arnold G. "Notes on Lope's El piadoso aragonés." HR, XXI(1953), 302-21.
    The publication of the autograph (ed. Greer, Austin, Texas, 1951) enabled Reichenberger to study the accuracy of the Academy edition, the handling of the original by censor and autor and some aspects of Lope's method of composing. This is a very valuable and necessary study, and the conclusions reached are interesting and convincing.

El piadoso veneciano

Kohler, E. "Lope de Vega et Giraldi Cintio" (1946). See Studies — Drama — General.

Los pleitos de Ingalaterra

See La corona de Hungría, ed. Tyler (1946): Editions — Drama — Individual Plays.

La pobreza estimada

Fradejas Lebrero, José. "Un cuento de Don Juan Manuel y dos comedias del Siglo de Oro." RL, VII(1955), 67-80.
    This article refers to Cuento XXV, Lope's La pobreza estimada and Calderón's El conde Lucanor.

Pobreza no es vileza

Saunal, Damien. "Autor des sources de Pobreza no es vileza." BH, XLVIII(1946), 239-46.

Saunal proves that in this play Lope followed very closely the
<u>Comentarios de las cosas sucedidas en los Países Baxos de
Flandes desde el año de 1594 hasta el de 1598, compuestos por
Don Diego de Villalobos y Benavides, capitán de caballos
lanzas españoles</u> (Madrid, 1612).

Los Porceles de Murcia

Morley, S. G. "Dos notitas..." (1961). See Studies — Drama —
    General.

Porfiar hasta morir

Pons, Joseph S. "Larra et Lope de Vega." <u>BH</u>, XLII(1940), 123-31.
    The article discusses the relationship of Larra's <u>Macías</u> and
    Lope's <u>Porfiar hasta morir</u>. The author affirms Larra's
    independence.

El postrer godo de España

Schulte-Herbrüggen, H. "El arte dramático de Lope de Vega..." (1950).
    See Studies — Drama — General.

El premio del bien hablar

Gómez de las Cortinas, José Frutos. "La génesis de <u>Las paredes oyen</u>
    de Ruiz de Alarcón." <u>RFE</u>, XXXV(1951), 92-105.
    The last part of the article analyses the analogous situations
    in the above play and Lope's <u>El premio del bien hablar</u> to
    illustrate the opposing visions of life and art held by Ruiz
    de Alarcón and Lope. (It is not to be inferred that the
    author implies any genetic relationship between the two plays.)

El premio riguroso y amistad bien pagada

Arjona, J. H. "Ten Plays Attributed to Lope de Vega" (1960). See
    Studies — Drama — General.

Los primeros mártires del Japón

Bernard, H. "Lope de Vega et l'Extrême-Orient" (1941). See
    Studies — Drama — General.

Nykl, A. R. "<u>Los (primeros) mártires del Japón</u>." <u>HR</u>, X(1942),
    160-62.
    Nykl points out two misstatements made by Morley and Bruerton in
    the <u>Chronology</u>: one concerns a statement made by Nykl in his
    study "<u>Los primeros mártires del Japón</u> and <u>El triunfo de la fe
    en los reinos del Japón</u>," <u>MP</u>, XXII(1925), 305-23; and the
    other a quotation used in the same study. In addition, Nykl
    here includes several other sources of information on Japan.

(On the page following this article, HR, X, 163, Morley and
Bruerton, in a "Rejoinder to Dr. Nykl," stand corrected on the
two points mentioned, but feel that their argument as to the
date of Los primeros mártires... is in no way invalidated by
these corrections.)

El príncipe despeñado

Hoge, Henry W. "Notes on the Sources and the Autograph Manuscript
of Lope de Vega's El príncipe despeñado." PMLA, LXV(1950),
824-40.
An excellent study intended as the Introduction to the author's
edition of Lope's play (dissertation, 1948; pub., 1955). Hoge
studies the manuscript (Nov. 27, 1602) and the printed editions
supplying precious information on dealings between autores and
printers gleaned from existing bibliography. The sources of
the play are clearly established, amplifying Menéndez Pelayo's
findings. The author sees in the play "for the most part no
more than a well-written typical comedia." The present
reviewer would rate it somewhat higher. In the passages
adduced to prove a reflection of the Lope-Micaela de Luján
relationship, one would be inclined to view them rather as
pre-Dorotea material or at least a blending of the two experi-
ences. The author discovered no self-plagiarism in "matters
of imagery, classical allusions, specialized vocabulary and
figures of speech" when comparing El cuerdo loco (Nov. 11,
1602) with El príncipe despeñado.

El príncipe inocente

González de Amezúa, A. Una colección manuscrita... (1945). See
Studies — Drama — General.

El príncipe melancólico

Arjona, J. H. "Did Lope de Vega Write the Extant El príncipe melancólico?" HR, XXIV(1956), 42-49.
The author rejects the authorship of Lope: a great abundance of
false and imperfect rhymes, an undue mixture of consonance and
assonance and the flagrant use of autorhymes.

El prodigio de Etiopía

Möller, W. Die christliche Banditen-Comedia (1936; review: 1938).
See Studies — Drama — General.

El prodigioso príncipe transilvano

Cioranescu, Alejandro. "El autor del Príncipe transilvano." In
Estudios de literatura española y comparada, La Laguna
(Canarias), Univ. de la Laguna, 1954, pp. 93-113.
"...todo ello parece indicar que Vélez de Guevara es el verdadero
autor...."

La prueba de los amigos

Morley, S. G. "Dos notitas..." (1961). See Studies — Drama — General.

Quien ama, no haga fieros

Morley, S. G. "Dos notitas..." (1961). See Studies — Drama — General.

La quinta de Florencia

Bruerton, Courtney. "La quinta de Florencia, fuente de Peribáñez." NRFH, IV(1950), 25-39.
    The term fuente is a misnomer. Bruerton shows the persistence and variation in structure and language of four plays dealing with the theme of the noble trampling upon peasant honour. It was first dramatized in La quinta de Florencia (1599-1603), based on a Bandello novella (II, xv). The article offers an analysis of asunto and versificación.

Leighton, Charles H. "La fuente de La quinta de Florencia." NRFH, X(1956), 1-12.
    The article studies the source in Bandello to ascertain the precise transmission of the subject, and compares French and Spanish translations of the Bandello original.

La reina doña María

Osma, José M. de. "Nota a Gustos y disgustos son no más que imaginación." Hisp, XX(1937), 47-54.
    The article includes a reference to La reina doña María, attributed to Lope.

Arjona, J. H. "Ten Plays Attributed to Lope de Vega" (1960). See Studies — Drama — General.

El remedio en la desdicha

González Ruiz, Nicolás. "Una visión caballeresca de moros y españoles." África: Rev. Española de Colonización, Nos. 77-78 (1948), 2-3.
    The article deals with El remedio en la desdicha.

El rey sin reino

Malkievics-Strzalkowa, Maria. "La Question des sources dans la tragi-comédie de Lope de Vega El rey sin reino." Polska Akademia Umiejetnosci, Archivum Neophilologicum (Cracow), III, No. 2 (1950). Pp. 26.

A detailed and reliable study. In addition to Pero Mejía's
Historia imperial y cesárea, and Aeneas Silvius Piccolomini's
Historia Bohemica, possible sources, the author finds many
details lacking in either history in Antonius Bonfinius' Rerum
Hungaricarum Decades. He was chronicler of Mathias Corvinus,
king of Hungary. The Decades were published between 1543 and
1568, but there were later editions (e.g., Hanoviae, 1606).
Bonfinius is the main source for Lope, if not the only one.
Lope documents this play very carefully. The Morley-Bruerton
dates for this play are 1597-1612.

El robo de Dina

Stanger, Jennie Abolafia. "El drama español, basado en el Viejo
    Testamento. El robo de Dina, comedia bíblica de Lope de Vega."
    Judaica, VII(1940), 191-99.
    This study is largely a paraphrase of Menéndez Pelayo's intro-
    duction to the play.

Roma abrasada

van Dam, C. F. A. "Doris." Correo Erudito, V(1959), 35-36, 199-201.
    The article concerns Roma abrasada.

El ruiseñor de Sevilla

Wilson, Edward M. "Ora vete, amor, y vete, / cata que amanece." In
    Estudios dedicados a Menéndez Pidal, V (Madrid, 1954), 335-42.
    An estribillo, from El ruiseñor de Sevilla, follows the tradi-
    tional pattern, and has two meanings, one for the lovers and
    another for the girl's father and the suitor he has chosen for
    her. An earlier melodrama with the same title by Cristóbal de
    Morales has a dawn-lyric, as does La Celestina, which is the
    principal source of the play.

El rústico del cielo

Tyler, R. W. "On the Dates..." (1950). See Studies — Drama —
    General.

San Isidro labrador de Madrid

Tyler, R. W. "Suggested Dates..." (1952). See Studies — Drama —
    General.

Salomon, Noël. "Sur la Date de San Isidro labrador de Madrid,
    comedia de Lope de Vega." BH, LXIII(1961), 5-27.
    Salomon dates the play as previous to Sept. 13, 1598.

San Segundo de Ávila

Baulier, F. "La Mise en scène dans deux pièces de Lope de Vega" (1945). See Studies — Drama — General.

Santiago el verde

Fichter, William L. "The Date of Lope de Vega's Santiago el verde." HR, XIII(1945), 243-44.
    Fichter notices that on the title-page of Lope's autograph MS there appears "in a very faint and in part almost illegible" (writing) the phrase "En Mad a 11 de dicyenbre." This is written "in a hand other than Lope's but quite certainly of the same century if not of the same period." Since the year, 1615, was already known, Fichter feels justified in accepting Dec. 11, 1615, as the date of composition of the play.

El secretario de sí mismo

Wade, G. E. "The Literary Sources..." (1953). See Studies — Drama — General.

La selva confusa

Hilborn, Harry W. "The Versification of La selva confusa." MLN, LIII(1938), 193-94.

Sloman, Albert E. "La selva confusa Restored to Calderón." HR, XX (1952), 134-48.
    The article controverts Heaton's conviction (PMLA, XLIV, 1929), supported by González Palencia (Acad. N., IX, 1930), that La selva confusa of Parte XVII — of which there was no known copy until Heaton's discovery of the Barcelona edition — is Lope's, and Calderón's MS a mere copy. After comparing the Parte text with Northup's edition of the MS, Sloman concludes that the text attributed to Lope is an amended version of the MS, which — with its alterations and added lines — is an earlier form of the text that "was pruned and shorn, perhaps by Calderón himself." Thus the Parte text is Calderón's and he is exonerated of the charge of plagiarism. The basic point of the argument is, briefly: the defective Parte text (incorrect verse forms, meaningless passages, missing scenes and characters) is clarified by the MS, which, "it follows, is the ultimate source of the printed text."

———. "El mágico prodigioso: Calderón Defended against the Charge of Theft." HR, XX(1952), 212-22.
    In an article published posthumously, in HR, XIX(1951), H. C. Heaton argued that Calderón's authorship of El mágico prodigioso remained to be proved. Sloman's purpose is to restore

the status quo: the Osuna MS is an autograph, therefore no
doubt can be cast on the authorship. He claims that Heaton
was prejudiced by his earlier study of La selva confusa.

Servir a señor discreto

Kohler, E. "Lope de Vega et Giraldi Cintio" (1946). See Studies —
    Drama — General.

La siega

Sanzoles, M. de. "La alegoría como constante estilística..." (1959).
    See Studies — Drama — General.

Los siete infantes de Lara

See El bastardo Mudarra (above).

El sufrimiento de honor

Arjona, J. H. "Ten Plays Attributed to Lope de Vega" (1960). See
    Studies — Drama — General.

Los Tellos de Meneses

Price, E. R. "The Peasant Plays..." (1937). See Studies — Drama —
    General.

La tragedia del rey don Sebastián y bautismo del príncipe de Marruecos

Arjona, J. H. "Dos errores de cronología lopesca" (1937). See
    Studies — Drama — General.

Los tres diamantes

Arjona, J. H. "Another Sonnet in Lope de Vega's Los tres diamantes."
    HR, XX(1952), 313-15.
    The identification of an emasculated sonnet in this play reopens
    the question of its date of composition, presumed to be
    1599-1603, in the M.-B. Chronology. The inclusion of the
    sonnet in La segunda parte de las Rimas de Lope de Vega (1602)
    would establish 1602 as the terminus ad quem, "since Montesinos
    and Jörder have shown that whenever a sonnet appears in a Lope
    play and in his Rimas, we can safely assume that the play
    version antedates the other." On autobiographical grounds
    (presence of the characters Belardo and Lucinda), Américo
    Castro had supposed that the play was written before 1602.
    Bruerton did not agree.

El triunfo de la fe en los reinos del Japón

Bernard, H. "Lope de Vega et l'Extrême-Orient" (1941). See Studies — Drama — General.

Nykl, A. R. See Studies — Drama — Individual Plays (Los primeros mártires del Japón).

El valor de las mujeres

Gillet, J. E. "Lucrecia-necia" (1947). See Studies — General.

Cisneros, Luis Jaime. "Preguntas sobre Lope." Mar del Sur, VIII, No. 22 (1952), 87.
"Al jardinillo quité los pájaros, porque venían de fuera a hurtarles el sustento, como ahora sucede a muchos poetas." This sentence in Lope's dedicatoria of El valor de las mujeres to his close friend Matías de Porras poses two questions: (a) Could it be that Lope's sonnet "Daba sustento a un pajarillo un día" alludes not to su vida amorosa but rather to su vida intelectual?; (b) the date? (Morley and Bruerton in the Chronology give 1615-18, perhaps 1615-16.) Cisneros refers to Lope's mention, in the dedication, of "la descalcez de Marta" which took place Feb. 12, 1622, and to the fact that "Lope cuenta el hecho como si la profesión tuviera cierta perspectiva." (The play was published in Parte XVIII, 1623, and listed in the Peregrino of 1616.) The author feels that Lope may have included the title in the Peregrino "cuando aún la obra no estaba sino en el proceso."

El vaquero de Moraña

Torner, E. M. "Índice de analogías..." (1946). See Studies — Poetry — General.

El vellocino de oro

Arjona, J. H. "Dos errores de cronología lopesca" (1937). See Studies — Drama — General.

Tiemann, H. "Über Lope de Vegas Bild..." (1947-48). See Studies — General.

La venta de la zarzuela (auto)

Wardropper, B. W. Introducción al teatro religioso... (1953). See Studies — Drama — General.

El verdadero amante

Morby, Edwin S. "Reflections on El verdadero amante." HR, XXVII (1959), 317-23.

In the light of La Dorotea, the author finds that Amaranta and Belarda of El verdadero amante equal, respectively, Marfisa and Dorotea of the acción en prosa. The plot of El verdadero amante "ends before La Dorotea begins, portraying the inception of a passion whose dissolution is the theme of La Dorotea."

La vida y muerte del rey Bamba

Schulte-Herbrüggen, H. "El arte dramático de Lope de Vega..." (1950). See Studies — Drama — General.

La villana de Getafe

Bataillon, M. "La desdicha por la honra..." (1947). See Studies — Prose — Individual Prose Works (La desdicha por la honra).

El villano en su rincón

Kohler, E. "Lope de Vega et Giraldi Cintio" (1946). See Studies — Drama — General.

Bataillon, Marcel. "El villano en su rincón." BH, LI(1949), 5-38. And, "Encore El villano en su rincón." BH, LII(1950), 397.
The comedia, taking place in France and strangely combining the menosprecio de la corte theme with that of the awe-inspiring position of the King (Act III), with its "ambiguité d'atmosphère poétique entre France et Espagne," is explained as a pièce de circonstance written between Feb., 1614, and Oct. 25, 1615, before the "double voyage d'Anne d'Autriche, petite reine de France, et d'Elisabeth de France, future reine d'Espagne, dont l'échange eut lieu à Béhobie en novembre 1615." Other elements entering into the creation of the play: a Spanish short story of ultimately French origin, the folklore figure of El villano en su rincón (see LII, 397); but in Act II royal grandeur and graciousness show the villano where real greatness is to be found. Bataillon studies also Valdivielso's version a lo divino and Matos Fragoso's refundición. An admirable piece of historical and esthetic interpretation.

Hesse, Everett W. "The Sense of Lope's El villano en su rincón." SP, LVII(1960), 165-77.
The play has many themes, but mainly that of "love in its several aspects." Among other things, it helps the King and Juan Labrador to understand each other, offsetting the pride of each, which had formerly made communication between them all but impossible.

Correa Calderón and Lázaro. Lope de Vega y su época... (1961). See Studies — General.

Entrambasaguas, Joaquín de. *Lope de Vega y su tiempo. Estudio especial de "El villano en su rincón." Estudios.* Barcelona, Teide, 1961. Pp. 431. (Col. Hilani, 12.)
    A biography of Lope for students of secondary school age. Authoritative, as is to be expected of the eminent lopista, its author. The last hundred pages are given over to a study of El villano en su rincón: its sources, its date, its literary characteristics.

------. *Lope de Vega y su tiempo. Estudio especial de "El villano en su rincón." Textos.* Barcelona, Teide, 1961. Pp. 352. (Col. Hilani, 13.)
    The companion-volume to the preceding monograph. This is a conventional comedia textbook (put in this section of our Bibliography to keep the set together), which has footnotes for secondary school students. The present volume ends with selections from Lope's other writings, mostly lyric poetry.

La viuda valenciana

Tyler, R. W. "Suggested Dates..." (1952). See Studies — Drama — General.

Fucilla, J. G. "Lope's Viuda valenciana and its Bandellian Source." BCom, X, No. 2 (1958), 3-6.
    A re-examination of the relation between this play and its Bandellian source shows that Lope takes from the Italian writer not only the dramatic kernel, as earlier critics had asserted, but all the essential elements of Bandello's story. "Perhaps in no other play does Lope show himself so indebted toward his model."

Los yerros por amor

Morley, S. Griswold. "The Date of the comedia Los yerros por amor." HR, VI(1938), 260-64.
    Morley reached the decision that Los yerros... was written probably in 1623-24, and, if by Lope, possibly as late as 1627.

C. THE ARTE NUEVO

Menéndez Pidal, R. *De Cervantes y Lope de Vega* (1940). See Studies — General.

Pons, Joseph S. "L'Art nouveau de Lope de Vega." BH, XLVII(1945), 71-78.
    In the first part of this interesting article, the author believes that Lope's Arte nuevo is an answer to Cervantes' canónigo's remarks about the Comedia (Don Quijote, I, 48). In the second part, which occupies the middle and most voluminous

part, the author glosses the Arte nuevo, and in the last part, Pons states that in this debate between academic art and free creation, the latter remained, while the former is all but forgotten. The article does not add anything new, but it restates the new attitude of modern critics in judging the Comedia.

Bolaño e Isla, Amancio. "En torno al teatro del Siglo de Oro." Filosofía y Letras, XII(1946), 303-14.
Deals mainly with the Arte nuevo.

Torre, Guillermo de. "Lope de Vega y su mundo" (1946). See Studies — General.

Oteiza, Alberto M. "El arte nuevo de Lope de Vega." Humanidades (La Plata), XXXIV(1954), 77-88.
The author analyses the Arte nuevo, shows that it was not true that all Italians and French considered Lope ignorant, as he said, and shows how Lope's style was defended by Alfonso Sánchez, Hugo and Lessing.

Soria, Andrés. "Notas sobre la métrica en el teatro de Lope y Calderón." El Molino de Papel (Granada), No. 2 (1954), 4-5.
Soria studies Lope's precepts for metrical form in the theatre as found in the Arte nuevo. He finds Lope both an innovator and a traditionalist, and also notes that he is not entirely consistent here with his own practice in his plays, since, for example, he does not mention quintillas. What he does give here are generalizations based principally on the practice of his closest predecessors. The latter half of this two-page article deals with Calderón and his metres.

Coyné, A. "Lope de Vega y sus ideas dramáticas" (1957). See Studies — Drama — General.

Sinicropi, Giovanni. "L'Arte nuevo e la prassi drammatica di Lope de Vega." QIB, No. 25 (1960), 13-26.
Disagreeing with Menéndez Pidal's stand (RFE, XXII, 1935, 337-98) that Lope was following the beaten path for Spanish popular poetry and was within the Platonic current of thought, the author examines several plays in the light of the Arte nuevo. Giving particular stress to the caso (first structural moment), conexión (or peripeteia) and solución (or anagnorisis), he finds that there is no real contradiction between the Arte nuevo and Lope's actual practices.

Morley, S. G. "Dos notitas..." (1961). See Studies — Drama — General.

Pérez and Sánchez Escribano. Afirmaciones... (1961). See Studies — Drama — General.

D. THE PEREGRINO LISTS

Sainz de Robles, F. C. Ensayo de un diccionario... (1949-50).
  See Studies — General.

Bruerton, Courtney. "Thornton Wilder and Lope's Peregrino Lists."
  BCom, III, No. 1 (1951), 1.
  Thornton Wilder, addressing the Romance Section of the MLA
  Meeting in New York in Dec., 1950, described his discovery of
  the order of titles in Lope's Peregrino lists; to wit, that
  they proceed according to the autores (Porres, Granados, etc.)
  to whom Lope sold his plays. Physical descriptions of Lope's
  characters, also, were found to fit, in a number of cases,
  similar rôles in known plays produced by a specific autor.
  Furthermore there is reason to believe that Lope listed the
  plays of each autor chronologically. In the second Peregrino
  list, selections from each published Parte, in order, are
  listed for each autor in succession. Mr. Wilder also announced
  the discovery of the names of Micaela and Diego Díaz in the
  reparto of the Gálvez copy of El blasón de los Chaves de
  Villalba (in the possession of Amezúa). This mention is the
  first in a discovered document concerning Micaela de Luján's
  activity as an actress. It also locates her husband in Spain
  some years after he was supposed to have left for Peru.

Castro de Zubiri, Carmen. "Lope en Nueva York, vía M.L.A." Clav,
  II, No. 8 (1951), 30-32.
  The article refers to Thornton Wilder's paper read at the MLA
  Meeting, New York, 1950.

Cisneros, L. J. "Preguntas sobre Lope" (1952). See Studies —
  Drama — Individual Plays (El valor de las mujeres).

Wilder, Thornton. "New Aids toward Dating the Early Plays of Lope
  de Vega." In Varia Variorum, Festgabe für Karl Reinhardt,
  Münster-Köln, Böhlau-Verlag, 1952, pp. 194-200.
  Keeping within the chronological framework provided by the M.-B.
  Chronology, the author concentrates close attention on small
  groups of approximately contemporaneous plays in an attempt to
  arrive at a still more precise chronology. The basic procedure
  depends on the considerable body of information that has been
  assembled — and which Wilder has thoroughly assimilated —
  concerning the organization of the theatrical companies to whom
  Lope sold his plays and of a new use to which the Peregrino
  lists may be put. He shows that the apparently incoherent list
  printed at the beginning of the 1604 Peregrino is not as hap-
  hazard as it first seems. The titles there are listed —
  although there are puzzling exceptions — according to the
  manager to whom Lope sold them. The order of the titles in the
  second Peregrino list does not reveal as much relative to the
  autor. (See Wilder's address to the MLA as reported by Bruerton, above.)

POETRY

A. GENERAL

Aaron, Sister M. Audrey. *Christological Concepts in the Non-Dramatic Lyric Poetry of Lope de Vega.* Unpub. doct. diss., Johns Hopkins Univ., 1951.

Alonso, Dámaso. "Lope despojado por Marino." — "Adjunta a 'Lope despojado por Marino'." — "Otras imitaciones de Lope por Marino." *RFE*, XXXIII(1949), 110-43; 165-68; 399-408.
  Marino was profoundly indebted to Spanish literature, a fact of which Italian scholars were already aware in the 17th century. Alonso discusses fifteen sonnets, thirteen from the *Rimas* (1602) and one from *La Arcadia*, imitated more or less closely by Marino in his "Amori," in *La Lira*, *Parte Terza*, 1614, without indicating the source. The similarities of the fifteenth sonnet were explained by Fucilla (*Hisp*, XV, 1932) through a common source, Ariosto. Dámaso Alonso shows that Marino imitated Lope, and not vice versa, despite Marino's dubious assertions. At the same time Alonso discusses the vague borderlines between translation, imitation and plagiarism. This article has the liveliness and human touch which Dámaso Alonso so admirably fuses with vigorous scholarship.

------. "Lope en vena de filósofo." *Clav*, I, No. 2 (1950), 10-15.
  The sonnet, "La calidad elemental resiste," philosophizing about *fuego elementar*, *celestial* and *angélico*, appeared first in *La dama boba* (1613), then in the *Novena parte* (1617), *La Filomena* (1621) and *La Circe* (1624); twice, 1613 and 1624, with Lope's own commentary. Lope, stung by Góngora's prestige in Madrid's leading literary circles, wanted to compete with him in the field of esoteric (or rather would-be esoteric) poetry.

------. *Poesía española. Ensayo de métodos y límites estilísticos. Garcilaso, Fray Luis de León, San Juan de la Cruz, Góngora, Lope de Vega, Quevedo.* 1st ed.: 1950. 2nd ed.: "aumentada y corregida, con un copioso índice alfabético de materias." Madrid, Gredos, 1952. Pp. 667. (3rd ed.: 1957.) (Bib. Románica Hispánica, 2. Ensayos y Estudios.)
  Rev: 1st ed.: J. L. Cano, *Ínsula*, No. 61 (1951), 4-5.
  The above-mentioned *índice*, occupying pages 633-67, of the second edition, gives it a greatly added value not possessed by the first edition. It becomes a kind of reference work for Lope's poetry. Two pages of analytical sub-headings make it possible for the user to conveniently locate any specific aspect of Lope's poetry that the author deals with. A good many of the sub-headings are titles of *comedias* and longer poems. First lines are listed for poems without a title. In the *Nota para esta segunda edición*, Dámaso Alonso says that he has made some amplifications or changes, corrected known errors, added

bibliographical data and has endeavoured to "castigar el estilo (que siempre se resentirá de su origen: un 'curso de conferencias')."

------. "Lope y el *Adone* de Marino." RFE, XXXV(1951), 349-51.
At the time of writing "Lope despojado por Marino," RFE, XXXIII (1949), the author had not read several articles on Lope and Marino written by Fucilla. Later, having done so and having found corroborative testimony in "Canción lírica en la muerte de Frey Lope Félix de Vega Carpio," *Fama Póstuma*, 1636, he is certain that Marino used Lope material in his *Adone*. As though speaking to Lope, Gabriel de Roa ends the fourth stanza of the *Canción* as follows: "Pero, ¿de qué me espanto, / si de episodios que tu idea previno / edificó su Adonis el Marino?"

------. "Poesía de Navidad de Fray Ambrosio Montesino a Lope de Vega." In *De los siglos oscuros al de oro*, Madrid, Gredos, 1958, pp. 137-43.
Some quotations of Lope's Christmas verse strung together with a rapid running commentary.

------. "La correlación poética en Lope (de la juventud a la madurez)." RFE, XLIII(1960), 355-98.
Dámaso Alonso studies *correlación*, or parallelism of corresponding elements, in Lope's poetry (especially sonnets, though some *canciones*, etc. are analysed), basing himself mainly on the *Rimas* of 1602. He also pays considerable attention to *La Arcadia*, *La Dragontea*, *La hermosura de Angélica* and *La Jerusalén conquistada*, as well as the much later *Rimas de Burguillos*.

Borghini, Vittorio. *Poesia e letteratura nei poemi di Lope de Vega*. Genoa, Scia, 1949. Pp. 542.
This work offers a valuable introduction to Lope's epic poems, giving a summary of their content and an esthetic evaluation, guided by the Crocean contrast of *poesia e non-poesia*. Most of the time he finds *non-poesia*. The best poems are those in which Lope's lyrical and religious emotions are happily fused: *El Isidro* and *Los pastores de Belén*. *La Gatomaquia* is "dei suoi poemi ... fra tutti, il più sobrio ed armonioso," but still no real "capolavoro."

Cirot, Georges. "Coup d'oeil sur la poésie épique du Siècle d'Or." BH, XLVIII(1946), 294-329.
In this excellent synthesis of Golden Age epic poetry, the last one written by Cirot, Lope de Vega's contributions to the *genre* are dealt with in various parts of the essay. The most important remarks concerning Lope's epic poetry are found on page 307, dealing with Lope's knowledge of Latin and even Greek poets; page 310, dealing with *El Isidro*; pp. 318-19, with *La Dragontea*, *La hermosura de Angélica*, *La Jerusalén conquistada*,

<u>La corona trágica</u>, <u>La Andrómeda</u>, <u>La Circe</u> and <u>La Gatomaquia</u>. There is not, however, sufficient critical comment, and the value of the article is limited.

Clarke, Dorothy Clotelle. "A Note on the <u>décima</u> or <u>espinela</u>." <u>HR</u>, VI(1938), 155-58.
   A reply to J. Millé y Giménez, "Sobre la fecha de la invención de la décima o espinela," <u>HR</u>, V(1937), 40-51. See below.

Croce, Benedetto. "Poesia di Lope." <u>La Critica</u>, XXXV(1937), 241-55. (Reprinted in <u>Cursos y conferencias</u>, Buenos Aires, VI, 1937, 663-79.)

Díaz-Plaja, Guillermo. <u>La poesía lírica española</u>. Barcelona, Labor, 1937. Pp. 441. (2nd ed.: <u>Historia de la poesía lírica española</u>, 1948. Pp. 456.)
   Lope de Vega: pp. 153-57, and <u>passim</u>.

Elwert, W. T. "Le varietà nazionali della poesia barocca." <u>Convivium</u>, XXV(1957), 670-79; XXVI(1958), 27-42.
   Along with other poets of his age, Lope is drawn upon for exemplification of the distinctive traits of Spanish baroque verse: its religious and burlesque motifs and its moral tone.

Farinelli, Arturo. <u>Poesía y crítica: Temas hispánicos</u>. Madrid, CSIC, 1954. Pp. 278.
   Rev: Rudolfo Oroz, <u>AUC</u>, CXIV, No. 102 (1956), 118-19.
   Lope de Vega: pp. 7-13.

Fichter, William L. "More 'Forgotten' Verse by Lope de Vega." <u>HR</u>, X(1942), 251-54.
   The author calls attention to a sonnet entitled "Lope de Vega al Príncipe," and to some lyric stanzas attributed to Lope by the Prince, both published in <u>Las obras en verso</u> (Madrid, 1648, but with <u>aprobación</u> and other preliminaries dated 1639) of Francisco de Borja, Prince of Esquilache. He argues, on the basis of the mutual respect held by Lope and the Prince for each other's poetry and on the basis of the contemporary convention of including works of authors in volumes not their own (specifically, in <u>Las obras en verso</u>, there is a sonnet by Bartolomé Leonardo de Argensola), that it is safe to attribute the authorship of these two compositions to Lope.

Frenk, Margarita. <u>La lírica popular en los siglos de oro</u>. Mexico, Private, 1946. Pp. 76.
   Rev: José F. Montesinos, <u>NRFH</u>, II(1948), 292-95.
   Montesinos says in his review: "...la Srta. Frenk nos sorprende con una porción de curiosísimas muestras de la vitalidad de canciones muy frágiles en apariencia. Letrillas divulgadas por Lope o por Góngora, tal vez obras suyas, perduran hoy en un área extensísima, desde Santander o Salamanca a Buenos Aires

o el Istmo de Tehuantepec." The volume is a "Tesis de la Universidad Nacional Autónima de México publicada por su autora."

Frieiro, Eduardo. "O maior poeta de Espanha." In O alegre Arcipreste e outros temas de literatura espanhola, Belo Horizonte, Nicolai, 1959, pp. 94-101.
  The article dates from 1943. Routine praise of Lope, in disagreement with Altoaguirre's naming of Garcilaso as the greatest Spanish poet. Narrowing the field to Lope and Góngora, the author quotes Azorín as considering Lope the greatest of all, and states that this was also the judgment of Lope's contemporaries.

García, Alonso (ed.). Al Santissimo Sacramento, en su fiesta; Iusta Poetica que Lope de Vega Carpio, y otros insignes Poetas de la Ciudad de Toledo y fuera del tuvieron en la Parrochial de San Nicolás de dicha Ciudad, a veynte y cinco de Iunio de 1608. Toledo, 1609. Ed. Antonio Pérez Gómez. Valencia, Tipografía Moderna, 1951. 88 folios.
  Rev: M. B., BH, LIII(1951), 339.
  On handsome paper and in type of a perfection seldom seen, the princeps is reproduced with absolute exactness. The volume contains some of the finest devotional poetry of Lope's time.

Hatzfeld, Helmut. "Poetas españoles de resonancia universal." Hisp, XL(1957), 261-69.
  Of the most general nature, this article devotes about two and one half columns to Lope, one of the six poets in question.

Jameson, A. K. "The Sources of Lope de Vega's Erudition." HR, V (1937), 124-39.
  The article deals specifically with the historical and scientific (geography, natural history and astronomy) allusions in the Jerusalén conquistada, Isidro, Dragontea and Hermosura de Angélica. The author concludes that "Lope is entitled to be reckoned among the learned poets as well as among the popular. It would be an exaggeration to describe him as an intellectual poet.... There is no profundity in his thought, his ideas on all the subjects of which he treats are trite and he accepted what he found without reflection and without criticism."

Milazzo, Elena. La lirica di Lope de Vega. Rome, Signorelli, 1954.
  A generally judicious analysis of Lope's poetry, including references to the dramatic. Additional documentation required in the first chapter. There is little attention to dates, which would seem important in a study of poetic and metrical form.

Millé y Giménez, Juan. "Sobre la fecha de la invención de la décima o espinela." HR, V(1937), 40-51.
  Pp. 42-46 deal mainly with Lope; references to Lope elsewhere in the article. See above for Clarke's reply, HR, 1938.

Nogueira, Goulart. "Lope de Vega, poeta nacional." Tempo Presente: Rev. Portuguesa de Cultura, No. 7 (1959), 63-70.
    The article contains general references to Golden Age literature, and references to Lope as both national and universal, with quotations from Vossler and Entrambasaguas.

Panarese, Luigi. Lope de Vega e Giambattista Marino. Maglie, Donadeo, 1935. Pp. 21.
  Rev: J. G. Fucilla, HR, V(1937), 192.

Peers, E. Allison. "Mysticism in the Religious Verse of the Golden Age." BHS, XXI(1944), 133-45, 217-23; XXII(1945), 38-43.
    Lope is dealt with in section IV, pp. 217-23, and in the following year, on pp. 38-43. The statement is made that "with very few exceptions, in his lyric verse as a whole, (Lope) was about as unmystical a religious poet as his age produced."

------. "Mysticism in the Poetry of Lope de Vega." In Estudios dedicados a Menéndez Pidal, I (Madrid, 1950), 349-58.
    The author examines all of the major religious poetry by Lope in the light of a strict theological definition of mysticism, and concludes that Lope "was as unmystical a religious poet as his age produced," as stated above. The dominant theme is repentance, and it "is scarcely possible to question his sincerity." Peers does not deny the profundity of Lope's love of God and the fervour of his aspiration. But it is an aspiration to "service and worthier living," rather than to mystical union. Peers recognizes "a semi-mystical quality" in the Rimas sacras. An important, well-documented study.

Pierce, Frank. La poesía épica del Siglo de Oro. Trans. J. C. Cayol de Bethencourt. Madrid, Gredos, 1961. Pp. 391. (Bib. Románica Hispánica, 2. Estudios y Ensayos, 51.)
    Pp. 297-305, on "Las poesías de Lope," contain important reference to La Dragontea, El Isidro de Madrid, La hermosura de Angélica, La Jerusalén conquistada, La corona trágica and La Gatomaquia.

Reid, John T. "Notes on the History of the verso esdrújulo." HR, VII(1939), 277-94.
    The article contains various references to Lope.

St.-Amour, Sister Mary Paulina. A Study of the "Villancico" up to Lope de Vega: Its Evolution from Profane to Sacred Themes and Specifically to the Christmas Carol. Washington, Catholic Univ. of America Press, 1940. Pp. x, 131.
  Rev: Joseph E. Gillet, HR, IX(1941), 410-11.
    Placing her emphasis on content rather than form, the author has examined in turn the villancico of the "courtly" poets from Santillana onwards, the more abundant popular villancicos and then the religious ones, some definitely relating to church

festivals, others dealing with moral or dogmatic topics. She reserves a special chapter for the Christmas-villancico, which provides a basis for the monograph's most original and valuable part, the chapter on "The Villancico in Religious Services." This doctoral dissertation, presented at the Catholic University of America, is called by Gillet "a clear and careful survey of the Spanish villancico in the sixteenth century."

Segura Covarsí, Enrique. La canción petrarquista en la lírica española del Siglo de Oro (Contribución a la métrica renacentista). Madrid, CSIC, 1949. Pp. 333. (Cuad. de Lit., Anejo 5.)
 The monograph includes a study of Lope as a link between the 16th and 17th centuries in the development of the Petrarchan canzone. The statement is made that Lope's canciones "mantienen la estructura petrarquista en un grado de pureza difícil de encontrar en otros poetas coetáneos," and that they "brindan un equilibrio estructural perfecto." Pp. 299-303 contain the analysis of the rhyme scheme of 23 canciones.

Steiger, Arnald. "Zur volkstümlichen Dichtung Lope de Vegas." In Hortulus Amicorum (Fritz Ernst zum 60 Geburtstag), Zurich, (1949), pp. 159-74.

Torner, Eduardo M. "Índice de analogías entre la lírica española antigua y la moderna." Symposium, I(1946), 12-33. (Continues in later issues.)
 The article deals in part with Lope. The well known lyric form zejel invented by the Spanish Muslims is found in the cantar de siega in Lope's play El vaquero de Moraña. Seguidillas are also quoted from Al pasar del arroyo (Act III) and El cardenal de Belén (Act III), for example.

Vossler, Karl. La poesía de la soledad en España. Trans. Ramón de la Serna y Espina. Buenos Aires, Losada, 1946. Pp. 398.
 Lope's poetry and his comedias are not noted for "loneliness," but certain examples are pointed out in a section entitled "Los motivos de la soledad...." The volume had appeared as La soledad en la poesía española, trans. José Miguel Sacristán, Madrid, Rev. de Occidente, 1941. Pp. vii, 348. The Ramón de la Serna translation follows the second German edition of Munich, 1940 (Poesie der Einsamkeit in Spanien). The first publication was in The Actas of the Bavarian Academy of Sciences, 1935-38.

B. INDIVIDUAL POEMS

A mis soledades voy...

Fichter, W. L., and F. Sánchez y Escribano. "The Origin and Character of Lope de Vega's A mis soledades voy...." HR, XI(1943), 304-13.
    The article rejects the theory advanced by Vossler, then Spitzer, that Lope's poem is related to a mystic tradition or formula. Rather, it is patterned on a popular cantarcillo printed in the Romancero general of 1604.

Amarilis (égloga)

Giraldo Jaramillo, Gabriel. Estudios históricos. Bogotá, Edit. Santafé, 1954. Pp. 387.
    The volume includes a study of Lope's Amarilis.

La Andrómeda

Cirot, G. "Coup d'oeil..." (1946). See Studies — Poetry — General.

Mazzara, Richard. "Saint-Amant's L'Andromède and Lope de Vega's La Andrómeda." KFLQ, VIII(1961), 7-14.
    The article studies Lope's use in 1621 of the Perseus-Andromeda myth of Ovid's Metamorphoses, and the use made by Saint-Amant of both Ovid and Lope for his version of the story.

Canción a la muerte de Carlos Félix

Croce, Alda. "La Canción a la muerte de Carlos Félix, di Lope de Vega." In Estudios dedicados a Menéndez Pidal, IV (Madrid, 1953), 391-404.

La Circe

Cirot, G. "Coup d'oeil..." (1946). See Studies — Poetry — General.

Alonso, D. "Lope de Vega en vena de filósofo" (1950). See Studies — Poetry — General.

La corona trágica

Cirot, G. "Coup d'oeil..." (1946). See Studies — Poetry — General.

Menéndez Pidal, R. El P. de las Casas... (1958). See Studies — General.

Pierce, F. La poesía épica... (1961). See Studies — Poetry — General.

La Dragontea

Jameson, A. K. "The Sources of Lope de Vega's Erudition" (1937). See Studies — Poetry — General.

------. "Lope de Vega's La Dragontea: Historical and Literary Sources." HR, VI(1938), 104-19.
 With regard to Lope's distortion of the facts in elevating the subordinate Amaya to the position of a national hero and denying credit to the Spanish commander Sotomayor, the author concludes: "One would welcome a fuller knowledge of the circumstances of the case, if only for the possibility that it might exhibit Lope's action in a less equivocal light."

Buchanan, M. A. "Cervantes and Lope de Vega..." (1942). See Studies — General.

Balbín Lucas, Rafael de. "La primera edición de La Dragontea." RBN, VI(1945), 355-56.
 Balbín Lucas prints a curious communication written by Antonio de Herrera, a cronista de Indias, in which he objects to Lope's treatment of history, and in which it is stated that Lope had printed the work in Valencia and wanted to have it reprinted in Seville. Although this communication is a curious document kept in the Archivo de Indias in Seville, it does not offer any serious scholarly proof to support Balbín Lucas' contention that the 1598 Madrid edition was never made.

Cirot, G. "Coup d'oeil..." (1946). See Studies — Poetry — General.

Hoffman, Dorothy. "Lope de Vega's La Dragontea: Sources and Models." Florida State Univ. Studies, I, No. 3 (1951), 31-39.
 For form and style, Lope's epic poem is indebted to Ariosto and Tasso and its immediate literary ancestors, La Araucana and the Arauco domado. The poem is based on information contained in the Real Audiencia de Panamá. Despite Lope's prejudice and some falsifying of facts, he follows the document so closely that "his pen is an excellent historical record."

Alonso, D. "La correlación poética en Lope..." (1960). See Studies — Poetry — General.

Pierce, F. La poesía épica... (1961). See Studies — Poetry — General.

La Filomena

Entrambasaguas, J. de. *Estudios sobre Lope de Vega* (II, 1947). See Studies — General.

------. "Un pasaje lopista de Salas Barbadillo." *Cuad. de Lit.*, I (1947), 377-91.
Entrambasaguas believes that a passage in a narration, La peregrinación sabia, inserted in the last work of Salas, Coronas del Parnaso y platos de las musas (1635), making fun of literary academies and ridiculing Suárez de Figueroa, among others, was influenced by the passage in Lope's La Filomena about the quarrel between el ruiseñor and el tordo. Since the latter was published in 1621, E. believes that La peregrinación was written soon afterwards and before 1627. He points out Salas' regard for Lope. An interesting additional note to the guerra literaria with which Entrambasaguas has so preoccupied himself.

Ureta, Alberto. "El enigma de Amarilis." *Rev. de América*, XIV(1948), 313-21.
The article deals with the Peruvian poetess who addressed a silva to Lope, which, with his reply, was included in his Filomena. Ureta believes, along with Luis Alberto Sánchez, that she was María Tello de Lara y de Arévalo y Espinosa. He considers the poem the most beautiful of colonial Peruvian poetry. See also Studies — General (Leonard).

Alonso, D. "Lope en vena de filósofo" (1950). See Studies — Poetry — General.

Marín, Diego. "Culteranismo en La Filomena de Lope." *RFE*, XXXIX (1955), 314-23.
The article states that "el uso de recursos culteranos es muy moderado."

La Gatomaquia

Mele, Eugenio. "Lope de Vega, Merlin Cocai e Luciano." *GSLI*, CXII (1938), 323-28.
Reference to Silva 7, La Gatomaquia.

Cirot, G. "Coup d'oeil..." (1946). See Studies — Poetry — General.

Borghini, V. *Poesia e letteratura...* (1949). See Studies — Poetry — General.

Macdonald, Inez. "Lope de Vega's Gatomaquia." *Atlante*, II(1954), 27-44.
Inez Macdonald analyses this work, which she calls not a classical parody, like those of Góngora, but a mock epic ridiculing

passionate love and jealousy as found in Ariosto and Boiardo, and in Lope's own plays. According to the writer of the article, the parallel between the behaviour of the cats and that of those characters is very close. She analyses the satiric and comic effects of this work, and suggests that Lope may possibly have learned from Cervantes to laugh at human love.

Pierce, F. La poesía épica... (1961). See Studies — Poetry — General.

La hermosura de Angélica

Jameson, A. K. "The Sources of Lope de Vega's Erudition" (1937). See Studies — Poetry — General.

Schevill, Rudolph. "Lope de Vega and the Year 1588." HR, IX(1941), 65-78.
    Serious doubt is cast on two affirmations made by Lope: (a) that he composed La hermosura de Angélica in the midst of the battle between Drake's forces and the Armada Invencible, and (b) that he did actually participate in the jornada against England. Lack of textual or biographic corroboration for these statements and contradictory evidence lead Schevill to believe that the Angélica was written in its entirety after 1598, and that, if Lope did enlist in Lisbon, he either remained ashore there when the expedition departed, or, at most, went only as far as La Coruña, where he may have been put ashore with the sick before the Armada continued north.

Cirot, G. "Coup d'oeil..." (1946). See Studies — Poetry — General.

Molinaro, J. A. R. Angélica and Medoro... (1954). See Studies — General.

Alonso, D. "La correlación poética en Lope..." (1960). See Studies — Poetry — General.

Pierce, F. La poesía épica... (1961). See Studies — Poetry — General.

El Isidro

Jameson, A. K. "The Sources of Lope de Vega's Erudition" (1937). See Studies — Poetry — General.

Cirot, G. "Coup d'oeil..." (1946). See Studies — Poetry — General.

Borghini, V. *Poesia e letteratura...* (1949). See Studies — Poetry — General.

Morby, Edwin S. "A Pre-Dorotea in *El Isidro*." HR, XXI(1953), 145-46.
An interesting note on the possibly earliest version of the Dorotea story, a version which gives it "a slight coloring of immediate reality."

Pierce, F. *La poesía épica...* (1961). See Studies — Poetry — General.

La Jerusalén conquistada

Jameson, A. K. "The Sources of Lope de Vega's Erudition" (1937). See Studies — Poetry — General.

Pierce, Frank. "*La Jerusalén conquistada* of Lope de Vega: a Reappraisal." BHS, XX(1943), 11-35.
The author concludes that although Lope's poem "possesses few if any of the main requirements of an epic the poet has been able to employ his talents to produce passages of sincere and noble feeling and an imagery of rare force and striking beauty."

Cirot, G. "Coup d'oeil..." (1946). See Studies — Poetry — General.

Lapesa, Rafael. "La *Jerusalén* del Tasso y la de Lope." BRAE, XXV (1946), 111-36.
Lapesa's essay was originally delivered as a lecture at the University of Salamanca on the occasion of the fourth centenary of Tasso's birth. Tasso's work is thoroughly analysed, and Lapesa points out the Spanish influence which Tasso received from the *libros de caballería* through Bernardo Tasso, his father, who had close personal and literary contacts with Spain. He then studies Tasso's influence on Lope's *Jerusalén*, and Lope's motives in writing the poem ("la ambición literaria," to "ganar la estimación de los letrados"). The two poems are carefully compared and contrasted; and the conclusion is that "las mejores y más originales cualidades de la *Jerusalén* lopesca se deben ante todo a los elementos potencialmente dramáticos trasvasados en ella."

Pierce, Frank. "Some Themes and their Sources in the Heroic Poem of the Golden Age." HR, XIV(1946), 95-103.
Lope de Vega's *Jerusalén*, together with the epic poems of Ercilla, Balbuena, Hojeda and Camões, are discussed with regard to classical, Christian and Italian Renaissance influences. For Lope's epic, this article finds an excellent companion-piece in Lapesa's study in BRAE, XXV, 1946 (see above).

Diego, Gerardo. *Una estrofa de Lope*. Santander, 1948. Pp. 36.
"Discurso leído el día 5 de febrero de 1948 en su recepción como académico de la Real Academia Española de las Lenguas. Contestaba a su intervención, en nombre de la Academia, don Narciso Alonso Cortés." The *discurso* discusses the beauties of an *octava real* of the *Jerusalén conquistada*.

Entrambasaguas, J. de. "Blair y Munárriz..." (1950). See Studies — General.

Allue y Morrell, F. "La 'Raquel hermosa'..." (1954). See Studies — General.

Willis, Raymond S. "Lope de Vega's *Jerusalén conquistada*." *PULC*, XV(1954), 159-61.
Willis writes for the patrons of the Princeton University Library about Lope de Vega and his epic poem on the occasion of the acquisition by the Library of a first edition of the *Jerusalén conquistada*.

Pierce, Frank. "The Literary Epic and Lope's *Jerusalén conquistada*." *BHS*, XXXIII(1956), 93-98.
Reference to Entrambasaguas' edition of the poem (Madrid, 1951-54).

Lida de Malkiel, M. R. "Alejandro en Jerusalén" (1956-57). See Studies — General.

Alonso, D. "La correlación poética en Lope..." (1960). See Studies — Poetry — General.

Pierce, F. *La poesía épica...* (1961). See Studies — Poetry — General.

Las lágrimas de la Magdalena

Powers, Perry J. "Lope de Vega and *Las lágrimas de la Madalena*." *CL*, VIII(1956), 273-90.
The article studies Lope's poem in the tradition of poetry written about Mary Magdalen and the larger tradition of the "tears of repentance." It compares Lope's imagery with other poems in the tradition, including those by English and Italian metaphysical poets.

El laurel de Apolo

Alonso Cortés, Narciso. "Los poetas vallisoletanos celebrados por Lope de Vega en el *Laurel de Apolo*." *Escorial*, IV(1941), 333-81.
In the poem, toward the middle of *silva* III, the section reserved for Valladolid, Lope praises six poets of the Pisuerga,

including don Francisco de la Cueva, who actually was a <u>natural</u> of Medina del Campo. Alonso Cortés provides valuable biographic information on the six literary figures, all contemporaries of Lope: Miguel Sánchez, Gabriel de Corral, Fernando Manojo de la Corte, Francisco de la Reguera, Gabriel de Henao and the above-mentioned Francisco de la Cueva.

Herrero, Miguel. "Una variante de un verso célebre." <u>Correo Erudito</u>, II, No. 11 (1941), 29.
    So well known in the time of Lope must have been the <u>octava</u> attributed to Fr. Pedro de los Reyes that the <u>Fénix</u> uses the last verse ("Loco debo de ser, pues no soy santo") as part of a poetic tribute to the poet-priest in <u>El laurel de Apolo</u> (<u>silva</u> VII). Herrero also points out a variant of the same verse in a work of Fr. Antonio de Arés, <u>Diálogos de la Naturaleza, de Raimundo Sabunde</u> (Madrid, 1616).

<u>El Orfeo en lengua castellana</u>

Entrambasaguas, J. de. <u>Estudios sobre Lope de Vega</u> (II, 1947). See Studies — General.

Cabañas, P. <u>El mito de Orfeo...</u> (1948). See Studies — General.

Parker, J. H. "Lope de Vega, the <u>Orfeo</u> and the <u>estilo llano</u>." <u>RR</u>, XL(1953), 3-11.
    If Lope did not write the <u>Orfeo en lengua castellana</u>, it was at least written with his approval, and it exemplified his stand on the question of the purity of the language as opposed to the <u>estilo culto</u>. As a reply to Jáuregui's "culto" <u>Orfeo</u>, it avoids excesses but is also "culto" itself, although to a lesser degree. The author concludes that Lope, who so often criticized <u>culto</u> language with great violence, in practice entered into a moderate use of its devices. Similar studies of other poetry of the period would be useful.

Marasso, A. "Humanismo de Lope de Vega" (1955). See Studies — General.

<u>Rimas</u> (1602)

Alonso, D. "Lope despojado por Marino" (1949). See Studies — Poetry — General.

Arjona, J. H. "Another Sonnet..." (1952). See Studies — Drama — Individual Plays (<u>Los tres diamantes</u>).

Glaser, Edward. "<u>Ir y quedarse, y con quedar partirse</u>: Una guirnalda de comentarios." In <u>Estudios hispano-portugueses: Relaciones literarias del Siglo de Oro</u>, Valencia, Castalia, 1957, pp. 97-130.

Rev: (of the volume): I. S. Révah, BEPIF, XXI(1959), 320; José
Ares Montes, RFE, XLIII(1960), 225-28; P. G., LR, XIV(1960),
356-58; Gerald M. Moser, HR, XXVIII(1960), 63-65.
The article on Lope deals with Sonnet 61, Rimas, Madrid, 1602.
The studies in the volume are highly praised by the reviewers
for the author's care and orderliness, abundant bibliography
and evident mastery of the material.

Alonso, D. "La correlación poética en Lope..." (1960). See
Studies — Poetry — General.

Rimas (1615)

Glaser, Edward. "A Biblical Theme in Iberian Poetry of the Golden
Age." SP, LII(1955), 524-48.
Reference to the Rimas, Lisbon, 1615: "Sirvió Jacob los siete
largos años..." ("Seven years a shepherd Jacob served...").

Rimas humanas y divinas de Tomé de Burguillos (1634)

Entrambasaguas, Joaquín de. "Envilecimiento de un soneto de Lope de
Vega." Correo Erudito, II, No. 13 (1941), 81-82.
Upon the death of his first wife, Isabel de Urbina, Lope commissioned the painter Felipe de Liaño to paint the deceased as
she was when still alive. Lope records this in a sonnet
("Duerme el Sol de Belisa en noche oscura..."), probably
composed in 1595, but published for the first time in Rimas
humanas... (1634). Entrambasaguas discovers thematic parallelism between Lope's sonnet and an anecdote from Francisco
Asensio's Floresta española, formed in the second half of the
seventeenth century. A line from the anecdote ("...la hizo
retratar el día que mejor le pareció") distorts Lope's poetized
love and anguish into an attempt at low humour. Entrambasaguas
feels that the creator of the anecdote altered Lope's ideas in
an insensible and cruel manner.

Blecua, José Manuel. "Un poema desconocido de 'Tomé de Burguillos'."
BBMP, XXII(1946), 177-83.
Blecua found in Antonio Sánchez Tortolés' El entretenido,
Zaragoza, 1701, a long poem in octavas, which Blecua attributes
to Lope; but not with certainty by him.

Gillet, J. E. "Lucrecia-necia" (1947). See Studies — General.

Alonso, D. "La correlación poética en Lope..." (1960). See
Studies — Poetry — General.

Rimas sacras

Vega, Lope de. Romancero espiritual (1941). See Editions —
Poetry — Individual Poems.

Peers, E. A. "Mysticism in the Religious Verse..." (1944, 1945). See Studies — Poetry — General.

------. "Mysticism in the Poetry of Lope de Vega" (1950). See Studies — Poetry — General.

Areny Batlle, R., and A. Porqueras Mayo. "Lope de Vega en Lérida" (1957). See Studies — General.

Romance(s)

Goyri de Menéndez Pidal, María. "Para el Romancero de Lope de Vega." Mediterráneo, No. 5 (1944), 209-15. (Reprinted in De Lope de Vega y del Romancero, 1953. See below.)

Fucilla, Joseph G. "A Classical Theme in Lope de Vega and G. B. Marino." MLN, LX(1945), 287-90.
  The theme of "Cupid and the bee" in Marino's sixth canto of the Adone, stanzas 188-92, derives from Lope's romance which reappears in Lope's play Adonis y Venus (II, x).

Zabala, Arturo. "Sobre una fisonomía inicial del romance de Lope De pechos sobre una torre." RBN, VI(1945), 311-24.
  In this interesting article, Zabala proposes a reconstruction of what might have been the original physiognomy of Lope's romance "De pechos sobre una torre...." He makes use of the Romancero General, a version found by Foulché-Delbosc in a pliego suelto (see RH, XLV, 1919, 519 and 608), and a version which was made by Catalán de Valeriola ("Silencio"), a member of the Valencian Academia de los Nocturnos.

Barbazán, Julián. "Una edición ignorada de un romance de Lope de Vega." Bibliografía Hispánica, V(1946), 157-67.
  Barbazán provides a two-page introduction and a facsimile of a romance, "Alabanças al Glorioso Patriarca / San Ioseph,..." (Seville, 1628).

Zabala, Arturo. Versos y pervivencia de Lope de Vega en el siglo XVIII. Madrid, CSIC, 1948. Pp. 14. (Suplemento I de la Rev. Bibliográfica y Documental, II, No. 3.)
  Among some manuscripts of the Biblioteca General of the University of Valencia are to be found four verses of a romance by Lope, attesting to the long popularity and pervivencia of the ballad.

Álvar, Manuel. "Romances de Lope de Vega vivos en la tradición oral marroquí." RF, LXIII(1951), 282-305.
  In Tetuán, during the summers of 1949 and 1950, the author heard versions of "Mira, Zaide, que te aviso..." and "Gallardo pasea Zaide..." (also known by its variant as "Por la calle de su dama...").

Goyri de Menéndez Pidal, María. "El duque de Alba en el Romancero de Lope de Vega." Filología, III(1951), 185-200.
    The author sets forth the most pertinent autobiographical circumstances concerning the youthful fifth Duke of Alba at the time Lope took service with him. Then, against this background she examines five romances that she would add to the authentic works which Lope devoted to don Antonio. For collateral reading, see José F. Montesinos, NRFH, VI(1952), 352-78.

------. De Lope de Vega y del Romancero. Zaragoza, 1953. Pp. 195. (Bib. del Hispanista, 1.)
  Rev: Manuel Álvar, RF, LXVII(1955), 188-89.
    This is a collection of essays already published by the author at various times. The majority of them relate to Lope's romancero. The volume contains: "La difunta pleiteada" (pp. 7-59), on ballads dealing with the subject, an article printed in 1909; "El Amor niño en el Romancero de Lope de Vega" (pp. 61-77), an article printed in Fénix, 1936; "Un romance pastoril de Lope de Vega" (pp. 80-87), an article printed in Mediterráneo, 1944, as "Para el Romancero de Lope de Vega" (see above); "Con motivo del reajuste de unas fechas. La muerte de Isabel de Urbina" (pp. 89-101), an article printed in NRFH, 1949 (see Studies — General); "La Celia de Lope de Vega" (pp. 103-74), an article printed in NRFH, 1950 (see Studies — General); "El duque de Alba en el Romancero de Lope de Vega" (pp. 175-94), an article printed in Filología, 1951 (see above).

Montesinos, José F. "Para la historia de un romance de Lope: Una estatua de Cupido." Symposium, IX(1955), 1-18.
    The article studies the artistic evolution of the romance.

Entrambasaguas, Joaquín de. "Acerca del autor del romance ¿De qué sirve, hermosa Lisis...?" RL, IX(1956), 148-51.
    The conclusion reached is that the romance is not by Lope, but by Luis de Vargas Manrique.

Romancero espiritual

Guarner, Luis. "Autenticidad y crítica del Romancero espiritual de Lope de Vega." RBN, III(1942), 64-79.
    All 32 romances contained in the Romancero espiritual were composed by Lope and published previously in two of his works (31 in Rimas sacras and 1 in Pastores de Belén). Guarner seems to show conclusively that Lope had nothing to do with the actual compilation and publication of this Romancero. The article includes an analysis of the poems themselves, praising their deep religious sensitivity and their popular expression.

------. "La cuestión bibliográfica referente al Romancero espiritual de Lope de Vega." RBN, III(1942), 198-207.

Guarner here supports Vicente Salvá's affirmation that a 1619 first edition of the <u>Romancero espiritual</u> was published in Pamplona. Guarner then lists chronologically the several editions of the work.

Peers, E. A. "Mysticism in the Religious Verse..." (1944). See Studies — Poetry — General.

<u>Soliloquios (Cuatro)</u>

Leonard, Irving A., and William L. Fichter. "Two Unrecorded Lorenzana Editions of Lope de Vega." <u>HR</u>, X(1942), 345-47.
  <u>Cuatro soliloquios de Lope de Vega</u> (1612) and Lope's <u>Coloquio pastoril</u> (1615) are the two hitherto unrecorded editions by the little-known Bartolomé de Lorenzana, who worked as a printer in Valencia before establishing his press in Granada, where these two editions were printed.

<u>Soliloquios amorosos de un alma a Dios</u>

Hatzfeld, Helmut. "Problemas estilísticos en los <u>Soliloquios amorosos de un alma a Dios</u> de Lope de Vega." <u>Thesaurus</u>, XIII(1958), 11-23.

<u>Sonnet(s)</u>

Jörder, Otto. <u>Die Formen des Sonetts bei Lope de Vega</u>. Halle, Niemeyer, 1936. (<u>ZRP</u>, Beiheft 86.)
  Rev: William C. Atkinson, <u>MLR</u>, XXXII(1937), 476-77; G. Cirot, <u>BH</u>, XXIX(1937), 276-77; W. L. Fichter, <u>HR</u>, VI(1938), 21-34 (see next item).

Fichter, William L. "Recent Research on Lope de Vega's Sonnets." <u>HR</u>, VI(1938), 21-34.
  A detailed review of <u>A Critical Index of Sonnets in the Plays of Lope de Vega</u>, by Lucile K. Delano (Toronto, Univ. of Toronto Press, 1935) and of <u>Die Formen des Sonetts bei Lope de Vega</u>, by Otto Jörder (see above).

------. "Two Sonnets Attributed to Lope de Vega." <u>HR</u>, VI(1938), 345-46.
  Fichter gives the texts of the two sonnets, not republished since 1612, beginning "A quien la bella Francia ver desea..." and "Pártese aquella luz del francés suelo...."

------. "More 'Forgotten' Verse by Lope de Vega" (1942). See Studies — Poetry — General.

Lafuente Ferrari, Enrique. "Un curioso autógrafo de Lope de Vega." <u>RBN</u>, V(1944), 43-62.
  The article concerns the sonnet "Ya no quiero más bien que sólo amaros..."

González Echegaray, C. "Soror Juana y Frey Lope..." (1948). See
	Studies — Drama — Individual Plays (La moza de cántaro).

Cisneros, L. J. "Preguntas sobre Lope" (1952). See Studies —
	Drama — Individual Plays (El valor de las mujeres).

Françon, M. "Sur le sonnet du sonnet" (1952). See Studies —
	Drama — Individual Plays (La niña de plata).

Serís, H. "Un soneto del autor..." (1953). See Studies — Drama —
	Individual Plays (La Estrella de Sevilla).

Spitzer, Leo. "No me mueve, mi Dios...." NRFH, VII(1953), 608-17.
	Spitzer begins by expressing agreement with Bataillon on reasons
	for believing in the anonymity of the sonnet and for not
	believing Lope to be the author. The remainder of the article
	analyses the sonnet, and does not refer again to Lope.

Jörder, Otto. "Luis Martín de la Plaza pro y contra Lope de Vega:
	Eine harmloshintergründige Sonettenrache." ZRP, LXX(1954),
	98-103.
	The author studies a sonnet written in praise of Lope by Luis
	(Pedro?) Martín de la Plaza on the occasion of Lope's visit to
	Antequera in 1602 or 1603, and a second version of the same
	sonnet, in which the words of praise are altered to refer to
	Southern Spain — a kind of Southern revenge against an
	ungrateful Castilian poet.

Spitzer, Leo. "Al triunfo de Judit." MLN, LXIX(1954), 1-11.
	Lope's sonnet, like medieval paintings on the same subject,
	depicts two different scenes of the story of Judith: the tent
	scene, a spectacle of human depravity; and in the last tercet,
	the Trionfo of Judith. Spitzer asks whether Lope described
	paintings he had actually seen, or produced the sonnet by
	means of his imagination, using the medieval trionfo as a
	pattern. Spitzer's answer: probably the latter. This article
	was reprinted in Spitzer's Romanische literaturstudien (1959).
	See Studies — General.

Fradejas Lebrero, José. "De Lope de Vega y E. M. de Villegas." RL,
	VIII(1955), 334-36.
	The article studies Lope's sonnet "Zaphiro blando, que más
	quejas tristes..." and Villegas' Oda sáfica in the light of
	Saphic tradition. Villegas is the imitator.

Fucilla, J. G. "Sonetti sul sonetto in Italia" (1956). See
	Studies — Drama — Individual Plays (La niña de plata).

Lázaro, Fernando. "Lope, pastor robado: Vida y arte en los sonetos
	de los mansos." In Neubert Festschrift, Berlin, 1956, pp.
	209-24.
	Rev: P. Moreau, RLC, XXXI(1957), 440-42.

Verspoor, Dolf. "Twee Sonnetten van Lope de Vega." In Homenaje a
J. A. van Praag, Amsterdam, 1956, pp. 138-39.

Dunn, P. N. "Some Uses of the Sonnets in the Plays..." (1957).
See Studies — Drama — General.

Glaser, Edward. "Cuando me paro a contemplar mi estado: Trayectoria
de un Rechenschaftssonett." In Estudios hispano-portugueses,
Valencia, Castalia, 1957, pp. 59-95.
  For reviews of the volume, see Studies — Poetry — Individual
    Poems (Rimas, 1602).
  There are echoes of Garcilaso's first sonnet in three of Lope's.
    The tone in each case varies from that of the model. The
    author's exposition is penetrating and illuminating.

------. "Ir y quedarse..." (1957). See Studies — Poetry — Individual Poems (Rimas, 1602).

Ryan, H. A. "A Note on Lope de Vega's Soneto de repente"
(1957). See Studies — Drama — Individual Plays (La niña
de plata).

Gallegos Valdés, L. "Del plagio literario." Cultura (San Salvador),
No. 14 (1958), 116-22.
  This is an article of a general nature on what constitutes plagiarism. Lope's sonnet "Desmayarse, atreverse, estar furioso..."
    is compared to a similar one by Quevedo.

Porqueras-Mayo, Alberto. "Un soneto olvidado de Lope de Vega." HR,
XXIX(1961), 332-34.
  The author transcribes a Lope sonnet from the rare editions of
    1614 and 1617 of Fray Antonio Daza's Historia: Vida y milagros ... de ... Sor Juana de la Cruz.

Los triunfos divinos

Müller-Bochat, Eberhard. Der allegorische Triumphzug. Ein Motiv
Petrarcas bei Lope de Vega und Rubens. Krefeld, Scherpe-Verlag,
1957. Pp. 30. (Schriften und Vorträge des Petrarca-Instituts
Köln, 11.)
  Rev: K.-L. Selig, BHR, XX(1958), 483-84.
  A study of the relation of Lope's Triunfos divinos to its prinpal forerunners in the short allegorical poem based on the
    victory procession: Petrarch, Trionfi, and Tasso, Il mondo
    creato, the latter a spiritualization of this originally
    Roman motif. Lope's poems are shown to be counterparts and
    supplements, not merely imitations. Notice is taken of parallel representation in the pictorial arts (effectively illustrated), and Rubens' cartoons for the tapestry series Triumph
    of the Eucharist are considered a derivation of Lope's work.

Villancicos a los Misterios del Rosario

Entrambasaguas, Joaquín de. "Unos villancicos a los Misterios del Rosario atribuidos a Lope de Vega." RJ, V(1952), 275-84.
(With no mention of previous publication, this study reappeared in RL, VII, 1955, 3-18.)
The author possesses a copy of Villancicos..., Salamanca, 1794. The portada attributes the first villancico to each of the misterios to Lope, the second to an unnamed Dominican friar, and the third to Miguel de S. Clemente.

------. "Más sobre unos Villancicos a los Misterios del Rosario, de Lope de Vega." RL, IX(1956), 72-81.

La Virgen de la Almudena

Entrambasaguas, Joaquín de. "Sobre un supuesto poema y unas olvidadas glosas lopianas de Lope de Vega." Rev. Bibliográfica y Documental, I(1947), 83-90.
The article states that five octavas beginning "La estrella de Antiochia en breve ermita...," which Millé y Giménez thought to be a separate poem, belong to La Virgen de la Almudena, and that they could not have appeared in an edition of 1607, as M. y G. asserts, since the longer poem was not written until after 1621.

PROSE

A. GENERAL

Avalle-Arce, Juan Bautista. La novela pastoril española. Madrid, Rev. de Occidente, 1959. Pp. xi, 249.
Rev: J. Ares Montes, Anales Cervantinos, VIII(1959-60), 409-10; Daniel Devoto, BH, LXIII(1961), 287-89; Edward Glaser, Renaissance News, XIV(1961), 28-30; Otis H. Green, HR, XXIX (1961), 246-49; Helmut Hatzfeld, MLN, LXXVI(1961), 85-88; R. O. Jones, BHS, XXXVIII(1961), 167-69; R. D. F. Pring-Mill, MLR, LVI(1961), 152-53.
Contains references to La Arcadia, pp. 131-39, and to Los pastores de Belén, pp. 239-40.

B. INDIVIDUAL PROSE WORKS

La Arcadia

Kany, Charles E. The Beginnings of the Epistolary Novel in France, Italy and Spain. Berkeley, Univ. of California Press, 1937. (UCPMP, XXI, 1.)
La Arcadia, pp. 77-78.

Alonso, Dámaso. "Lope despojado por Marino..." (1949). See Studies — Poetry — General.

López Estrada, Francisco. "La Arcadia de Lope en la escena de Tirso." In *Tirso de Molina por Revista Estudios*, Madrid, 1949, pp. 303-20.
    A study of Tirso's *La fingida Arcadia* of only marginal importance for Lope's bibliography. The author concludes: "*La fingida Arcadia* pertenece a la forma tradicional del teatro según la herencia de Lope, y presenta la originalidad de recoger las formas de la narración pastoril por medio de la *Arcadia* de Lope, y en general la influencia de la tradición pastoril de la novela española...."

Wellington, Maria Z. *The Influence of Sannazaro on Spanish Renaissance and Golden Age Literature*. Unpub. doct. diss., Northwestern Univ., 1951.

Areny Batlle, R., and A. Porqueras Mayo. "Lope de Vega en Lérida" (1957). See Studies — General.

Avalle-Arce, J. B. *La novela pastoril española* (1959). See Studies — Prose — General.

Alonso, Dámaso. "La correlación poética en Lope..." (1960). See Studies — Poetry — General.

Ricciardelli, Michele. *Studio estetico-comparativo sul romanzo pastorale: Sannazaro e Lope de Vega*. Unpub. doct. diss., Univ. of Oregon, 1961. (*DA*, XXI, 2720.)
    The dissertation is "primarily an aesthetic study of Lope's work in direct relation to Sannazaro's work, showing the artistic qualities and beauties of (the latter's) *La Arcadia*. (The dissertation) intends to be a reaction to critical opinion and an attempt to revaluate this pastoral novel."

La desdicha por la honra

Bataillon, Marcel. "*La desdicha por la honra*: Génesis y sentido de una novela de Lope." *NRFH*, I(1947), 13-42.
    Lope acquired from the *Nuevo tratado de Turquía*, by Octavio Sapiencia, not only his knowledge about the Turks, but also essential data for his plot. Other details he acquired from the *repertorio cervantino*. Lope desired to compete with Cervantes on his own ground (that is, the novel), and lacking Cervantes' adventures, he supplied a grace of narrative sprinkled with aphorisms and wit. Bataillon points out a similarity between an incident in the novel and one in *La villana de Getafe* (the hero's Moorish descent). He discusses briefly the question of honour and Lope's attitude toward it. In his appendices, of which there are three, he gives passages

from the Nuevo tratado of which Lope availed himself for his
novel, the passages dealing with the "Historia de don Jerónimo
de Urrea," which he (Bataillon) believes to be the model for
Lope's hero, Felisardo, and an osbscure passage in the novel,
which he discusses ("Anotaciones a un paréntesis"). This
article is a valuable addition to our knowledge of Lope's
sources.

La Dorotea

Oñate, María del Pilar. El femenismo en la literatura española
(1938). See Studies — General.

Croce, Alda. "La Dorotea" di Lope de Vega. Studio critico. Seguido
dalla traduzione delle parti principali dell'opera. Bari,
Laterza, 1940. Pp. 352.
  Rev: Ángel J. Battistessa, RFH, III(1941), 381-83; A. A. Parker,
  MLR, XXXVI(1941), 138-40.
  The critical study, which comprises half the book, is considered
  by reviewers to be of significance. (It is pointed out that
  the translation of "principal parts" is the first of La Dorotea
  into Italian.) For Alda Croce, La Dorotea is Lope's "spiritual
  testament," too mature and too deeply infused with the serene
  spirit of his old age for any youthful first draft not to have
  been completely rewritten and transformed. Signorina Croce
  differs radically with Vossler in interpreting the significance
  of the mass of humanistic erudition scattered throughout the
  work. She does not believe that Lope is satirically condemning
  a craze for culture, but rather that he is perfectly sincere
  in paying homage to a culture for which he had the most profound veneration. A. A. Parker praises particularly the
  sensitive analysis of the characters, but feels that the
  critic's high opinion of the literary quality of La Dorotea is
  unconvincing.

Torre, G. de. "Prisma de Lope de Vega..." (1947). See Studies —
General.

Durand, René L. F. "La intromisión de lo literario en la vida en
La Dorotea de Lope de Vega." RNC (Caracas), XI, No. 77 (1949),
65-79.
  "...hay en La Dorotea un sentido paródico que hace falta recalcar
  fuertemente. Pero al mismo tiempo amor de lo parodiado." The
  author does not raise the question of chronology, and takes
  La Dorotea as a work of old age. He does not mention the
  studies of Spitzer and Alda Croce.

Morby, Edwin S. "Persistence and Change in the Formation of La
Dorotea." HR, XVIII(1950), 108-25; 195-217.
  The author studies "the complex of motives constituting the
  argument of La Dorotea" and shows "its tenacity of survival

and its adaptability." He is not interested in all possible reflections of the Elena Osorio experience, but only in those in which Lope works toward the final form which this love affair assumed in La Dorotea as published in 1632. Morby discusses six "pre-Doroteas," and isolates ten or eleven leitmotifs which recur with variations in them. This article is a thorough analytical study of the growth of the "matter of Dorotea" on the way to the "wonderful detachment" of La Dorotea. Yet, La Dorotea itself remains a "striking, sudden phenomenon."

Sainz de Robles, F. C. Ensayo de un diccionario de la literatura... (1949-50). See Studies — General.

González de Amezúa, Agustín. "En el tercer centenario de La Dorotea (1632-1932)." In Opúsculos histórico-literarios, II, Madrid, CSIC, 1951, pp. 255-67. (Previously pub. in BRAE, XIX, 1932.)

Trueblood, Alan S. Substance and Form in "La Dorotea." A Study in Lope's Artistic Use of Personal Experience. Unpub. doct. diss., Harvard Univ., 1951. Pp. 355.
A very valuable and fruitful investigation, which has led to later publications on La Dorotea.

Morby, Edwin S. "Levinus Lemnius and Leo Suabius in La Dorotea." HR, XX(1952), 108-22.
Another elusive and contradictory aspect of Lope is found in his cherished rôle of scholar. Morby has been confronted with this problem in La Dorotea, noted and criticized for its display of pedantry. In this article he selects Lemnius and Suabius to illustrate Lope's devices for glossing the learning of impressive authorities and shows how these devices become an integral part of the central technique of composing the dialogue.

------. "A Footnote on Lope de Vega's barquillas." RPh, VI(1953), 289-93.
This is a short note on four poems in praise of Marta de Nevares in La Dorotea. All are barquillas or romancillos piscatorios, in which Fabio laments his departed Amarilis. They belong to a tradition which probably derives from Sannazaro.

------. "A Pre-Dorotea..." (1953). See Studies — Poetry — Individual Poems (El Isidro).

------. "Proverbs in La Dorotea." RPh, VIII(1956), 243-59.
The article deals with the identification of proverbs in La Dorotea and with speculation regarding the particular use of proverbs in the light of baroque procedure.

Trueblood, Alan S. "The Case for an Early *Dorotea*: A Reëxamination." *PMLA*, LXXI(1956), 755-98.
    In this major article, the author discusses Lope's creative process in the artistic formation of *La Dorotea*.

Monge, F. "*La Dorotea* de Lope de Vega." *VR*, XVI(1957), 60-145.
    The most original part of this study concerns the relation between *La Dorotea* and the *Comedia*. This involves differences of degree rather than of kind: the conventions of feeling are the same, only more extensively and intensively analysed. *Literarisierung*, less extreme, is to be found in the *Comedia* and in Lope's life. Rhetorical expression and erudite adornment, Lope's standard idiom, are satirized in *La Dorotea* only when improperly applied.

Trueblood, Alan S. "Espacio, tiempo y género en *La Dorotea*." *NRFH*, XI(1957), 189-93.
  Rev: R. Baes, *LR*, XV(1961), 65.
    Lope has paradoxically used the "más libre teatro" given by this work's form to confine himself more closely than ever to realistic conditions of time and space. The reason lies in his acute sense of time's passage. He sets chronological time against a lyric sense of evanescence; the inner form of the work grows out of their interrelation.

Morby, Edwin S. "*Oro potable* and *confección de alquermes*." *RPh*, XI(1957-58), 368-70.
    Two pharmaceutical footnotes to *La Dorotea* which bring together material scattered through several notes of Morby's edition of the work.

Trueblood, Alan S. "The *Officina* of Ravisius Textor in Lope de Vega's *Dorotea*." *HR*, XXVI(1958), 135-41.
    Textor's work, a handbook and index to a great variety of classical instances and lore, was drawn on by Lope to give a showy, exotic flavour to his characters' talk and to underscore certain prominent themes and key moments of *La Dorotea*.

------. "Plato's *Symposium* and Ficino's Commentary in Lope de Vega's *La Dorotea*." *MLN*, LXXIII(1958), 506-14.
    The fundamental artistic pattern of *La Dorotea*, centring on the interaction between the worlds of art and actuality, is reinforced by the use made of Ficino's commentary and occasionally of the *Symposium* itself, which are drawn on for both idealized and earthy views of love.

Guerrieri Crocetti, Camillo. "Per la *Dorotea* di Lope de Vega." In *Studi in onore di Angelo Monteverdi*, I, Modena, Soc. Tip. Editrice Modenese, 1959, pp. 303-12.

> The author sees La Dorotea not as an autobiographical work, but
> as one of "ammaestramento morale," to a large extent lacking
> in spontaneity, and in the last act conveying a pervasive
> sense of nothingness and disillusionment.

Morby, E. S. "Reflections on El verdadero amante" (1959). See
Studies — Drama — Individual Plays (El verdadero amante).

Snyder, Isabel. "A Twentieth Century Adaptation of Lope de Vega's
La Dorotea." Hisp, XLII(1959), 325-29.
> A play, wholly in verse, by Marquina, performed in Jan., 1935,
> at the Teatro Cómico in Madrid. In general, the characters
> are less picaresque than Lope's, the servants less graciosos,
> and the whole work more restrained, with a more idealistic
> ending.

Iventosch, Herman. "The Elaboration of an Episode from the Quijote
in the Dorotea." HR, XXVIII(1960), 215-19.
> Bandurrio, the shepherd of a burlesque sonnet in La Dorotea,
> seeks his lost beloved, and mistakes some white mares for
> souls. Here, Lope turns inside out Cervantes' chapter on
> Rocinante and the "desalmados yangüeses." While ridiculing
> Góngora, Lope also glorifies him, his style and the age, per-
> haps as Cervantes parodies, yet also exalts, the chivalric.

Los pastores de Belén

Guarner, L. "La cuestión bibliográfica..." (1942). See Studies —
Poetry — Individual Poems (Romancero espiritual).

Borghini, V. Poesia e letteratura... (1949). See Poetry —
Studies — General.

Areny Batlle, R., and A. Porqueras Mayo. "Lope de Vega en Lérida"
(1957). See Studies — General.

Avalle-Arce, J. B. La novela pastoril española (1959). See
Studies — Prose — General.

El peregrino en su patria

See Studies — Drama — The Peregrino Lists.

Reyes, Alfonso. "El peregrino en su patria de Lope de Vega." Bol.
de la Acad. Argentina de Letras, V(1937), 643-50. (Reprinted
in Capítulos de literatura española, primera serie, Mexico,
La Casa de España, 1939, pp. 99-110; and in Cuatro ingenios,
Mexico-Buenos Aires, Espasa-Calpe, 1950, pp. 59-69; in each
case preceded by "Silueta de Lope de Vega" — see Studies —
General.)

Cirot, G. "L'Allégorie des tireurs à l'arc" (1942). See Studies — Drama — Individual Plays (Las bodas entre el Alma...).

Horne, Ruth Nutt (Mrs. A. David Kossoff). Lope de Vega's "Peregrino en su patria" and the Romance of Adventure in Spain before 1604. Unpub. doct. diss., Brown Univ., 1946. Pp. viii, 290.
In Part I, the author studies editions and translations, date of composition, contemporary notices and modern criticism, and gives a summary of plot, with a careful consideration of structure, style and literary theory in the work, characterization, erudition, autobiographical elements and interpolated plays and poetry. Part II deals with suggested sources, and the romance of adventure throughout its history in many countries as well as Spain.

Tiemann, H. "Über Lope de Vegas Bild..." (1947-48). See Studies — General.

Cossío, José María de. "Una noticia de América en Lope." Finisterre (segunda época), I(1948), 89-92.
The reference is to a passage in quintillas in an auto inserted in the first book of El peregrino en su patria. The Devil invites the Will to accompany him in his ship "Pleasure" to the nuevo mundo, and the Will replies with a series of questions about the New World. As Cossío points out, as a literary exhibition it is curious and very brilliant, but as a test of knowledge, it could not be more inexact.

THE QUADRICENTENNIAL YEAR 1962

Commentary

1 9 6 2

As we close our survey (December, 1963), it cannot be said that the Quadricentennial Year is yet over. Publications bearing the date 1962 are still appearing, and many works inspired by the Anniversary of Lope's birth are coming forth with the date 1963. (Good examples are Hispanófila, No. 18, and Cuadernos Hispanoamericanos, Nos. 161-62, both homenajes of significance.) But it is necessary to bring our investigation to a conclusion; otherwise it would be unending. And that last thought is in itself a tribute to our great Spanish dramatist: interest in him is continous and continuing.

The Quadricentennial Year has given birth to a good deal of new and valuable scholarship. It is true, on the other hand, that there have been reprintings of old materials (e.g., Sainz de Robles' Retrato, horóscopo, vida y transfiguración) and many publications of a general nature, due to a desire to participate in the occasion. But it is heartening to note world response to such an important event — by scholars themselves, by periodicals, by learned institutions and by printing presses.

As James A. Castañeda has so rightly said in the preface to his critical edition of Las paces de los reyes, "the revaluation of Lope de Vega that has been one of the features of the new critical approach to Spanish Literature since Menéndez Pelayo cannot bear full fruit until most of his major works have been critically edited." Many of the major works do still remain in an unsatisfactory condition, but the Quadricentennial Year has done something to correct a lamentable state of affairs. Castañeda's own publication is the remedying in one case of a great need; Arnold G. Reichenberger's critical edition of Carlos V en Francia (the Stetson autograph, now in the Library of the University of Pennsylvania) and El galán de la Membrilla, edited critically by Diego Marín and Evelyn Rugg (published by the Royal Spanish Academy) are also excellent contributions. Noteworthy too in drama are the "edición conmemorativa" of Las ferias de Madrid (Instituto Nacional del Libro), a paleographic edition of La nueva victoria de D. Gonzalo de Córdoba by Henryk Ziomek (publication of doctoral thesis, Minnesota, 1961), an abridged edition of La moza de cántaro by Melissa A. Cilley, and translations of La dama boba by Willis Knapp Jones (in Poet Lore) and of La fianza satisfecha, attributed to Lope, by Willis Barnstone (in Tulane Drama Review). In adaptations, Joaquín de Entrambasaguas has given us a version of El nuevo mundo and Sainz de Robles one of El perro del hortelano. For poetry, the Aubrun-Muñoz Cortés edition of La Circe stands out, and in prose, regrettably neglected, the Morby edition of La Dorotea (Berkeley, 1958) continues to be the recipient of enthusiastic reviews.

Some biographies had already appeared in 1961 (Zamora Vicente's, very well reviewed in 1962, for example), but for the Quadricentennial Year, Juan Antonio Cabezas' Lope de Vega, and Baeza's and Zertuche's monographs of the same title (containing reprinted material) are the only general studies which have so far come to our notice. The more popular, but still scholarly, brief study is well represented by Alan S. Trueblood's "Lope de Vega: Four Hundred Years Ago and Now" (Brown Daily Herald) and by Bruce W. Wardropper's "On the Fourth Centenary" (Drama Survey). José Simón Díaz has provided a fascinating account of lopeana in Spanish bookstores, and four theatrical directors in their discussion in Primer Acto have commented on live production. Russian critics (Plavskin, et al.) have brought forth a bibliography of Lope de Vega materials in Russia, and other lopistas have studied in short monographs and in periodicals a variety of themes such as "La alabanza" in Lope (John Brooks in Hispanófila), humanism in Lope (Marcos Gordoa in Abside) and Lope's use of the retrato as a literary device (Myron A. Peyton in Romance Notes).

In drama in particular, well-known critics have extended the horizons in various directions: Arjona (rhyme as applied to authorship), Fichter (character names; inspired by Morley and Tyler), Kennedy (on mangas cortas applied to chronology), Marín (dramatic versification), McCready (heraldry), Rothberg (the agente cómico), Shergold and Varey (the dating of several plays), Villarejo (an ingenious but unsubstantiated questioning of established chronology),... For individual plays, Reichenberger has described the recently-acquired and hitherto-unknown autograph of Los Benavides, Glaser has discussed La creación del mundo, Pring-Mill Fuenteovejuna, Salomon the date of Peribáñez and Entrambasaguas El villano en su rincón (reprint of 1961). For poetry, Rozas has studied El laurel de Apolo, Fucilla sonnets and Blecua villancicos. For prose, the only study thus far of any importance has been Yndurain's brief (82-page) Lope de Vega como novelador. For Lope bibliography, Warren McCready and Robert Bishop have continued their current surveys in the Bulletin of the Comediantes and in Studies in Philology and José Simón Díaz his "Información bibliográfica" in Revista de Literatura.

As has been mentioned, learned institutions and publishing houses have cooperated to make the Quadricentennial worthy of the artist who inspired it. The British Museum's exhibit of Lope materials (It is not our intent to discuss any aspect but publication) inspired a most enlightening printed catalogue, as did those of the University of Pennsylvania, Rutgers, Toronto — to mention only a few. Periodicals, as has been noted also, have honoured Lope by special numbers (and here, contrary to this Bibliography's general policy, are included some newspapers). ABC, with a series of short articles in its Supplement of April 8, Arriba, with a "número especial" of the same date, Blanco y Negro, in its November 24 issue, Cuadernos de Bellas Artes, La Estafeta Literaria, Poesía Española,

Primer Acto, The Theatre Annual, The Tulane Drama Review, Villa de Madrid,... are but a few of the many, which like Hispanófila, already cited, recognized the importance of the occasion and encouraged scholars to avail themselves of their pages. The many lectures too, given over wide areas, are reflected on the printed page: José María Pemán's Lo tradicional y lo moderno en Lope de Vega... being, for instance, a "discurso leído el 27 de enero en el Instituto de España," and Professor Entrambasaguas' Góngora y Lope en la coyuntura del Renacimiento y del Barroco, being his opening lecture for the academic year 1962-63.

Space in this section does not permit an adequate discussion of the many contributions in print to the Lope Year; nor does it allow us to give due recognition to those who entered so vigorously into it. A special plea might be directed to recent recipients of doctoral degrees to bring their unpublished theses to the printed page. True it is that interlibrary loan, microfilming or other processes are helpful, but nothing takes the place of a volume at hand, and there are so many dissertations in less than easily accessible form in the libraries of colleges and universities in Europe, America and elsewhere. As examples of progress along this line one might cite Castañeda's above-mentioned Paces de los reyes, which was an unpublished thesis (Yale, 1958) until 1962, and Warren McCready's definitive study of La heráldica, originally a doctoral dissertation for the University of Chicago.

Time, and conscientious reviews, will ultimately pass judgment on the scholarly activities with which we have sought to honour the memory of the Fénix de los Ingenios. Lope de Vega scholarship is very much alive. The interval until the next centennial (1962-2035) is as long as Lope's lifetime, and will be for coming generations of critics to assess. We know that they will continue our work. Four hundred years after Lope's birth, we find him in the full bloom of a flourishing after-life and we look ahead to a fruitful future of Lopean scholarship.

Bibliography

EDITIONS

GENERAL

Vega, Lope de. Comedias (Fuenteovejuna, La dama boba, El arauco domado). Los pastores de Belén. Ed. C. Rivas Xerif. Mexico, El Ateneo, 1962. Pp. 282.

------. Lope en las escuelas. Antología. Ed. José Fradejas Lebrero. Ceuta, Inst. de Crédito de las Cajas de Ahorros, 1962. Pp. 81.

------. Obra selecta. I: Teatro (La gallarda toledana, El sembrar en buena tierra, La del abanillo). II: Prosa y verso (La desdicha por la honra, La prudente venganza, Guzmán el bravo, Soliloquios amorosos). 2 vols. Madrid, Pubs. Españolas, 1962. Pp. 347, 213. (Col. El Libro para Todos.)

------. Oda. Trans. A. Zarnescu. Las bizarrías de Belisa (Enrique's speech of Act I, Scene 8). Trans. Teodor Balș. Steaua (Bucharest), XIII, No. 11 (1962), 59.

------. Purecul. Noptii. Trans. Romulus Vulpescu. Cind iubesti fara să stii pe cine (Amar sin saber a quién). Trans. Tascu Gheorghiu. Gazeta Literară (Bucharest), No. 51 (1962), 8.

------. El villano en su rincón, seguido de una antología lírica y dramática (El caballero de Olmedo, Peribáñez). Ed. Guillermo Díaz-Plaja, Barcelona, La Espiga, 1961.
  Rev: F. López Montenegro, Religión y Cultura, VII(1962), 162-63.

DRAMA

A. GENERAL

Vega, Lope de. (Antología.) V Demostración sindical (Teatro, música y danza). Madrid, Obra Sindical de Educación y Descanso, 1962. Pp. 36.
  The published account of the act of homage held in the Santiago Bernabéu Stadium, Madrid, on May 1, 1962. Included, in addition to preliminary materials, are: "El amor picado" (from El galán de la Membrilla); "La discreción y el enredo" (from La discreta enamorada); "Cantar de vendimia" (from El heredero del cielo); "Un galán con dos damas" (from La prueba de los

amigos); "Tres canciones y danzas populares" ("Canción de boda" from El tirano castigado, "Canción de bautismo" from El piadoso aragonés, "Villano" from Al pasar del arroyo); "Un imposible amor" (from El castigo sin venganza); "El amor se ha vuelto indiano" (from La dama boba); "Muerte del caballero de Olmedo" (from El caballero de Olmedo); "Canto al nacimiento de la Virgen Nuestra Señora" (from La madre de la mejor); "Los desposorios de los Reyes Católicos" (from El mejor mozo de España); "Carrera de sortija" (from El capellán de la Virgen).

------. Ausgewählte Werke. Dt. Nachdichtungen von Hans Schlegel. Bd. 4. Emsdetten (Westf.), Lechte, 1962. Pp. 489.
Contains: Toledanische Nacht, Wenn Frauen keine Augen hätten, Die Liebesprobe, Tumult im Narrenhaus, Der verwirrte Hof, Die Torheit des Weisen.

------. Five Plays. Trans. Jill Booty. Ed. R. D. F. Pring-Mill. New York, Hill and Wang (London, McGibbon and Kee), 1961.
Rev: J. T. Boorman, BHS, XXXIX(1962), 256-57.

------. Historias de Lope de Vega (La Estrella de Sevilla, El mejor alcalde el rey, La dama boba). Adaptación para niños por María Luz Morales. 5th ed. Barcelona, Araluce, 1962. Pp. 122. (Las Obras Maestras al Alcance de los Niños.)

------. Fuenteovejuna, Peribáñez, El mejor alcalde el rey, El caballero de Olmedo. Ed. J. M. Lope Blanch. Mexico, Porrúa, 1962. Pp. xxiv, 229. (Col. "Sepan Cuantos...", 12.)

------. El mejor alcalde el rey, Fuenteovejuna. 7th ed. Madrid, Espasa-Calpe, 1962.

------. El perro del hortelano, El arenal de Sevilla. 3rd ed. Madrid, Espasa-Calpe, 1962. Pp. 158.

------. El villano en su rincón, Los melindres de Belisa. Ed. José María de Riquer y Palau. Barcelona, Mateu, 1962. Pp. 321. (Col. Todo para Muchos, 34.)

B. INDIVIDUAL PLAYS

Vega, Lope de. El acero de Madrid. Ed. Lázaro Montero de la Puente and Antonio Ayora. Madrid, Ministerio de Educación Nac., 1962. Pp. 78. (Nueva Bib. Teatral.)

------. Las almenas de Toro. Ed. Thomas Edward Case. Unpub. doct. diss., State Univ. of Iowa, 1962. (DA, XXIII, 4673-74.)
"Las almenas de Toro is the only play by Lope de Vega in which the Cid appears."

------. *El caballero de Olmedo*. Ed. Álvaro Arauz. Mexico, 1962. (Teatro Universal.)

------. *El caballero del milagro*. Refundición de Juan Germán Schroeder. In *Primer Acto*, No. 37 (1962), 29-56.

------. *Carlos V en Francia*. Ed. Arnold G. Reichenberger. Philadelphia, Univ. of Pennsylvania Press, 1962. Pp. 256.

------. *La dama boba*. Ed. Francisco Tolsada. 4th ed. Zaragoza, Ebro, 1962. Pp. 142.

------. *The Stupid Lady* (*La dama boba*). Trans. Willis Knapp Jones. In *Poet-Lore*, LVII, No. 3 (1962), 291-354.

------. *Las ferias de Madrid*. Ed. conmemorativa del IV Centenario del nacimiento del autor. Madrid, Inst. Nac. del Libro Español, 1962. Pp. 110.
"Edición no venal de 4.000 ejemplares numerados para ser repartida gratuitamente entre los compradores de la Feria Nacional del Libro, celebrada en Madrid en mayo-junio de 1962."

------. *The Outrageous Saint* (*La fianza satisfecha*). Trans. into English prose by Willis Barnstone. In *TDR*, VII(1962), 58-104.

------. *Fuenteovejuna*. Ed. Tomás García de la Santa. 5th ed. Zaragoza, Ebro, 1962. Pp. 108.

------. *Fuenteovejuna*. Trans. Ángel Flores and Muriel Kittel. In *Spanish Drama*, New York, Bantam, 1962, pp. 33-80.

------. *El galán de la Membrilla*. Ed. Diego Marín and Evelyn Rugg. Madrid, RAE, 1962. Pp. 267. (*BRAE*, Anejo 8.)

------. *El hijo pródigo*. In *Cuad. de Bellas Artes* (Mexico), III, No. 11 (1962), 33-52, and No. 12 (1962), 67-80.
The *auto* which was published in *El peregrino en su patria*.

------. *La moza de cántaro*. Ed. Melissa A. Cilley. Decatur, Georgia, Agnes Scott College, 1962. Pp. iv, 99.
An abridged version.

------. *La nueva victoria de D. Gonzalo de Córdoba*. Paleographic ed. by Henryk Ziomek. New York, Hispanic Inst., 1962. Pp. 211.
Doct. diss., Univ. of Minnesota, 1961.

------. *El nuevo mundo*. Ed. and "adaptación original" by Joaquín de Entrambasaguas. Madrid, Inst. de Cultura Hispánica, 1962. Pp. 153.

------. *Las paces de los reyes y judía de Toledo*. Ed. James A. Castañeda. Chapel Hill, Univ. of North Carolina Press, 1962. Pp. 265. (<u>Univ. of North Carolina Studies in Romance Langs. and Lits.</u>, 40.)
Doct. diss., Yale Univ., 1958.

------. <u>Peribáñez</u>. Barcelona, Edit. Juventud, 1962. Pp. 152. (<u>Col. Z</u>, 86.)

------. <u>El perro del hortelano</u>. Revisada por Federico Carlos Sainz de Robles. Madrid, Edit. Nac., 1962. Pp. 132. (<u>Obras del Teatro Español</u>.)

------. (<u>El perro del hortelano</u>.) <u>A Kertész kutyája</u>. Trans. Gáspar Endre. Budapest, Irodalmi Könyvkiadó, 1962. Pp. 136.

------. <u>La prudente venganza</u>. "Madrigal" from <u>La prudente venganza</u>. In <u>Cuad. de Bellas Artes</u> (Mexico), III, No. 11 (1962), 16.

------. <u>Los ramilletes de Madrid</u>. <u>Comedia</u>. In <u>Mundo Hispánico</u>, No. 171 (1962), 55-69.

------. <u>La siega</u>. Ed. Álvaro Arauz. Mexico, 1962. (<u>Teatro del Bolsillo</u>.)

------. <u>El villano en su rincón</u>. Ed. revisada por Alfredo Carballo. Madrid, Organización para el Fomento de la Enseñanza, 1962. Pp. 80.

------. <u>El villano en su rincón</u>. Ed. Joaquín de Entrambasaguas. See Studies — Drama — Individual Plays.

POETRY

A. GENERAL

Marín, Diego (ed.). <u>Poesía española</u>. <u>Estudios y textos</u> (<u>Siglos XV al XX</u>). New York, Las Américas, 1962. Pp. 496.
Lope de Vega: pp. 185-202.

Vega, Lope de. <u>Poemas</u>. In <u>Cuad. de Bellas Artes</u> (Mexico), III, No. 11 (1962), 7-13.

------. <u>Poesía escogida</u>. Ed. Roque Esteban Scarpa. Santiago de Chile, Zig-Zag, 1962. Pp. 148.
More than one hundred sonnets, <u>letras</u>, ballads and excerpts from Lope's epic and elegiac poetry.

———. *Poesías preliminares de libros*. Ed. Florentino Zamora Lucas. Madrid, CSIC, 1961.
Rev: Juan M. Rozas, <u>RL</u>, XXI, Nos. 41-42 (1962), 199.

———. *Selección poética*. Ed. Jorge Rangel Guerra. In F. M. Zertuche, <u>Lope de Vega</u>, pp. 63-132. See Studies — General.

B. INDIVIDUAL POEMS

Vega, Lope de. *La Circe*. Ed. Charles V. Aubrun and Manuel Muñoz Cortés. Paris, Centre des Recherches de L'Institut d'Études Hispaniques, 1962. Pp. lxxxviii, 96. (<u>Chefs-d'Oeuvre des Lettres Hispaniques</u>, 2.)

———. *Filis*. Madrid, Ministerio de Educación Nac., 1962. Pp. 48.

———. *Pasión de Cristo*. Ed. Fray José María Guervós. Villava, Pamplona, Edit. Ope, 1962. Pp. 171. (<u>Col. Ope</u>.)

———. "Seis sonetos de Lope de Vega." In <u>Temas de Lope de Vega. Miscelánea literaria. Homenaje a Lope de Vega en el cuarto centenario de su nacimiento</u>, ed. Manuel Ruiz-Lagos de Castro, Granada, Colegio Mayor Isabel la Católica, Univ. de Granada, 1962, pp. 121-26.
The text of six sonnets beginning "No queda más lustroso y cristalino," "Ir y quedarse y con quedar partirse," "¿Qué tengo yo que mi amistad procuras?", "Desmayarse, atreverse, estar furioso," "Si estáis enfermos, dulces ojos claros," and "Muere la vida y vivo yo sin vida."

———. "Tres sonetos a Cristo, Nuestro Señor." In <u>Cuad. de Bellas Artes</u> (Mexico), III, No. 11 (1962), 14-15.

PROSE

INDIVIDUAL PROSE WORKS

Vega, Lope de. *La Dorotea*. Ed. Edwin S. Morby. Berkeley-Los Angeles, Univ. of California Press, 1958.
Rev: Kenneth S. Reid, <u>Durham Univ. Journal</u>, LIV(1962), 70-74; P. E. Russell, <u>MLR</u>, LVII(1962), 119-21.
Russell praises Morby's scholarship and editing, but wonders whether the work merits all his efforts. Russell finds it boring in many places. "Considered as a work of art, it seems to me to be a curious hybrid grown in a literary cul-de-sac."

———. *El hijo pródigo*, from <u>El peregrino en su patria</u>. See Editions — Drama — Individual Plays.

------. Pastores de Belén. 2nd ed. Barcelona, Juventud, 1962. Pp. 158.
A re-printing of the 1941 ed.

STUDIES

GENERAL, INCLUDING BIOGRAPHY

(Anon.) "Lope Félix de Vega Carpio (1562-1635)." Cuad. de Bellas Artes (Mexico), III, No. 11 (1962), 21-26.

(Anon.) "Tesis doctorales de interés literario de la Universidad de Madrid." RL, XXI, Nos. 41-42 (1962), 107-16.
A very useful list, including several items on Lope.

ABC (Madrid), Apr. 8, 1962.
"Número extraordinario" dedicated to Lope de Vega. Includes photographs, with a portrait of Lope, and several short articles: José María Pemán, "El estreno de anoche;" Ángel Valbuena Prat, "Lope, en su vida y en su época;" Luis Morales Oliver, "Los caminos hacia Dios en la poesía de Lope;" M. Fernández Almagro, "Lope, nobleza y pueblo;" José Camón Aznar, "El paisaje en Lope de Vega;" Joaquín de Entrambasaguas, "Lope de Vega, autor de ballets;" Rafael de Balbín, "Lope de Vega, maestro de la estrofa;" José María Castro Calvo, "Amor, tan solo (Unas breves notas a La Dorotea);" José Manuel Blecua, "Las novelas cortas de Lope;" José Vega, "El madrileñismo de Lope de Vega;" F. Bonmatí de Codecido, "De cuándo y cómo fue preso Lope de Vega;" Alfredo Marquerie, "El Fénix renace cada día;" Arturo Zabala, "Lope de Vega y Valencia;" Pedro Rocamora, "Invocación a Lope."

Abreu Gómez, Ermilo. "Máscara y fisonomía de Lope de Vega." Anuario de Letras (Mexico), II(1962), 227-31.

(Academia Española.) Real Academia Española. La casa de Lope de Vega. Nota preliminar de F. J. Sánchez Cantón. Madrid, Atles, 1962. Pp. 186.

Albarracín Teulón, Agustín. "Teatro, sociedad y medicina: La medicina en la obra de Lope de Vega." Bol. de la Soc. Española de Historia de la Medicina, II, No. 3 (1962), (7-13).

Allué y Morer, Fernando. "En versos de diamantes." Poesía Española, No. 110 (1962), 22-25.

Alonso, Dámaso. "Lope en Antequera." In <u>Del Siglo de Oro a este siglo de siglas</u> (<u>Notas y artículos a través de 350 años de letras españolas</u>), Madrid, Gredos, 1962, pp. 47-54. (<u>Bib. Románica Hispánica</u>, 7. <u>Campo Abierto</u>.)
This article is reprinted from <u>Fénix</u>, No. 2, 1935.

------. "Lope, sobre su propio abismo." <u>Blanco y Negro</u>, No. 2638 (1962), 77-79.

Alperi, Víctor. "El amor en Lope de Vega." <u>Poesía Española</u>, No. 116 (1962), 31-32.

Arce, David N. "Lope entre nosotros." <u>Bol de la Bib. Nac</u>. (Mexico), 2nd series, XIII, No. 3 (1962), 11-36.
Works by and about Lope in the Biblioteca Nacional, Mexico.

<u>Arriba</u> (Madrid), Apr. 8, 1962.
Special number dedicated to Lope de Vega. Includes photographs, and several short articles: Domingo Paniagua, "La quiniela de Lope;" Joaquín de Entrambasaguas, "Lope, figura simbólica en el paisaje del barroco;" Eugenia Serrano, "El Dorotheum de los amores de Lope;" Gaspar Gómez de la Serna, "Lope y el nivel histórico;" Gonzalo Torrente Ballester, "¿Es el teatro histórico de Lope un teatro de evasión?"; José Simón Díaz, "Lope de Vega ante sus posibles lectores de hoy;" Manuel Gallego Morell, "Fuenteovejuna, todos a una;" José Manuel Blecua, "Perdiendo respeto a Aristóteles;" Enrique de Aguinaga, "Brevísimo padrón de un madrileño consecuente;" Enrique Franco, "Lope de Vega en la música;" Pedro Pascual, "Cinco personas definen a un autor."

Aubrun, Charles V. "Idées de Lope de Vega sur le système du monde." In <u>Mélanges offerts à Marcel Bataillon par les Hispanistes français</u>, Bordeaux, Féret, 1962, pp. 304-17. (<u>BH</u>, 64 bis.)
Aubrun discusses Lope's attitude toward the universe, particularly in <u>La Circe</u>. Lope expresses his ideas in his own way, "plus naïve que savante," in his poetical compositions, especially <u>La Circe</u> and <u>comedias</u>.

Baeza, José. <u>Lope de Vega</u>. <u>Vida y obra del genio</u>. 3rd ed. Barcelona, Araluce, 1962. (<u>Los Grandes Hechos de los Grandes Hombres</u>.)

Bajarlia, Juan Jacobo. "Revisión de Lope de Vega." <u>Comentario</u> (Buenos Aires), IX, No. 39 (1962), 40-54.

Bentata, J. "Lope de Vega humano." <u>RNC</u> (Caracas), No. 155 (1962), 98-103.

Berenguer Carísimo, Arturo. "Lope de Vega, ese desconocido." <u>Estudios</u> (Buenos Aires), No. 537 (1962), 533-36.

Bergamín, José. "Un verso de Lope y Lope en un verso." <u>Primer Acto</u>, No. 37 (1962), 12-14.

<u>Blanco y Negro</u>. LXXII, No. 2638 (1962). "El hombre Lope de Vega. Número especial dedicado al Fénix.... Panorama gráfico y literario de Lope de Vega y su tiempo."
    Contains 72 pages of pictures; short articles by living critics (listed separately); and passages from the writings of Menéndez Pelayo, Ortega y Gasset, Amezúa, etc.

Brooks, John. "La alabanza en las obras de Lope de Vega." <u>Hispanó</u>, No. 16 (1962), 91-99.

Cabañas, Pablo. "A Lope de Vega." <u>Poesía Española</u>, No. 115 (1962), 32.
    A sonnet in honour of Lope.

------. "La lima de Lope." <u>Poesía Española</u>, No. 114 (1962), 25-30.

Cabezas, Juan Antonio. <u>Lope de Vega: Su vida, sus mejores páginas, su época</u>. Madrid, Nuevas Edit. Unidas, 1962. Pp. 273. (<u>Genio y Figura</u>, 7.)

Camón Aznar, José. "La arquitectura española en tiempos de Lope de Vega." <u>Villa de Madrid</u>, IV, No. 18 (1962), 37-44.

Cantón, Wilberto. "Homenaje a Lope de Vega." <u>Cuad. de Bellas Artes</u> (Mexico), III, No. 11 (1962), 5-6.

<u>Caracola</u> (Málaga). Nos. 121-22 (1962). "Homenaje a Lope de Vega."
    Contains material by Joaquín Caso Romero, Carmen Conde, Concha Lagos, Rafael Laffón, Blas de Otero; with selections from Lope's works.

Casona, Alejandro. "Tres mujeres en la vida de Lope." <u>Cuad. de Bellas Artes</u> (Mexico), III, No. 12 (1962), 56-64.

Catalogues of Exhibitions of Works (selected)

    British Museum. <u>Lope de Vega, 1562-1635. Catalogue of an Exhibition Held in the King's Library, September, 1962</u>. Compiled by H. G. Whitehead. London, British Museum, 1962. Pp. 39.

    Pennsylvania, University of. <u>Lope de Vega Carpio, 1562-1635. A Quadricentennial Exhibition</u>, Charles Patterson Van Pelt Library, 12 December 1962 — 15 February 1963. Pp. 11 (mimeographed).

Rutgers University, Romance Language Department, Section of Spanish. *Lope de Vega; Fourth Centennial, 1562-1962: Bibliographic and Iconographic Exhibition.* Foreword by F. Toro-Garland. New Brunswick, New Jersey, 1962. 12 leaves (mimeographed).

Toronto, University of. *Lope de Vega, 1562-1635: Catalogue of an Exhibition Held at the University of Toronto Library,* October 29 — November 17, 1962. Compiled by Warren T. McCready. Toronto, Univ. of Toronto Library, 1962. Pp. 15.

Chueca Goitia, Fernando. "La Corte en tiempos de Lope." *Villa de Madrid,* IV, No. 18 (1962), 51-60.

Colegio Santa María de las Nieves. *Última lección del curso académico 1961-62, dedicada a Lope de Vega en ocasión del centenario de su nacimiento.* Madrid, José Vicente Hernández, 1962.

Comba, Manuel. "A Note on Fashion and Atmosphere in the Time of Lope de Vega." *The Theatre Annual,* XIX(1962), 46-51.

Cossío, José María de. "Lope y la Montaña." *BBMP,* XXXVIII(1962), 213-29.

Cuadernos de Bellas Artes (Mexico). III, Nos. 11 and 12 (1962). Dedicated to Lope de Vega. The numbers contain articles (listed separately), and two portraits.

Dicenta, Manuel. "Lope y sus versos." *Primer Acto,* No. 37 (1962), 10-11.

Diego, Gerardo. "Lope de Vega." *Mundo Hispánico,* No. 171 (1962), 36-39.

------. "Primores de Lope." *Villa de Madrid,* IV, No. 18 (1962), 45-49.

Durán, Manuel. "Lope de Vega y el problema del manierismo." *Anuario de Letras* (Mexico), II(1962), 76-98.

Entrambasaguas, Joaquín de. *Góngora y Lope en la coyuntura del Renacimiento y del Barroco.* Madrid, Estades, Artes Gráficas, 1962. Pp. 62.
An opening lecture of the academic year, 1962-63.

------. "El Madrid literario de Lope de Vega." *Villa de Madrid,* IV, No. 18 (1962), 5-12.

------. *La temática de Lope de Vega en la enseñanza media.* Madrid, Ministerio de Educación Nac., 1962. Pp. 15. (*Bib. Cátedra.*)

Espinós Orlando, Juana. "Lope y Orfeo. Perfil musical del Fénix de los Ingenios." RIE, XX, No. 80 (1962), 303-13.
Lope's interest in, and knowledge of, music.

La Estafeta Literaria (Madrid), May 15, 1962.
Special number dedicated to Lope de Vega. Includes short articles: R. M., "Cuatro siglos y vigencia de Lope;" Domingo Paniagua, "Lope en el Estadio;" José María Pemán, "Belisa, la melindrosa;" Santiago Arauz de Robles, "Lope y el Emperador;" Rafael Laffón, "Lope y unas uvas;" L. Jiménez Martos, "La Gatomaquia, último Lope;" Juan Emilio Aragonés, "A Lope lo que es de Lope;" Luis Sastre, "Cerca y lejos de Lope;" Leopoldo Rodríguez Alcalde, "Lope en la tierra y en el cielo;" José María Otero, "Lope de Vega, autor de películas;" Joaquín de Entrambasaguas, "La pasión amorosa de Lope y la lira erótica del Fénix;" Mariano Baquero Goyanes, "Narración y diálogo en Lope de Vega;" Juan Ruiz Peña, "Lope, poeta de la soledad;" José Hierro, "Lope en el corral de comedias;" José Castellano, "Lope y el teatro poético;" Federico Carlos Sainz de Robles, "Madrid en el teatro de Lope."

García Nieto, José. "Lope de Vega, estilo español." Villa de Madrid, IV, No. 18 (1962), 19-27.

Gordoa, Marcos. "Lope de Vega considerado como humanista." Abside, XXVI(1962), 375-408.

Gringoire, Pedro. "Portento y recordación de Lope de Vega." Horizontes (Mexico), V, No. 27 (1962), 9-11.

Hornedo, R. M. de. "Lope y los jesuitas." Razón y Fe, CLXVI(1962), 405-22.

Icaza, Francisco A. de. Lope de Vega, sus amores y sus odios y otros estudios. Ed. E. Abreu Gómez. Mexico, Porrúa, 1962. Pp. xxxvi, 348. (Col. de Escritores Mexicanos, 82.)

López, M. "Lope, ausente y presente." Rev. de la Institución Teresiana (Madrid), L(1962), 3.

------. "El dolor en la vida y en la poesía de Lope." Rev. de la Institución Teresiana, L(1962), 5-6.

López Ibor, J. J. "La fiera melancolía, la tristeza, los celos." Blanco y Negro, No. 2638 (1962), 75-76.

Lozoya, El marqués de (Juan Contreras y López de Ayala). "Lope de Vega y el arte de su tiempo." Villa de Madrid, IV, No. 18 (1962), 13-18.

Luis, Leopoldo de. "Una mujer." Poesía Española, No. 114 (1962), 30.
A sonnet in honour of Lope.

Mancini, Guido. "Lope de Vega." Cultura e Scuola, I, No. 3 (1962), 65-69.

Marquerie, Alfredo. "Soneto a Lope de Vega." Villa de Madrid, IV, No. 18 (1962), 28.

Martín Calpena, Miguel. "El arrepentimiento como elemento de creación en Lope de Vega." In Temas de Lope de Vega. Miscelánea literaria, Granada, Univ. de Granada, 1962, pp. 79-92.

Molnar, Gal Peter. "A négyszáz éves Lope de Vega (1562-1635)." Népszabadság (Budapest), Nov. 25, 1962, p. 12.
The fourth centenary of Lope's birth.

Monleón, José. "Acabando el IV centenario de Lope de Vega." Primer Acto, No. 37 (1962), 2-4.

Montoliu, Manuel de. "El beato Juan de Ávila y Lope de Vega." Miscelánea Filológica dedicada a Mons. A. Griera, II (Barcelona, 1962), 153-58.

Nandino, Elías. "El Fénix de los Ingenios." Cuad. de Bellas Artes (Mexico), III, No. 11 (1962), 17-20.

Ocampo, Fernando. "Lope de Vega, lírico humano (1562-1635)." Revista Javeriana (Bogotá), LVIII, No. 209 (1962), 675-80.

Oliver, Antonio. "El arte y la naturaleza en Lope de Vega." Poesía Española, No. 114 (1962), 31-32.

------. "Lope de Vega como padre." Poesía Española, No. 116 (1962), 28-31.

Oostendorp, H. Th. El conflicto entre el honor y el amor en la literatura española hasta el siglo XVII. The Hague, Inst. de Estudios Hispánicos ... de la Univ. de Utrecht, 1962. Pp. 215.
A useful study leading up to Lope.

Orozco, Emilio. "Las Soledades y Lope de Vega." Ínsula, XVII, No. 190 (1962), 1.
The subtitle is "Aspectos desconocidos de una polémica y nuevo índice de textos inéditos."

Pemán, José María. Lo tradicional y lo moderno en Lope de Vega: Edad Media y Renacimiento. Madrid, Edit. Magisterio Español, 1962. Pp. 22.
An address delivered in the Instituto de España, Jan. 27, 1962.

Pérez de Montalván, Juan. "Fama póstuma a la vida y muerte del Dr. Frey Lope Félix de Vega Carpio." In Temas de Lope de Vega. Miscelánea literaria, Granada, Univ. de Granada, 1962, pp. 105-20.

Peyton, Myron A. "The Retrato as Motif and Device in Lope de Vega." RomN, IV, No. 1 (1962), 51-57.
References to miniatures by Felipe de Liaño, and to portraits mentioned and described in some of Lope's works.

Plavskin, Z. I., V. G. Joltsova, L. A. Shur and D. E. Mijalshi. Lope de Vega: Bibliografiia russkikh perevodov i kriticheskoi literatury na russkom iazyke 1735-1961. Moscow, Izdatel'stvo Vsesoiuznoi Knizhnoi Palaty, 1962. Pp. 139.
Russian translations and critical literature on Lope. The volume contains 746 items.

Pulbere, Ion. "Lope de Vega. 400 ani de la naşterea lui." Tribuna (Bucharest), VI, No. 48 (1962), 12.
Lope de Vega 400 years from his birth.

Reichenberger, Arnold G. "Competitive Imagery in Spanish Poetry." Annali dell'Istituto Universitario Orientale (Sezione Romanza), IV (1962), 83-97.
This was a paper read at the FILLM, Liège, Sept., 1960. An abstract was printed in Langue et Littérature, FILLM, VIII Congress, 1962, pp. 265-66. The study contains brief references to Lope's dramatic and non-dramatic poetry.

Rocamora, Pedro. "Lope de Vega o la estética del optimismo." Arbor, LII, Nos. 199-200 (1962), 5-15 (or 275-85; double pagination).
Lope's joie de vivre.

Rozas, Juan M., and Antonio Quilis. "El lopismo de Jiménez Patón (Góngora y Lope en la Elocuencia española en arte)." RL, XXI, Nos. 41-42 (1962), 35-54.
The author of the Elocuencia (Toledo, 1604) is the first lopista-rhetorician and admired Lope as "dramaturgo, culto, lírico y épico." The writers of the article list the works of Lope cited by Jiménez. Although Jiménez cites various poets from Juan de Mena on, he cites Lope by far the most frequently. "Góngora y Quevedo no le hacen sombra."

Ruiz Fornells, Enrique. "IV Centenario del nacimiento de Lope de Vega. Celebración del aniversario (1562-1962)." RL, XXI, Nos. 41-42 (1962), 117-53.
An important listing of commemorative events.

------. "IV Centenario del nacimiento de Lope de Vega. Celebración del aniversario (1562-1962)." RL, XXII, Nos. 43-44 (1962), 211-53.

"Habiéndose publicado ya en el número anterior la relación de los hechos más importantes de los seis primeros meses del año 1962, sobre el IV Centenario del nacimiento de Lope Félix de Vega Carpio (1562-1635), se continúa con los seis meses restantes. Con ello termina este orden cronológico que sin ser exhaustivo refleja los actos de más relieve celebrados en honor del Fénix." A second, most important article on the Quadricentennial Year, giving, above all, newspaper references to the Year's events.

Sainz de Robles, Federico Carlos. Lope de Vega: Retrato, horóscopo, vida y transfiguración. Madrid, Espasa-Calpe, 1962. Pp. 423.
  The reprinting of the "Estudio preliminar" of the Madrid, Aguilar, 1946 ed. of Lope's Obras escogidas, I, Teatro. (It also appeared in 1958.) One new item of bibliography is added: the Simón Díaz-José Prades Ensayo de una bibliografía....

Salvá, Jaime. "Aclarando un texto epistolar de Lope." RL, XXI, Nos. 41-42 (1962), 77-78.
  The author seeks to elucidate a reference to Góngora by Lope in one of his letters to the Duke of Sessa. Salvá believes that he is punning on the name and unrepentance of Herrezuelo, a Lutheran of Toro, who was burned as a heretic in 1559.

Sánchez, José. Academias literarias del Siglo de Oro español. Madrid, Gredos, 1961.
  Rev: Ramón Esquer Torres, Arbor, LII, Nos. 199-200 (1962), 111-13 (or 381-83).

Sánchez, Rafael. "La biblioteca del profesor Entrambasaguas." El Libro Español, V, No. 52 (1962), 103-08.
  A brief description of Joaquín de Entrambasaguas' private library, including his Lopeana.

Sánchez Escribano, Federico. "Lope de Vega según una alusión de John Dryden." Hispanó, No. 16 (1962), 101-02.

Shepard, Sanford. El Pinciano y las teorías literarias del Siglo de Oro. Madrid, Gredos, 1962. Pp. 227. (Bib. Románica Hispánica. Estudios y Ensayos, 58.)
  Lope de Vega: pp. 194-95. Includes reference to the Arte nuevo.

Simón Díaz, José. "Lope de Vega en las librerías españolas." El Libro Español, V, No. 52 (1962), 97-101.

Simón Díaz, José, and Juana de José Prades. Ensayo de una bibliografía de ... Lope de Vega. Nuevos estudios. Madrid, CSIC, 1961.
  Rev: Juan M. Rozas, RL, XXI, Nos. 41-42 (1962), 19.

Tasis, Rafael. "Lope de Vega, el autor peregrino en su vida." Horizontes (Mexico), V, No. 27 (1962), 6-8.

Trueblood, Alan S. "Lope de Vega: Four Hundred Years Ago and Now." *Brown Daily Herald*, VII, No. 8, Supplement (Dec. 10, 1962), 9-10, 14-16.

Varela, José Luis. "Lope recibe a Celestina." *Blanco y Negro*, No. 2638 (1962), 85-87.

Vásquez Dodero, José Luis. "Biografía minúscula de un español pasmoso." *Blanco y Negro*, No. 2638 (1962), 58-65.

Villa de Madrid. IV, No. 18 (1962).
    Special number in honour of Lope. See separate items. Includes an "Editorial" by José María Díaz-Guijarro, and also photographs of Lope's house.

Vosters, S. A. "Lope de Vega y Titelmans (Cómo el Fénix se representaba el universo)." *RL*, XXI, Nos. 41-42 (1962), 5-33.
    Frans Titelmans, a native of the province of Limburg and a Franciscan, became famous for his violent attacks against Erasmus. "Como la ortodoxia de Titelmans, quien glorificó a Carlos V como defensor de la iglesia, y cuyo hermano era inquisidor, estaba fuera de duda, no había inconveniente para que Lope de Vega, familiar de la Inquisición, mencionara la obra de este flamenco 'amigo de Dios y del Rey'." Vosters locates nineteen of Lope's citations from Titelmans. He concludes by showing that Titelmans "más que nadie, es quien nos enseña cómo el Fénix se figuraba el universo."

------. "Dos adiciones a mi artículo 'Lope de Vega y Titelmans'." *RL*, XXII, Nos. 43-44 (1962), 90.
    Vosters adds a note on the works of Titelmans in the Biblioteca Nacional and gives two instances in the *Isidro* of Lope's indebtedness to him.

------. "Lope de Vega y Hadriano Junio. La geografía como expresión del ansia de mandar." *RL*, XXII, Nos. 43-44 (1962), 29-47.
    Adriaen de Jonghe (Hoorn, Holland, 1511-1575). Lope quite frequently cites his *Nomenclator omnium rerum*, and makes use of material contained therein.

Wardropper, Bruce W. "On the Fourth Centenary of Lope de Vega's Birth." *Drama Survey*, II(1962), 117-29.

Whitehead, Harold G. "Lope de Vega, 1562-1635. An Exhibition Held in the King's Library, September, 1962." *British Museum Quarterly*, XXV(1962), 70-74.
    See Catalogue, above.

Zamora Vicente, Alonso. *Lope de Vega, su vida y su obra*. Madrid, Gredos, 1961.
    Rev: J. L. Cano, *Ínsula*, No. 182 (1962), 8-9; S. G., *PSA*, XXVII (1962), 88-92; M. D. M., *Letras Hispánicas* (São Paulo), II

(1962), 45-46; E. Martino, <u>Humanidades</u> (Colmillas), No. 31 (1962), 132; Edwin S. Morby, <u>Hisp</u>, XLV(1962), 824-25; Mario Pinna, <u>Belfagor</u>, XVII(1962), 610-13; J. A. van Praag, <u>Neophilologus</u>, XLVI(1962), 245.

From the Morby review (p. 824): "As announced on the cover flap, Zamora Vicente's <u>Lope de Vega</u> inaugurates a Gredos series of works by specialists for a popular audience. It is an auspicious beginning. Unpretentious as it is, it should also prove one of the real contributions to the quadricentennial. It is not, as the timing might suggest, an improvisation, but a systematic introduction, based to a refreshingly large extent on a direct reading of Lope, of the recognized authorities, and many of the latest findings and critical assessments...."

Zertuche, Francisco M. <u>Lope de Vega</u>. Monterrey, Univ. de Nuevo León, 1962. Pp. 132.

This volume is a <u>número extraordinario</u> (Nos. 3-4) of Vol. V, segunda época, of <u>Armas y Letras</u>, Rev. de la Univ. de Nuevo León. It contains a collection of works by Zertuche, published over a period of years. The studies are followed by a selection of Lope's poetry prepared by Jorge Rangel Guerra. The divisions of the work are as follows: I. "Vida y literatura" (pp. 9-26); II. "El caudal dramático" (pp. 27-45); III. "<u>La Dorotea</u>" (pp. 47-61); "Selección poética" (pp. 63-132).

DRAMA

A. GENERAL

Arjona, J. H. "Improper Use of Consonantal Rhyme in Lope de Vega and its Significance Concerning the Authorship of Doubtful Plays." <u>Hispanó</u>, No. 16 (1962), 7-39.

Arozamena, Jesús María de. <u>Algunos aspectos del teatro de Lope de Vega</u>. Madrid, Private, 1962. Pp. 35.

Baader, Horst. "Die Eifersucht in der spanischen <u>Comedia</u> des goldenen Zeitalters." <u>RF</u>, LXXIV(1962), 318-44.
Includes references to Lope.

"<u>Encuesta</u>. Responden cuatro directores de obras de Lope: José Tamayo, José Luis Alonso, Adolfo Marsillach, Ángel F. Montesinos." <u>Primer Acto</u>, No. 37 (1962), 5-9.

Entrambasaguas, Joaquín de. "La convivencia de Lope de Vega y Tirso de Molina." <u>Estudios</u>, XVIII(1962), 387-97.

Fichter, William L. "The Probable Sources of Certain Character Names Used by Lope de Vega." <u>HR</u>, XXX(1962), 267-74.

Froldi, Rinaldo. *Il teatro valenzano e l'origine della commedia barocca*. Pisa, Edit. Tecnico-Scientifica, 1962. Pp. 112.
Rev: E. Juliá Martínez, RL, XXI, Nos. 41-42 (1962), 181-83.
The reviewer gives a brief summary of the contents of the volume, which includes an examination of "the true position of Lope in his time." The monograph consists of three chapters, to serve as a basis for a later study of Guillén de Castro.

Gatti, José Francisco (ed.). *El teatro de Lope de Vega: Artículos y estudios*. Buenos Aires, Edit. Universitaria de Buenos Aires, 1962. Pp. 221.
The volume contains the reprinting of several earlier studies: Amado Alonso, "Lope de Vega y sus fuentes" (pp. 193-220) — reprinted from Thesaurus, VIII, 1952; Charles V. Aubrun and José F. Montesinos, "Peribáñez" (pp. 13-49) — a reprint of the prologue to their ed. of Paris, 1943, and translated by Ricardo J. Velzi; Marcel Bataillon, "El villano en su rincón" (pp. 148-92) — reprinted from BH, LI, 1949 and LII, 1950, and translated by Elsa Tabernig; G. W. Ribbans, "Significado y estructura de Fuenteovejuna" (pp. 91-123) — reprinted from BHS, XXX, 1954, and translated by Horacio Martínez; Leo Spitzer, "Un tema central y su equivalente estructural en Fuenteovejuna" (pp. 124-47) — reprinted from HR, XXIII, 1955, and translated by Ricardo J. Velzi; Edward M. Wilson, "Imágenes y estructura en Peribáñez" (pp. 50-90) — reprinted from BH, LI, 1949, and translated by Rafael Ferreres.

Georgescu, Paul Alex. "Teatrul lui Lope de Vega în lumina actualității (la 400 de ani di la nașterea lui Lope de Vega)." Rev. de Filolgie Romanica și Germanică (Bucharest), VI(1962), 335-72.
Lope's theatre in the light of today.

Heidenreich, Helmut. *Figuren und Komik in den spanischen "Entremeses" des Goldenen Zeitalters*. Doct. diss., Ludwig Maximilians Univ., Munich, 1962. Pp. 221.

Hudson, Herman Cleophus. *The Development of Dramatic Culture in England and Spain during the Elizabethan Period and the Golden Age*. Unpub. doct. diss., Univ. of Michigan, 1962. (DA, XXIII, 235.)
"The discussion is arbitrarily limited to commentators roughly contemporary with William Shakespeare (1564-1616) and Lope de Vega (1562-1635). An effort has been made to include the most articulate exponents of all major points of view."

Kennedy, Ruth Lee. "Las mangas cortas in Lope's Theatre (1611-1616): Their Importance as a Tentative Norm for Chronology." In *Homage to Charles Blaise Qualia*, Lubbock, Texas, Texas Technological College, 1962, pp. 89-104.

> This change in fashion, in which the long tight sleeve gave way to a shorter, looser one, took place in 1611, and is reflected in some of Lope's plays.

Koremblit, Bernardo Ezequiel. "Cuadrugentésimo jocundo y dramático de Lope de Vega." Comentario (Buenos Aires), No. 34 (1962), 27-39.

Lefebvre, Alfredo. La fama en el teatro de Lope (Un aspecto en la elaboración dramática). Madrid, Taurus, 1962. Pp. 74. (Cuad. Taurus.)

MacCurdy, Raymond R. "Homage to Lope de Vega." The Theatre Annual, XIX(1962), i-vi.

Marín, Diego. "The Rôle of Dramatic Versification in Lope de Vega." The Theatre Annual, XIX(1962), 27-42.

------. Uso y función de la versificación dramática en Lope de Vega. Valencia, Castalia, 1962. Pp. 120. (Estudios de Hispanó, 2.)

McCready, Warren T. La heráldica en las obras de Lope de Vega y sus contemporáneos. Toronto, Private, 1962. Pp. xii, 470.
Rev: Juan M. Rozas, RL, XXI, Nos. 41-42 (1962), 195-96.
> McCready's dissertation, Chicago, 1961, in published form. It considers heraldry in Lope for its significance for Lope's biography, for its meaning for the people of Lope's time and for its value as an indication of Lope's authorship of doubtful plays. McCready read almost a thousand comedias of Lope and other dramatists. The study is obviously a very thorough one. Having determined Lope's distinctive use and manner of description of heraldry, the author claims for Lope nineteen plays that Morley and Bruerton (Chronology) consider doubtful; he rejects from the same Morley and Bruerton list sixteen others in which the passages on heraldry indicate an author other than Lope.

Miramón, Alberto. "El Nuevo Mundo en el universo dramático de Lope de Vega." Bol. Cultural y Bibliográfico (Bogotá), V(1962), 943-50.

Montero Padilla, José. "Teatro clásico español." Arbor, LIII, No. 203 (1962), 132-40 (or 344-52).
> The article is inspired by Sainz de Robles' Lope de Vega: Retrato, horóscopo..., Madrid, 1962; and also makes reference to several other recent works on the Spanish theatre of the Golden Age, including Entrambasaguas' Lope de Vega y su tiempo, 2 vols., Barcelona, 1961, Zamora Vicente's Lope de Vega: Su vida y su obra, Madrid, 1961, and Juan Antonio Cabezas' Lope de Vega: Su vida, sus mejores páginas, su época, Madrid, 1962.

Morley, S. G., and R. W. Tyler. *Los nombres de personajes en las comedias de Lope de Vega.* 2 vols. Berkeley, Univ. of California Press, 1961.
Rev: R. Baehr, *NS*, No. 5 (1962), 246-47; W. Bahner, *Deutsche Literaturzeitung*, LXXXIII, Nos. 7-8 (1962), 636-37; J.-L. Flecniakoska, *RLR*, LXXV (1962), 84-85; Raymond R. MacCurdy, *Hisp*, XLV (1962), 584-85; Arnold G. Reichenberger, *HR*, XXX (1962), 160-62; J. E. Varey, *BHS*, XXXIX (1962), 122-23.
From the Reichenberger review (p. 162): "The evaluation of this mass of material is essentially still to be done...." (The review had stated above: "The authors are, of course, aware of the fact that their 'someras notas' are far from exhausting the research possibilities opened up by their work....") "Yet, beyond its immediate purpose, the study of Lope's nomenclature, *Los nombres* has its importance as a tool. The list of *categorías* is imposing in its variety and Lope's presentation of various types, from *rey* to *villano*, can now be studied. Furthermore, the book can be useful, as it actually was in a recent case, in identifying manuscripts lacking a title page or *arrachements* of *sueltas* or *partes* through the combination of the characters. The editor of an annotated play can now search for appearances of such rare fictitious names as Bisanzón or he can easily verify how often and in what capacity a given historical character has been brought on the stage by Lope."

Olmos, Francisco. "García Lorca, el teatro clásico y Lope de Vega." *Primer Acto*, No. 37 (1962), 15-27.

Orozco Díaz, Emilio. "Teatro y barroco (Notas para un ensayo)." In *Temas de Lope de Vega. Miscelánea literaria*, Granada, Univ. de Granada, 1962, pp. 9-22.

Palacios, Leopoldo. "Lope de Vega y el vulgo necio." *Blanco y Negro*, No. 2638 (1962), 89-90.

Pulbere, Ion. "Lope de Vega, și dramaturgia Renașterii." *Steaua* (Bucharest), XIII, No. 11 (1962), 60-65.
Lope de Vega and the theatre of the Renaissance.

Reese, Lowell Grant. *Lope de Vega and Shakespeare: A Comparative Study of Tragicomic Style.* Unpub. doct. diss., Univ. of Washington, 1962. (*DA*, XXIV, 285-86.)
"Lope de Vega's and Shakespeare's dramaturgies are mainly dissimilar, but they both seem to have used the classical dramatic precepts widely current during the Renaissance in constructing their plays and to have used drama as an imitation of the reality they each perceived."

Rothberg, Irving P. "El agente cómico de Lope de Vega." *Hispanó*, No. 16 (1962), 69-90.

Ruiz-Lagos de Castro, Manuel. "Algunas notas de estilística pictórica para los autos sacramentales de Lope de Vega." In *Temas de Lope de Vega. Miscelánea literaria*, Granada, Univ. de Granada, 1962, pp. 23-55.

Shergold, N. D., and J. E. Varey. "Notas sobre la cronología de seis comedias de Lope de Vega." *Hispanó*, No. 16 (1962), 1-5. The plays are: 1. *La boba para los otros y discreta para sí*; 2. *El labrador venturoso*; 3. *La merced en el castigo*; 4. *La moza de cántaro*; 5. *Por la puente, Juana*; 6. *Los Tellos de Meneses* (2ª. parte).

Very, Francis George. *The Spanish Corpus Christi Procession: A Literary and Folkloric Study*. Valencia, Castalia, 1962. Pp. xii, 160. (*Estudios de Hispanó*, 1.)

Villarejo, Oscar M. "Fechas auténticas de varias comedias compuestas y autografiadas por Lope de Vega." *Hispanó*, No. 16 (1962), 41-68.

B. INDIVIDUAL PLAYS

El acero de Madrid

Fichter, W. L. "Un ejemplo del genio creador de Lope de Vega: *El acero de Madrid*." *MLN*, LXXVII(1962), 512-18.

Monleón, José. "IV Certamen Nacional de Teatro Universitario. Una sola representación elogiable: *El acero de Madrid*, bajo la dirección de Eugenio García Toledano." *Primer Acto*, No. 34 (1962), 57-58.

El arauco domado

Toda Oliva, Eduardo. "*El arauco* de Lope de Vega." *Nuestro Tiempo* (Madrid), XVII(1962), 48-71.

La bella malmaridada

Díez Crespo, M. "*La bella malmaridada* en el María Guerrero." *Arbor*, LII, No. 197 (1962), 90-92.

Monleón, José. "Crítica de *La bella malmaridada* de Lope de Vega." *Primer Acto*, No. 32 (1962), 41-42.

Los Benavides

Reichenberger, Arnold G. "The Autograph Manuscript of Lope de Vega's Play *Los Benavides*." *The Library Chronicle*, XXVIII(1962), 106-08.

La boba para los otros y discreta para sí

Shergold and Varey. "Notas sobre la cronología...." See Studies — Drama — General.

El Brasil restituido

Sánchez, Alberto. "Ante un centenario: *El Brasil restituido* de Lope de Vega." *Rev. de Cultura Brasileña,* I(1962), 203-15.

El caballero del milagro

Schroeder, Juan Germán. "Sobre la refundición de *El caballero del milagro*." *Primer Acto,* No. 37 (1962), 28.

La creación del mundo

Glaser, Edward. "Lope de Vega's *La creación del mundo y primera culpa del hombre*." *Annali dell'Istituto Universitario Orientale* (Sezione Romanza), IV(1962), 29-56.
  Glaser believes that the play is Lope's, and that its central theme does not turn around "death's sway over mankind," as Menéndez Pelayo would have it, but that Lope "grafts upon the opening chapters of Genesis an entirely different eschatological message, namely the great Christian promise of life eternal."

La fianza satisfecha

Barnstone, Willis. "Lope's Leonido: An Existential Hero." *TDR,* VII(1962), 56-57.
  Barnstone, whose translation of *La fianza satisfecha* is in this same issue of *TDR*, states that "Leonido is a natural existential hero," for he finds the world absurd and "embarks on a wild journey of rejection and destruction" in which he commits numerous vile acts, indulging in the sinful desire for self-knowledge that was the impelling motive of Lear, Oedipus, Faust. (It might be noted that the M.-B. *Chronology,* p. 286, lists the play as one of doubtful authenticity.)

Rank, Otto. "The Incest of Amnon and Tamar." *TDR,* VII(1962), 38-43.
  Rank, the famous psychiatrist, discusses the use of the motif of sibling love in *La fianza satisfecha* especially. The translation is by Bayard Q. Morgan, and the essay is taken from an earlier volume by Rank. (Rank published in Leipzig, 1926, a monograph on *Das Inzest-Motiv in Dichtung und Sage: Einer Psychologie des dichterischen Schaffens*.)

Valbuena Prat, Ángel. "A Freudian Character in Lope de Vega." *TDR*, VII(1962), 44-55.
    This is the reprinting of an essay first written in 1931, as the editor of *TDR* reminds us. The essay deals with Leonido of *La fianza satisfecha*.

Fuenteovejuna

(Anon.) "*Fuenteovejuna*: The Anatomy of a Drama." *Brown Daily Herald*, Supplement, VII, No. 8 (Dec. 10, 1962), 12-13.

Alonso, Dámaso. "*Fuenteovejuna* y la tragedia popular." In *Del Siglo de Oro a este siglo de siglas*, Madrid, Gredos, 1962, pp. 90-94.

Casalduero, Joaquín. "*Fuenteovejuna*." In *Estudios sobre el teatro español. Lope de Vega, Guillén de Castro, Cervantes, Tirso de Molina, Ruiz de Alarcón, Calderón, Moratín, Duque de Rivas*, Madrid, Gredos, 1962, pp. 9-44. (*Bib. Románica Hispánica*, 54.)
    This is the article published in 1943 (*RFH*, V) and in the English translation of Ruth Whittredge in 1959 (*TDR*, V).

Gallego Morell, Manuel. "Fuenteovejuna, todos a una." See Studies— General (*Arriba*).

Green, Ronald. "Karl Marx and Lope." *Brown Daily Herald*, Supplement, VII, No. 8 (Dec. 10, 1962), 12-13.

Miserocchi, Manlio. "Festival internazionale del teatro di prosa a Venezia." *Nuova Antologia*, CDLXXXVI(1962), 280-84.
    Reference to a performance of *Fuenteovejuna*.

Monleón, José. "Crítica de *Fuenteovejuna* de Lope de Vega." *Primer Acto*, No. 34 (1962), 45; and No. 37 (1962), 61-62.

Pring-Mill, R. D. F. "Sententiousness in *Fuenteovejuna*." *TDR*, VII (1962), 5-37.
    The author discusses sixty-three *sentencias* of the play as he shows how "Lope uses such aphoristic commonplaces to point out the relationship between the general and the particular — between abstract universal principles and the particular situations facing the characters in the play."

Ribbans, G. W. "Significado y estructura de *Fuenteovejuna*." See Studies — Drama — General (Gatti).

Spitzer, Leo. "Un tema central y su equivalente estructural en *Fuenteovejuna*." See Studies — Drama — General (Gatti).

El gran duque de Moscovia

Lawson, Richard H. "*El gran duque de Moscovia*: A Likely Source for Lessing." RomN, IV, No. 1 (1962), 58-62.
   Das Horoskop.

La Imperial de Otón

Strzalkowa, Maria. *Studia Polsko-Hiszpanskie*. Cracow, Nakladem Uniwersytetu Jagiellonskiego, 1960.
   Rev: J. M. Díez Taboada, RL, XXII, Nos. 43-44 (1962), 272.

El labrador venturoso

Shergold and Varey. "Notas sobre la cronología...." See Studies — Drama — General.

La mayor desgracia de Carlos V

María y Campos, Armando. "Temas lopianos. Hernán Cortés en *La mayor desgracia de Carlos V*." *Cuad. de Bellas Artes* (Mexico), III, No. 12 (1962), 53-55.

Los melindres de Belisa

Pemán, José María. "Belisa, la melindrosa." See Studies — General (*Estafeta Literaria*).

La merced en el castigo

Shergold and Varey. "Notas sobre la cronología...." See Studies — Drama — General.

La moza de cántaro

Shergold and Varey. "Notas sobre la cronología...." See Studies — Drama — General.

El nuevo mundo descubierto por Cristóbal Colón

Rodríguez Bachiller, Ángel. "Lope de Vega y el Nuevo Mundo." *Mundo Hispánico*, No. 175 (1962), 28-31.

Las paces de los reyes y judía de Toledo

Schweitzer, Jerome W. "The Jewess of Toledo: Three Unstudied Dramatic Adaptations of the Raquel-Alfonso VIII Legend." RomN, IV, No. 1 (1962), 21-29.
   Chevalier, *Rachel, ou la Belle juive* (1803), Lucas, *Rachel* (1849) and Lázaro Montero de la Puente, *Doña Fermosa* (1955).

Soons, C. Alan. "The Emblematic Technique in <u>Las paces de los reyes</u>." <u>The Theatre Annual</u>, XIX(1962), 43-45.

<u>Peribáñez y el comendador de Ocaña</u>

Aubrun and Montesinos. "<u>Peribáñez</u>." See Studies — Drama — General (Gatti).

Salomon, Noël. "Toujours la date de <u>Peribáñez y el comendador de Ocaña</u>." In <u>Mélanges offerts à Marcel Bataillon par les Hispanistes français</u>, Bordeaux, Féret, 1962, pp. 613-43. (<u>BH</u>, 64 bis.)
    Salomon changes his mind about the date of the play (cf. <u>BH</u>, LXIII, 1961). He believes that the model of the Comendador was Rodrigo Calderón, who became Comendador de Ocaña and a Caballero de Santiago in Nov.-Dec., 1611. In 1612, it was claimed that Calderón was not the son of Francisco Calderón but the bastard son of the Duque de Alba, don Fadrique. Because of these facts and the reference in the <u>comedia</u> to <u>grandeza</u> (verse 873) in connection with Calderón's aspirations to <u>grandeza</u>, Salomon puts the date between the autumn of 1612 and Dec., 1613, the date of the earliest <u>aprobación</u>.

Wilson, E. M. "Imágenes y estructura en <u>Peribáñez</u>." See Studies — Drama — General (Gatti).

<u>El perro del hortelano</u>

Díez Crespo, M. "<u>El perro del hortelano</u> en el Español." <u>Arbor</u>, LIII, No. 204 (1962), 109-11 (or 473-75).

<u>Por la puente, Juana</u>

Doménech, Ricardo. "Crítica de <u>Por la puente, Juana</u>." <u>Primer Acto</u>, No. 34 (1962), 48.

Shergold and Varey. "Notas sobre la cronología...." See Studies — Drama — General.

<u>Los Tellos de Meneses</u> (segunda parte)

Shergold and Varey. "Notas sobre la cronología...." See Studies — Drama — General.

<u>El triunfo de la fe</u>

Hornedo, R. M. de. "Lope historiador: <u>El triunfo de la fe</u>." <u>Humanidades</u> (Colmillas), XIV, No. 33 (1962), 313-44.

El villano en su rincón

Bataillon, M. "El villano en su rincón." See Studies — Drama — General (Gatti).

Entrambasaguas, Joaquín de. *Lope de Vega y su tiempo. Estudio especial de "El villano en su rincón." Estudios.* 2nd ed. Barcelona, Teide, 1962. Pp. 431. (*Col. Hilani*, 12.)

------. *Lope de Vega y su tiempo. Estudio especial de "El villano en su rincón." Textos.* 2nd ed. Barcelona, Teide, 1962. Pp. 352. (*Col. Hilani*, 13.)
  The second edition of the same title published in 1961. The two volumes form companion volumes.

C. THE *ARTE NUEVO*

Oliver, Antonio. "El arte y la naturaleza." *Poesía Española*, No. 114 (1962), 31-32.
  Makes reference to the *Arte nuevo*.

Shepard, S. *El Pinciano y las teorías literarias....* See Studies — General.

POETRY

  A. GENERAL

Alonso, Dámaso. *Poesía española. Ensayo de métodos y límites estilísticos.* 4th ed. Madrid, Gredos, 1962.

Pierce, Frank. *La poesía épica del Siglo de Oro.* Madrid, Gredos, 1961.
  Rev: Wolfram Krömer, *RF*, LXXIV(1962), 458-60; Winston A. Reynolds, *Hisp*, XLV(1962), 826-27; Edward M. Wilson, *BHS*, XXXIX(1962), 196-99.

Simón Díaz, José, and Luciana Calvo Ramos. *Siglos de Oro: Índice de justas poéticas.* Madrid, CSIC, 1962. Pp. 111. (*Cuad. Bibliográficos*, 5.)
  A list of 139 works having to do with *justas poéticas* and similar matters. Includes Lope.

Subirá, José. "El villancico literario-musical. Bosquejo histórico." *RL*, XXII, Nos. 43-44 (1962), 5-27.
  Passing reference to Lope.

Víctor, Antonio. "Lo humano y lo divino en la poesía de Lope de Vega." <u>Poesía Española,</u> No. 115 (1962), 30-32.

B. INDIVIDUAL POEMS

La Circe

Aubrun, Charles V. "Idées de Lope de Vega sur le système du monde." See Studies — General.

La Dragontea

Rodríguez Gómez, Juan Carlos. "Crítica impresionista de <u>La Dragontea</u>." In <u>Temas de Lope de Vega. Miscelánea literaria,</u> Granada, Univ. de Granada, 1962, pp. 57-78.

La Gatomaquia

Jiménez Martos, L. "<u>La Gatomaquia,</u> último Lope." See Studies — General (<u>Estafeta Literaria</u>).

El Isidro

Vosters, S. A. "Dos adiciones..." (1962). See Studies — General.

El laurel de Apolo

Rozas, Juan M. "Lope de Vega y los escritores ciudad-realeños elogiados en <u>El laurel de Apolo.</u>" <u>Cuad. de Estudios Manchegos,</u> XII(1962), 75-87. (Ciudad Real, Inst. de Estudios Manchegos, 1962. Pp. 16.)

Romance(s)

Laza Zerón, Manuel. "Algo más sobre un romance morisco de Lope: La autobiografía y la novela morisca." In <u>Temas de Lope de Vega. Miscelánea literaria,</u> Granada, Univ. de Granada, 1962, pp. 93-103.

Méndez de Asturias, Luz. <u>Estudio de los manuscritos de los "Romances de la pasión" de Lope de Vega y Carpio, recogidos por el Santo Oficio de Nueva España en el año de 1613.</u> Guatemala, Fac. de Humanidades, Univ. de San Carlos, 1962. Pp. 114.

Sonnet(s)

Allué y Morer, Fernando. "Un soneto de Lope." <u>Poesía Española,</u> No. 147 (1962), 29-32.

Entrambasaguas, Joaquín de. "La creación poética de Lope de Vega en uno de sus sonetos." <u>Blanco y Negro</u>, No. 2638 (1962), 81-83.

Fucilla, Joseph G. "Two Sonnets Ascribed to Lope de Vega." <u>Hispanó</u>, No. 16 (1962), 103-09.

<u>Villancicos</u>

Blecua, José Manuel. "Villancicos de Lope a Santa Teresa." In <u>Strenae. Estudios de Filología e Historia dedicados al profesor Manuel García Blanco</u>, Acta Salmanticensia, Iussu Senatus Universitatus Edita, Filosofía y Letras, Tomo XVI, Salamanca, 1962, pp. 97-100.
    The author offers six <u>villancicos</u> written by Lope for the celebration in Barcelona in 1624 of the canonization of Teresa de Jesús.

PROSE

A. GENERAL

Ynduráin, Francisco. <u>Lope de Vega como novelador</u>. Santander, Pubs. de la Univ. Internacional Menéndez Pelayo, 1962. Pp. 82.

B. INDIVIDUAL PROSE WORKS

<u>La Dorotea</u>

Castro Calvo, José María. "Amor, tan solo (Unas breves notas a <u>La Dorotea</u>)." See Studies — General (<u>ABC</u>).

Guerrieri Crocetti, Camillo. "Per la <u>Dorotea</u> di Lope de Vega." In <u>Studi in onore di Angelo Monteverdi</u>, I, Modena, 1959, pp. 303-12.
    Rev (of the two vols. of the <u>Studi</u>): Antonio Alatorre, Margit Frenk Alatorre and M. Lope Blanch, <u>NRFH</u>, XVI(1962), 132-34.

Zertuche, F. M. <u>Lope de Vega</u>. See Studies — General.

www.ingramcontent.com/pod-product-compliance
Lightning Source LLC
Chambersburg PA
CBHW051351070526
44584CB00025B/3718